A WOMAN'S
GUIDE TO
MEN AND SEX

A Woman's Guide to Men and Sex

*How to understand
a man's sexual and
emotional needs*

DR. ANDREW STANWAY

Carroll & Graf Publishers, Inc.
New York

First Carroll & Graf edition 1988

We are grateful to the following to use the photographs in this book:

Tony Stone Worldwide (pages 7, 54, 71, 130)
Marshall Cavendish Ltd (pages 16–17, 60, 81, 179, 204)
Nancy Durrell-McKenna/The Hutchison Library (pages 32–33)
Image Bank (pages 37, 116)
Stockphotos (pages 42–43, 182–183)
Photo Co-op (pages 64–65)
Barnaby's Picture Library (pages 74, 91)
Pictor International (pages 83, 84)
Sally and Richard Greenhil (page 92)
Adam Woolfitt/ Susan Griggs Agency (page 110)
Art Director's Photo Library (page 183 (inset))
A.P. LaserPhoto (pages 9, 63, 108–109)
Library Picture Collection (page 86)
Picture research by Sara Driver

Carroll & Graf Publishers, Inc.
260 Fifth Avenue
New York, NY 10001

LIBRARY OF CONGRESS
Library of Congress Cataloging-in-Publication Data

Stanway, Andrew.
   A woman's guide to men and sex / Andrew Stanway.
      p.   cm.
   Includes index.
   ISBN 0-88184-440-3 : $17.95
   1. Men—United States—Sexual behavior.   2. Men—United States-
-Psychology.   I. Title.
HQ28.S82   1988
305.3'1—dc19   88-20978
                                                                      CIP

Manufactured in the United States of America

CONTENTS

PREFACE

Over the last thirty years much has been written about women, their place in society, and their sexuality. Without a doubt such a blossoming of interest in matters to do with women was long overdue and there can be few people, of either sex, who have remained untouched by what has been written and said.

During this same period things have also been happening to the world of men, some of which are the result of the revolution that has taken place in society's attitudes to women. Both these factors have so altered men's position in our culture and the way that they are treated both by other men and by their partners and families that it is hardly surprising that many women are as confused about the current situation as are most men.

In the space of a generation age-old tenets have been turned upside down with the result that society as a whole is often at a loss to know how to cope with the changes.

Over recent years I have worked mainly with female patients and it appeared to me that most of them were confused, at least to some extent, as to how to come to terms with their new-found 'liberation' in the context of men who were wary of it or even disadvantaged by it. This called for a new look at men in the light of recent history as their roles as fathers and partners have changed.

But it is not just social attitudes that have changed. With the coming of AIDS, promiscuity has become even more unpopular than ever and couples are trying to understand one another better so that they can live together in greater harmony. This 'new monogamy' has changed the nature of many couples' relationships and has, in a way, put both sexes under at least some pressure to make things work better. This kind of stable, loving and long-lasting relationship can only be successful with considerable understanding on both sides coupled with a great deal of communication.

This book tries to help women understand men's psychological and emotional make-up better so that such communication can occur. Most women know that their sex lives are geared to the nature and style of their whole relationship rather than to the state of genital 'play' at any time yet few men appear to be as aware of this link. This puts a strain on many a man-woman relationship as both misunderstand one another for much of the time.

I have tried throughout the book to paint a broad picture of male sexuality as it affects them and their partners day-by-day in their lives. This means taking a far broader view of 'sex' than most people immediately think of yet it is vital to do so if one is to understand men better. It is probably only through such an increased understanding of their men that many women can hope to enjoy their lives to the full, if only because so many women have believed men's own publicity that equates their sexuality with their genital sexual activity. Of course this

A new look at men

RIGHT: *Many's the woman who is attracted by this sort of stereotypical maleness – yet the emotional side of such a man often leaves her disappointed.*

is fallacious and leads both men and women into all kinds of trouble.

Throughout the book I have, understandably, concentrated almost exclusively on men and their sexuality. In the second and third parts of the book this might at first appear to suggest that women should do everything to please their men at the expense of their own pleasures. Of course this is not what I am saying. Many books throughout the last three decades have schooled men as to what women most want and enjoy when it comes to sex. This book tries to do the same for women so that they can rebalance the equation at a time when, as we have seen, couples are looking to one another increasingly to answer all their needs for closeness, sex, and love.

There have been several books written about male sexuality, though to be fair, not nearly as many as there have about female sexuality. I have collected together the main titles in this area in the Bibliography on page 232. The reasons for this relative disinterest in the sexuality of men are three-fold. First, the recent focus has, rightly, been on women after thousands of years of ignoring them; second, both sexes are more interested in learning about female sexuality than about that of the male; and third, men tend not to buy books, or indeed anything much, that deals with their emotional lives. The truth is that there has never been a mass-market best-seller about men in the way there has been about women. The only exception perhaps, is the *Hite Report* on men but this is a factual 'scientific' report detailing the findings of a massive questionnaire rather than a practical, discursive book.

For all these reasons I have targeted this book unashamedly at women. Women buy most books about sex and relationships, which is hardly surprising because women are more interested, or perhaps feel that they can more easily show their interest in, matters to do with human relationships and sexuality. I have no doubt that men are every bit as interested but from a different standpoint.

The other main reason that the book is aimed at women is that women can, by understanding their men better, make changes that men would be unlikely to make for themselves. This appears to put the onus on women to 'sort their men out' and this is quite deliberate. Men are pretty ignorant about themselves and so often cannot begin to seek help from their, often quite able and willing, partners. Women, on the other hand, being more in touch with feelings and generally more insightful, are used to building a body of self-knowledge which they then call upon personally or socially to make the world a better place for them and their families. Women spend much of their life studying people and putting their knowledge and insights to use but men, in general, do not.

Having said this, however, I hope that at least some men will buy this book and that many more will take the opportunity of having it around the home to read it and so learn more about themselves.

Gradually, over the *next* thirty years, I hope we shall find men's consciousness raised in these matters so that they will cast off the oppressive stereotypes just as women have done over the *last* three decades.

Disinterest in the sexuality of men

RIGHT: *Men such as these feel truly 'male' only when indulging in macho activities. But how easy is it to turn off and become a sensitive partner and lover?*

PART ONE

UNDERSTANDING MEN

The study of men and their sexuality is rather different from that of women and theirs. For example, work means something very different to the sexes, with a man having a vital part of his masculinity invested in it. Women are, by and large, not as violent or aggressive as men and few use pornography or go to prostitutes. Such subjects therefore assume a prominence in a book about men and sex whereas they'd hardly feature at all in a similar book about women.

It is said that we all need love and this is profoundly true yet men and women are often very different in what they mean by love and men remain likely to fall in love throughout their lives whereas women tend to be much more resistant to the 'love bug'.

Although women work, play, live with, make love to, and bear the children of men, most of them know very little about what makes them tick. A 1987 UK survey, for example, found that more than half of the women asked said they did not know enough about the men in their lives. In the South-West of England the figure rose to three quarters.

Of course some of the differences between the sexes are genetic and others cultural but, as we see in this part of the book, it is the biological differences that have important effects on our daily lives and affect the way we relate to one another at work, at home and at play. They also show men as the rather second-class sex – a fact which helps explain why so many men spend most of their lives asserting their superiority. They need to because of the unconscious realisation that they are, in many ways, inferior, if only in biological terms.

This part then looks at men in their everyday lives and sees how they function in terms of their sexuality rather than their genitality. Of course, the two are inextricably inter-linked but for most of the time women deal with men not in genital situations but as males with a rather different sexuality to their own.

I have not spelled out the practical solutions to many of the situations I describe because this would fill a whole book in itself. Rather I have tried to outline many of the more pressing areas of

It's easy to be vulnerable if you can trust your partner not to take advantage of your lowered defences. Many men go a whole lifetime unable to be truly themselves with their partner.

concern together, I hope, with some insights gained from other people's lives in the hope that with common sense and by applying the general principles upon which this book is founded the average reader will, with some thought and effort, be able to find her own way through to an answer that suits her particular life.

I hope that this section of the book will be a thought-provoking mine of useful material for women to discuss with their partners. In a sense this is how I run my practice – not by telling people what to do or how to run their lives but by opening the field to discussion so as to enable the couple to do the really valuable work in between their sessions with me.

THE SECOND-CLASS SEX?

T hroughout history, and in most societies today, men have tended to be the dominant sex socially and most of the good things that have been available have been appropriated by men for themselves. This behaviour, however it originated, has made men appear superior in that they seem to have called the shots for countless thousands of years. It was against this kind of background that the women's movement of the last thirty years was set.

Although it is impossible to deny such trends and tendencies in societies all over the world, as we learn more about the sexes it has become clear that men, rather than being so superior, are almost certainly the 'inferior' sex, at least in biological terms. This fact has made men over-assert themselves in relation to women with the result that male domination appears to be the norm almost everywhere.

Men the 'inferior' sex

At some very obvious levels men and women are very different biologically. For example, males snore more; probably masturbate more; are more aggressive; have many measurable differences in their body structures; are more likely to be colour-blind, left-handed, or haemophiliac; are more likely to die from cot death; feel less pain than women; age earlier; die younger; express their emotions less readily; and worry about themselves more. The list is endless.

Whatever the significance of these differences between the sexes what has actually happened is that facets of maleness have been portrayed, by men, as being desirable and valuable whereas those of femaleness have been undervalued or even denied.

In emotional terms we are all a mixture of masculine and feminine personality traits. Most of us know men who are caring, nurturing, calm, emotional, and so on, and women who are aggressive logical and competitive. Largely depending on how we were brought up and on the masculine and feminine profiles of our parents, we come to behave in ways that are a mixture of masculine and feminine that are unique to us and our personalities.

Of course, however masculine or feminine our personalities our gender identity, be it male or female, remains the same. As we shall see later, men who exhibit feminine characteristics, however few, are thought poorly of by other men and this understandably makes them reluctant to exhibit feminine personality traits. Women on the other hand, are encouraged to display masculine characteristics, in a culture that values them, provided that they do not interfere with men and the way they run the world.

Overall, masculine attributes have been favoured as being more valuable, as I have pointed out, but some feminine traits are more valued than are certain masculine ones. On balance then it appears that men have, over the centuries, looked at their attributes and rated them as being of value while at the same time ignoring or denying feminine ones.

While it is a gross over-generalisation it is probably true to say that we tend to marry someone whose masculinity and femininity profiles broadly match the mirror image of our own. So it is that a man with a large feminine part to his character will tend to marry a woman whose masculine characteristics are dominant. In this way one partner makes up for the personality defects of the other, if only to some extent.

Masculinity and femininity profiles

So in behavioural terms at least we try, however unconsciously, to balance out the characteristics in our personalities to make life not only pleasant but workable. That many couples do not realise that they are playing this unconscious 'game' is often at the heart of marital disharmony as one or the other behaves in a way that their partner sees as inappropriate but which often matches very well what the other unknowingly lacks.

But none of this takes away from the fact that men still tend to over-value themselves and their masculine characteristics at the expense of those of their partners. This usually involves denying the feminine characteristics in their own personality. If we are to understand why this should be we have to look at the true situation in men and see why it is that they are so defensive. Of course the story is a complex one involving genetic and environmental influences but even at the most basic of biologically observable and measurable levels the sexes are very different and different in ways that affect their behaviour towards one another.

In the beginning all fetuses are female until something happens to change things. In a fetus that is destined to become a male a tiny parcel of protein called the H-Y antigen triggers the growing fetus into developing testes, the first sign of maleness. Once they are formed they start to produce male hormones (along with female ones, incidentally) that in turn make the growing fetus become recognisably male.

But femaleness is very persistent, as several laboratory experiments have shown. If the testes are removed from a male rat embryo it turns into a female even though genetically it is still a male. Male rats castrated at birth later exhibit female sexual behaviour.

This fragile grip on maleness is just the start of a pattern that soon develops in which male fetuses, and later babies and men, end up being more delicate in biological terms than females. Of all fetuses that are lost spontaneously as miscarriages the majority are male; male babies fare worse at and after birth than do female ones; and at almost every age fewer women die than men. Nature seems to have tried to compensate for this male loss and frailty by creating a situation in which there are just slightly more male babies born than female ones.

No reasonable scientist looking dispassionately at the evidence would assert that men were the stronger sex, except in terms of muscular strength. Studies have, for example, found that women survive shipwreck, starvation, fatigue, illness, and shock better than men and few men would dispute that their partners have greater staying power than they do.

Men and women do not think in the same way

It is a truism to say that men and women do not think in the same way and over the centuries scientists have tried to fathom the differences between male and female brains. There is now a body of scientific evidence that shows that men and women do, in fact, have different brains which function somewhat differently.

The human brain is divided into two halves. The left hemisphere is the verbal brain controlling language and reading. This is the logical part of the brain that processes information and helps us perform intellectual tasks.

The right hemisphere governs the way we perceive space and how we think about design, shape and form. This half of the brain also works more intuitively.

In boys the right brain develops earlier than in girls whose left brain develops sooner. Whilst it is difficult to be certain it seems that men use both their brain halves together to deal with life whilst women tend to use their left brains more. Male brains, it appears, are more specialised which gives them certain advantages in problem solving. Unfortunately a major disadvantage inherent in this is a loss of flexibility. However it is arguable that the world is becoming a less physical place and that women's superior skills in the intuitive and emotional areas might be what is needed for the future.

Against this background it should now become clear why it is that men are so defensive in their stance against women. And based on the age-old maxim that the best form of defence is attack, it is easy to see how men have for thousands of years gone all out to assert their superiority.

Ironically, though men know only too well how weak they are, as we shall see throughout the book, they are also greatly in awe of women and femaleness in general. This is perfectly understandable because they realise, however unconsciously, that women hold many of the trump biological cards and that many of them affect men and their lives very deeply.

But what has all of this got to do with sex?

Clearly the way men and women think and function emotionally so differently has profound effects on the man-woman relationship but in more physical terms too men are somewhat second best when it comes to sex.

It is usually claimed that women are less interested in sex. This is because our culture has made it unacceptable for women to express their sexual interests. However women are almost permanently think-ing, however unconsciously, about something to do with their sexual-ity and even genital sex is never far from their minds. Women are never far from the realities of sexuality in all its forms. Their monthly cycles keep them in close touch with their sexual bodies; and their closeness to family and other emotions keep them in touch with the realities of the interactions between the sexes not only in their own homes but in those of others, and at work. Historically women have spent a large proportion of their reproductive lives pregnant or breast-feeding and this too has kept them in daily touch with their sexuality in a way that men are not. The sales of romantic fiction match those of male 'pornography' and there are those who claim that in all its forms, including the millions of women's magazines sold every week, they outstrip it.

When it comes to physical sex women are more active too. It is always thought that men masturbate more than women. However clinical experience shows that about a third of all women claim that they cannot remember a time when they have not masturbated, ever since they were very young. Most boys stop masturbating as young pre-schoolers and start again at puberty. Some girls never stop from babyhood.

The areas of a woman's body that are sexually arousing for her to touch or stroke are far more numerous than those of a man. And when a woman does have an orgasm it is much like a man's but, unlike all but the very youngest of men, she can have several in quick succession.

Clearly a female's sexual repertoire is vast compared with that of a man and there is no doubt in my mind that this is why male-dominated societies have, very successfully, controlled female sexu-ality, or rather its expression, throughout the ages. Women, it has been held for thousands of years, well before Judeo-Christian society finally reinforced the notion, were a distraction to men and the real business of life as defined by men. They represented all that is base and animal in humankind and needed controlling lest the whole human machine go off the rails. Or so the message went.

But if female sexuality has always been seen as rampant and in need of control male sexuality has always been a confusing affair. This is hardly surprising because it seems to be so full of contradictions and dilemmas. Biologically speaking males would like to impregnate as many females as possible so as to be sure that their genetic line would continue. Of course a man can't be sure that any one mating will make his female pregnant and he cannot be sure that the woman, once pregnant with the baby, will be content to look after it until it is ready to become independent – a very long time in humans compared with other animals.

Male sexuality is a confusing affair

Some sort of male-female bonding is common in almost every human society. As we look around the world the pattern is that men offer a kind of parental caring system for their women and their children in return for the women's sexual fidelity. This fidelity ensures that he is not having to care for and support children fathered by other men. Her sexual exclusivity buys him peace of mind.

But this trade off had disadvantages for the man in that there is at least some conflict between his demands that his partner remain faithful and his desires to have other partners. One study of human cultures found that of 849 only 137 were monogamous.

No one knows why men are interested in having many partners but the observation is not solely a human one as any farmer knows.

Men, it appears, also seem to tire of the same sex partner much more easily than women do. This has been called the Coolidge Effect after a story about President and Mrs Coolidge. During a guided tour of a US government farm, Mrs Coolidge expressed curiosity about how often a rooster performed its duty. 'Dozens of times a day,' she was told. 'Tell that to the president,' she said.

Most men, it appears, never tire of sexual novelty. His encouraging body language has not been missed by the girl – or by his wife!

On being told of this feat, President Coolidge was initially dismayed, then a thought occurred to him. 'Wait a minute,' he said, 'is that with the same hen each time?'

'Oh no, Mr President, a different hen each time.'

'Tell that to Mrs Coolidge.'

Man is unusual among the primates in having a female that is always sexually receptive. This was originally thought to be a biological device to strengthen the pair bond between a man and his partner in that unlimited copulation would tend to reward the man and keep him around to look after the young that take so long to mature. However, on more reflection this notion is now thought to be somewhat unlikely. After all, why should ever-available sex keep a man and a woman together? Of course it doesn't, as other animal species prove. Males of other species stay around so as to ensure that their genetic offspring survive – they don't need any other rewards. Also, research has found that other long-term pair-bonded animals are actually *less* active sexually and have more defined reproductive cycles than do those that don't form pair bonds.

The lesser apes, gibbons and siamangs, which are monogamous for life, are sexually very *in*active, with siamangs copulating only during four months every two and a half years. In fact it appears that for many animals constantly available sex is a distraction from the important business of staying alive and raising their offspring.

Another more modern view of the ever-ready human female is that by being so she can conceal her ovulatory state. If women were like most animals and were interested in having intercourse only when they were fertile their males would not stay around to help with the rearing of children, they would be off looking for other women who were available to mate with. A woman who is sexually available when she is not fertile will ensure that she is protected and her children supported by the man who has sole rights to sire her. A woman's mate is also kept around to support her because by not knowing when she is ovulating he cannot know when she is at her most valuable to him in reproductive terms. He thus has to stay around all the time and have sex with her on an unlimited basis if he wants to fulfil his reproductive duty.

It is my view that men know, however unconsciously, that they are in fact the 'weaker' sex and that in many, if not most, areas of human endeavour women can outshine them. The only way that men persistently and consistently outshine women is in pursuits that require physical strength but today even this very real attribute is no longer as prized as it was historically.

Men on the defensive

The realisation that women are, in reality, every bit as able as themselves and in addition have abilities and skills that they envy, puts most men on the defensive a lot of the time. This, in turn, makes them behave in ways that are less than attractive or helpful to themselves, their partners, or their families.

There are, hopefully, signs that things are changing in this respect. Increasing numbers of men are more aware of their feminine qualities and are happier to acknowledge the masculine qualities in their women. This re-balancing of the characteristics of the sexes is not only more *practical* when it comes to day-to-day living but also reduces the battles between the sexes.

The exciting thing about all of this for me, as a specialist in man-woman relationships, is that the seeds of such a major revolution in society lie within one-to-one bonded couples. Notions of global masculinity and femininity may be difficult to grasp, especially for men who, in historical terms, have not much concerned themselves with such matters. But within the security of a loving pair-bonded relationship a man can experiment with letting go of the old stereotypes and, in acknowledging his intrinsic 'weaknesses', become more aware of his intrinsic strengths.

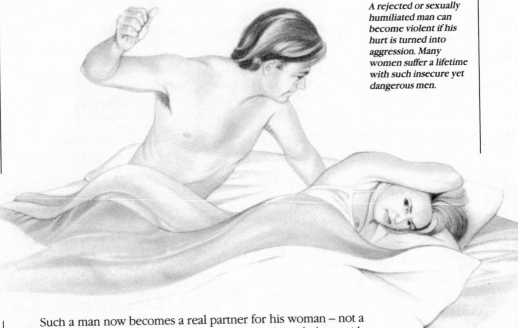

A rejected or sexually humiliated man can become violent if his hurt is turned into aggression. Many women suffer a lifetime with such insecure yet dangerous men.

Such a man now becomes a real partner for his woman – not a sparring partner but a love partner. He now acknowledges with pleasure her individual strengths and weaknesses, be they masculine or feminine and realises that she can hold both sets of qualities in balance within her personality. Having learned from her that this can happen many men can, I find, then do the same thing for themselves. This forms the basis not only for more stable and mature man-woman relationships but also for a more stable and mature world for our children to inherit.

Masculine and feminine stereotypes

When thinking about males and females it is helpful to bear in mind that the personality characteristics that we attribute to males are to be found also in females, if to a lesser extent, and vice versa. So it is that characteristics generally thought to be 'feminine' are found in almost all men.

Men are said to be aggressive, logical, active, worldly, skilled in business, adventurous, never to cry, able to lead others, ambitious, ideas centred, unaware of the feelings of others, sloppy in their habits, unable to express tender feelings, and so on.

Anyone with more than a fleeting knowledge of men will know that this stereotype, whilst perhaps broadly true for many men, does not apply to all, some of whom exhibit quite the opposite personality traits. Many women too, perhaps especially so today, act in a way that would or could be called masculine, if only some of the time.

We are all a complex mixture of masculine and feminine personality characteristics and we do one another untold harm if we label our partner 'masculine' and then expect him to live up to all the cultural stereotypes, some of which are unquestionably harmful within a loving relationship.

We marry a mirror image

The interesting thing one finds in therapy is that most couples have, quite unwittingly of course, married a kind of mirror image of the other when it comes to such matters. So it is that a man who shows mainly feminine characteristics in his personality structure will tend to marry a woman whose masculine traits are dominant. This does not mean that the man is a homosexual or a wimp or the woman a butch man-eater but rather that the couple have balanced out the sorts of things listed above in a way that seems to work for them.

Trouble brews though when the balance changes or needs changing. A not uncommon problem in marital practice is the couple where the man has so many feminine traits that the woman loses patience because he is unassertive both in and out of bed. She originally liked, and maybe still does like, his kindness, care-giving, loving, nurturing behaviour and values it but she finds she cannot cope with the lack of aggression, ambition, his excessive dependence and so on.

Thankfully, as society is changing couples are becoming more flexible about sharing their masculine and feminine qualities within the household. So it is that a man might do some of what used to be called 'mothering' whilst his wife earns a living and does other so-called masculine things. The happily married couple have a kind of on-going and shifting system in which the roles interchange from time to time, sometimes within a few hours. This certainly works well and acknowledges the fact that old-fashioned stereotypical ways of behaving and thinking do few couples much good. The main trouble with such models is that most of us drop all too readily into the mould we or our partner thinks should fit us. This shuts us out of whole areas of skill, ability, and pleasure not only for ourselves but for our families too. This arguably happens much more to men than to women who have, on balance, been able to be more flexible over such matters. It has for some time been more acceptable socially for a woman to behave in a 'masculine' way than it is for men to exhibit their feminine traits.

THE MYTHS
OF MALE
SEXUALITY

As if men were not already complex enough and quite clearly and recognisably different from women, as we have just seen, things are made even more difficult for both sexes because our culture has created a whole series of myths about male sexuality that have harmful effects on the man-woman relationship.

These myths, or messages have, for the most part, been learned quite unconsciously, often from the very earliest days of our lives. We pick them up from conversations overheard at home; from our peer group; from authority figures directly and indirectly; from our partners as we seek experience of the opposite sex; from literature and the media generally, and so on.

Most are unconsciously learned

It is worth looking at some of these myths here because they set the scene for understanding male sexuality in general. They assume an importance that is greater than any other cultural myths because they form the basis for a world of sexual fantasy that cannot be realised by any man or his partner. Unfortunately many, if not most, men do not really understand this and run their lives, usually unconsciously, as if the fantasy world were real. When it becomes plain that it is not they blame themselves or their partners.

The starting point in almost any discussion about male sexuality must be the penis. We look at the subject in considerable detail on page 136 but here let's just look at the myths surrounding the organ.

MYTH NUMBER ONE

If a man is to be successful at sex he must have a big penis that erects readily and stays erect

There are few more powerful myths than the 'bigger is better' myth of the penis. Most men actually believe that things would go better for them sexually if they had a bigger penis. Many men believe that their sex partners share this view and that if only they had a bigger organ they would please *them* better too. The fantasy woman, in this context, wants a vast organ that impales her so deeply that she nearly chokes to death on it.

This wonderland penis is not only gigantic but it jumps to attention at the slightest hint of a woman's body. 'Show him a square inch of female flesh and he's away,' is all part of this myth.

Along with its size and its readiness to 'perform' any time of day or night is the amazing hardness of the fantasy penis. It is like a pillar of rock and stays that way for hours on end.

She clearly wants sex but he is just not interested. Perhaps he is no less aroused than she is but without his erection intercourse cannot occur.

The effects of such a myth are all too apparent. Given that most men are always falling short of possessing such a fantasy penis they are exceptionally sensitive to any criticism from other men, or their partners. Unfortunately, many women believe these myths too, as we shall see as this section progresses and it is their beliefs that can also adversely affect their sex life with their partner.

Many's the woman who believes, for example, that all women need to do is to lie there and look gorgeous and their man will automatically go into the gigantic, hard, long-lasting, mode. The facts are that for all but the youngest of men the penis needs quite a lot of stimulation, even if much of it is mental rather than physical, if it is to become hard and stay that way.

Lie there and look gorgeous

And there are considerable influences on how big, how thick, how hard, how ever-ready, and how long-lasting any individual penis is which are controlled by a host of conditions in the man himself, his relationship, his surroundings, and much much more. Few women understand this and wonder how it is that their man's penis appears to be such a fickle organ.

The truth is that many a man's penis is burdened with weighty matters that simply do not always allow it to rise to the occasion and that, contrary to popular expectations, it is part of a rather sensitive set-up that is prone to failure at the cry of a baby, the yawn of a woman, or the thought of the mortgage.

By and large it is probably fair to say that men would enjoy sex more and so would women if their women took less notice of what the myth said and got on with stimulating their man on the basis that the penis needs all the help it can get.

Now we have introduced the man's partner let's look briefly at what she is like in the fantasy myth.

MYTH NUMBER TWO

Women are always ready for sex; are aroused quickly; respond to their man by having multiple orgasms; say 'no' when they mean 'yes'; resist sex until it is forced upon them; and express ecstasy much of the time

Although this is a book about myths that apply to men and *their* sexuality, it will not take the reader long to realise that a man who believes these myths about women will be in for a very disappointing time. The trouble is that so many men do not see this stereotype for what it is – a fantasy model.

As a result of this myth many men think that sex can only be ideal if the woman is preferably young, physically superb, without blemish, and in all other ways behaves like the true fantasy model. Such a man is permanently dissatisfied unless he is with one. He never hears what his woman says when, for example, she asks him to be more gentle with her breasts, because to him all women need to be handled roughly and 'forced' to do things they say they do not want. This is

Is this the start of a real relationship or will he expect her to behave like the fantasy myth?

further enhanced by the way we bring up girls to declare few or none of their real sexual needs for fear of appearing tarty. The way out of this dilemma is, of course, to bring up girls to be honest about their needs for sex so that men can take them seriously.

The fantasy woman must, of course, always be orgasmic and preferably multiply so. Given that most men see their partner's orgasm as a validation of their abilities and skills as lovers the better, the quicker, and the more of them she has the better he must be as a lover. And given that for many a man love-making is largely a matter of making love to his own ego this is somewhat important. For such a man the woman he is with is almost of secondary importance provided that he fulfils his own unconscious needs to impress himself.

This is a particularly cruel myth because some women enjoy sex generally and intercourse in particular yet do not have orgasms at all, even in masturbation, and others are orgasmic during masturbation yet never climax during penis-in-vagina intercourse and do not much mind if they do. In clinical practice I see this myth working away in the lives of couples every day, much to their detriment. Whatever the man actually says to his partner he really believes that things would be better if she were orgasmic with penile thrusting alone. Not only is this myth harmful when the woman doesn't behave as expected but it is used by the man either to put his partner down as inadequate or himself down as a failure for not being able to 'make things happen' as they should. Either way he loses.

But back to more male myths.

MYTH NUMBER THREE

A woman who doesn't do what I want sexually doesn't love me

As we shall see throughout the book, men make a major investment in their partner as a love-object. Most men claim that their partner is their most loved person and that the thing they most enjoy about being married is the loving relationship they share with their wife.

Because men have all their emotional eggs in one basket they are exceptionally vulnerable to the loss of them. Almost anything can be taken as a sign that this love is being withdrawn and sex is the biggest and most fertile ground for misunderstandings. This comes about because in our culture love and sex are inextricably inter-linked. Girls are brought up to exaggerate their loving feelings so as to justify their need for sex – and men believe them. But such behaviour also leads men to believe that their partner does not have sex because she *needs* it for herself but rather because she loves him. Obviously, should she not want sex, for whatever reason, he is open to believing that it has something to do with his lovability rather than anything else. This is especially likely to be the conclusion given his insecurity about his love-worthiness anyway.

Many men believe that a woman who 'really loves' a man will do anything for him. But a woman rarely sees her love as being able to be judged in this way. In fact many women see it as ridiculous that their willingness to indulge in say, oral sex, should be taken as any indication at all of their love for their man. He though, and for reasons that I've explained, sees things very differently.

MYTH NUMBER FOUR

Men know what to do without being told

This is an especially harmful myth because it is patently untrue and destroys countless marriages. The truth is that men have *more* to learn about sex than women do. Women are very much more varied in their sexual responses than men are and even a very experienced man will not necessarily be able to predict what a new sex partner will most enjoy. Most women say that it annoys them when they are treated in the way their *man* wants rather than in the way *they* want. Yet they won't show him what they best like for fear of appearing tarty. Men

Emotional eggs in one basket

complain that they get too few cues and that, short of telepathy, they cannot seem to win.

The only way around all this is for the woman to share with her man what makes her excited, aroused and pleased and for him to take his cues from her. If she sees herself as too 'nice' to help him to help her then she has only herself to blame, whatever the outcome.

Who will blame who in the morning? In a loving relationship no blame is required – both learn from the failure and comfort one another in other ways.

MYTH NUMBER FIVE

Men are always ready for sex

As we saw earlier, many women believe that they have only to want sex or just to look sexy to make their man have an erection. Some men too

believe this, or rather believe that they *should* be able to have an erection just by looking at their lover or being in her presence.

If the man is much over twenty-five, and especially if he is over forty, things are somewhat different in practice. Men, as they get older need a lot more stimulation, be it physical or emotional. The follow-up myth to this is 'If he really fancied me/wanted me/loved me he'd get an erection double-quick'. Whilst it is true that, biologically speaking, the most flattering thing a man can do for his partner is to have an erection for her a failure to do so doesn't necessarily mean that he is critical of her. The reasons may date back into his childhood; long before they even met.

The confusion about all this starts because a woman needs only to be willing enough to lie there with her legs open if she is to have intercourse, or rather to copulate (for the differences between the two see page 155) whereas a man has to be fairly aroused before anything much can happen. Also, don't forget that a man can feel very aroused and loving and not even have an erection at all. Some women find this difficult to believe yet they know very well that they can want to be made love to without feeling very aroused.

A woman needs only to be willing

MYTH NUMBER SIX

Men should not express any tender feelings

Men, it is held, by both the sexes, should display only a narrow range of emotions most of which are to do with competition, aggression and being in control. Signs of weakness, tenderness, softness, vulnerability, fear, compassion, and confusion are considered unmanly and only suitable for women to express.

This puts men in a quandary when making love because for many it is the only situation in which they feel sufficiently at ease to lose control and to display any of the so-called 'feminine' emotions. What men need is permission from their partner to be expressive in an emotional way that is normally taboo in other settings. This can, with luck, some encouragement, and hard work be extended with benefit into areas of the couple's life outside the bedroom.

The fantasy model of sex says that men should be doers. And 'do' is exactly what most men do. We shall see on page 178 how a woman can encourage her man to get out of this rut and to become at the least a feeling doer, or even sometimes not to *do* at all but simply to *be* and to *feel*.

Many men, eager to feel loved and wanted, or perhaps to express certain tender emotions, are so crippled by their upbringing that they resort to sex as the only vehicle by which such things can be expressed. As we shall see throughout this book this leads men to cry out for more sexual activity when what they really need is more loving or other tender behaviour. To ask directly for it though would be womanish or 'sissy' so they go for sex which is, as we all 'know', what real men do!

LEFT: *A loving man can often express tenderness to his beloved – even if he cannot do so elsewhere in life. It is this contrast of maleness and tenderness that so attracts – and confuses – many women.*

MYTH NUMBER SEVEN

All physical contact must eventually lead to intercourse

This is a myth widely circulated by both the sexes. In the fantasy model of 'girlie magazine' sex any physical contact with a woman is bound to end up in bed. Kissing, hugging, just being held, massaging, indeed any other form of sexual but non-genital love-making is always seen as a prelude to genital activity.

A prelude to genital activity

We touch so little in our culture that people have largely forgotten what it is like to be touched, stroked or massaged simply for the pleasure of it. The mythological, fantasy world says that any contact between a man and a woman *must* be the start of something genital. As a result many couples, and indeed many men and women who aren't pair-bonded, miss out on an enormous amount of physical and sensual pleasure.

Men are seen as being allowed only two forms of physical contact with human beings in our culture. One is violent, as in sports, and the other is while he is 'doing' something sexual with his partner.

For a man to ask to be held in bed and not to have it progress to genital activity is considered weird by most men and not a few women, but it is what some men want, at least on some occasions.

LEFT: This couple seem to be having fun but even a walk in the country can be transformed into hard work by a 'driven' male.

MYTH NUMBER EIGHT

Successful sex is about being a good performer

Men are brought up from early boyhood to value achievement and doing. A 'successful' man in the western world is one who achieves. Few men believe that good things just 'happen' – they have to be made to happen.

The impact of such beliefs on sex is all too obvious. Much of a couple's loving and even genital behaviour involves something happening, it is true, but there is no reason to suppose that it is the man who has to make it happen. Unfortunately, few women dare make things happen because they fear that they will appear cheap or tarty and that their man will thus reject them or think badly of them.

But whoever 'makes things happen' the man almost always sets out on a love-making episode with a goal in mind. This kind of approach relegates foreplay to being seen as the 'run up' to the 'real thing' rather than an end in itself.

Many men are so involved in the 'work' involved in intercourse that they miss out on all the pleasure. It is no surprise then that they want to do it all again very soon afterwards to try to get something more meaningful and rewarding out of it. By constantly aiming for the goal most men miss out on the journey to get to it – a journey, in the case of sex, that has its own unique pleasures.

Sex is hard work

Men seek advice from sex books, buy penis enlargers, dress their women up in sexy undies, and so on the better to enhance this journey but in truth if the goal were de-bunked the journey would of itself assume greater value. Men will no doubt continue to search for a better love-making position; an aphrodisiac; a new partner; or more sophisticated foreplay; but if they could take their eye off the goal and enjoy the journey for what it is, a perfectly valid end in itself, things would be a lot happier in the average bedroom.

The trouble with goal-setting is that if the individual who sets them fails to reach them he or she becomes anxious. And this is exactly what happens with men and sex. Most men in our culture are pretty anxious a lot of the time about many things that they are trying to 'achieve'. So it is with sex.

Many a man gets into bed with all kinds of anxieties about his performance, her performance, his expectations (however unrealistic) and her expectations. All this is loaded on his penis and it is hardly suprising that so many suffer sexual failure as a result. The penis is too heavily burdened.

But when discussing anything about this particular myth it is important to remember that sex is a form of pleasure and that to many men pleasure is something they should have to work at. For most men

OVERLEAF: For many men playing with their children is the only time when they really let their hair down and allow their inner child out to play.

their sporting activities, their hobbies, their children, and their homes are all 'work'. They simply don't know how to do something and not to work at it. This also applies to sex. They think that if it is to be 'successful' it must involve work. Therefore, the more they work at it the better it should be.

Women can greatly help their men to relax into sex and to make it as unlike work as possible by discouraging achievement and showing that, to them, the journey is every bit as good as the goal. A loving woman can give her man a gift beyond price by helping him to see that sex and possibly other pleasures in life, do not have to be worked for. Sometimes wonderful things just happen and can be enjoyed all the more for that.

Clearly she's not getting much out of it but for him, reading a sexy magazine together just had to end in sex.

MYTH NUMBER NINE

Sex means having intercourse

We look at this in more detail on page 152 but here it is worth just considering some of the damage that is done to relationships that are run on this basis.

When sex meant making babies obviously it had to include intercourse but today with most couples having only two babies in a

Sex is intercourse

sexually active lifetime the overwhelming majority of sexual events has nothing whatsoever to do with procreation – it is about recreation.

Having said this, the average man, especially, seems not to have got the message. 'Normal sex' whatever this means, is seen by most men to be intercourse. In fact, Shere Hite found that most men found it difficult to think of sex as being anything other than intercourse. This is linked to the goal-centred sex of the fantasy world in which all that matters is the final orgasm. Not only do men miss out on a whole range of wonderful activities as a result of this myth but so do their partners. The girlie magazine myth has it that all real women have an orgasm on penetration and do so noisily, with enormous gusto, moaning or shouting. In reality many women don't have orgasms at all during intercourse, unless they or their partners stimulate the clitoris directly and even then some do not do so, yet they are not allowed ever to enjoy oral sex, anal sex or even manual stimulation because the man thinks that 'normal sex' is all about penis-in-vagina thrusting.

Several studies have found that men, by and large, see clitoral stimulation as somewhat juvenile and many of my male patients have never learned where their partner's clitoris is; have never taken lessons from her in what to do to it to best excite her; and frankly don't seem all that concerned about anything other than penile thrusting.

That this is a tragedy for many women is not too harsh a statement, yet their men, sometimes to be fair aided and abetted by the women themselves, continue to treat the whole sexual arena as if it were only a matter of perfecting penile thrusting. We see on page 192 how a couple can greatly enlarge and enhance their pleasures by doing away with this myth.

MYTH NUMBER TEN

Really good sex happens spontaneously

This myth is perhaps held more by women than by men but it is nevertheless still very commonplace in men.

It is true to say that few people enjoy sex much first time around and most young people, when polled, say that they found their first experience rather disappointing. The truth is that the best sex occurs between those who care for one another; have a commitment to each other; know quite a lot about one another's personalities; have taken trouble to learn and re-learn what best suits one another both physically and emotionally; can communicate well; and so on.

For the man, or woman, who truly believes that sex must be spontaneous to be good or valid, life must seem pretty bleak because so often things do not work out well on their own yet to make things happen or to learn about sex, to study it in the context of one's partner, and to make an art of it are all seen as 'un-natural'. This can lead to the search for a partner with whom things *will* go well spontaneously, an often fruitless and certainly destructive search if it involves abandoning other partners or even families along the way. Somewhere at the

RIGHT: *The girlie magazine fantasy partner is always ready, willing and able. Varicose veins and PMT are not for her!*

end of some rainbow such men believe that they will find a woman with whom it will all happen without any effort. This woman is their Cinderella and if the slipper fits all will be well and they'll live happily ever after. Whilst this is undoubtedly an attractive myth to many men it creates havoc, broken families and lonely men and as such cannot be recommended.

I have dealt with these myths of male sexuality at some length because so many men believe them to be true and, often to the bafflement of their women, run their lives as if they *were*. Because so many women are dragged through life kicking and screaming against such myths, knowing them to be a nonsense, it is helpful to see them for what they are so as to be able to deal with them. For the woman who was not aware of what was going on in her relationship I hope this section has started to open the doors, however little.

But before we leave the subject of myths and fantasy sex and their effects not only on men but on their partners it is only fair to say that many of the myths we have looked at have a basis in fact. If they were totally mythological they could be easily dismissed – but they are not.

Some myths are based on fact

Some women *do* have orgasms on penetration alone; some women *do* become so carried away during sex that they cry out uncontrollably; some men *do* get their best pleasure from sex when their penis is at its biggest and hardest; some women *do* indeed like a larger penis than a smaller one; many women *in fact* have their best orgasms and enjoy sex most when they are 'forced' to do what their man wants; and so on.

The problem with the myths is that what is in reality the norm for only a few is extrapolated as if it were, or should be, the norm for all.

There is little doubt that for many men women who behave like those in girlie magazine fiction *are* more exciting in bed but it is equally true that others are greatly put off by a woman who is demanding, noisy, assertive, highly orgasmic, or whatever the fantasy model dictates. To a lot of men such a woman is more of a threat than a source of pleasure. This is not, of course, the woman's fault but rather that the man's sexual self-esteem is so weak that he fears being taken over by his partner.

Some women do, indeed, want to behave like the fantasy model, and not because they are trying to live up to it, they are often not aware of it, at least not in any detail. The sexuality, or at least its expression, of such women is sometimes held back by their men.

An example might help illustrate the point.

The mythological fantasy model has it that women should have orgasms and several of them, preferably as a result of penis-in-vagina thrusting alone. But when talking to men who have had experience of such women they sometimes say that they wish the woman just had one orgasm and enjoyed it rather than their having to go on and on stimulating them, especially if they, the men, have already climaxed. The multiply-orgasmic woman can be a considerable source of pleasure for a man but she can also be a nuisance because it puts her partner under pressure to help her, even if it is only by lasting long enough, to have more and more. Undoubtedly for some women more orgasms *will* mean better but unless such a woman can produce them herself at least some of her sexual partners will see her as just another chore in life that they have to work at.

The dilemma then is to know how to strike a balance with these myths of the fantasy world. Some of them will be attractive to one or other partner and others will actually apply to them – that is they won't be myths at all, they'll be reality. A couple who love one another, want to please each other and to grow together over the years will be constantly modifying and extending their love-making be it genital or non-genital. This policy of constant improvement is the surest way of combatting boredom and ensuring that other members of the opposite sex don't get a look in.

Many men would benefit hugely from their sex lives becoming more 'feminine' and many women would enhance their pleasure if they incorporated more 'masculine' features that they found attractive. In this way women would come to express their physical and genital needs in a more forthright way which would be helpful to those men who think that women are 'just a bag of emotions' and men would feel able to express their needs for emotional and non-performance love-making in the knowledge that they'd be met half-way on physical and genital matters by their partners. In this model neither sex would have the responsibility for, or the burden of, all the emotions or all the performance. This is true team-work and sharing – the heart of intercourse rather than copulation. This surely must be a valuable goal worth aiming for in any loving relationship between a man and a woman, especially if it is a committed and long-lasting one.

Such sharing is also of considerable value because it proves to the couple that divisive stereotypes are meaningless. As a man comes to see and enjoy his partner's delight in so-called masculine aspects of sexuality and realises that she has a strong biological drive for sex, he comes to value her more. Similarly, as a woman sees her man reveal his emotions and stop his unconscious pretences to a model of behaviour that is typically 'masculine' she can enjoy him as a more rounded and less defended personality. This letting down of the culturally imposed defences enriches both the individuals as they reveal their real selves. Now two *real* human beings start to inter-act with one another rather than the two cut-out cardboard characters they used to be.

Sharing personality characteristics

THE STAGES
IN A MAN'S LIFE

Boys will be boys

It is often said that boys will be boys but, as most women know only too well, many men remain boys throughout their lives. It is only a matter of how grown up they are in their boyishness.

This might at first appear a rather combative statement, especially bearing in mind that women too retain at least some of their girlishness and that many of their partners find this attractive. However, on balance it is probably fair to say that more men remain as 'boys' in adult life than women do as girls. This state of affairs probably comes about because females of all ages appear to have an inbuilt desire to care for and mother others whatever their age or sex. Of course this is a generalisation but it seems to hold good for most women in our western culture. This leads many women to behave in a 'motherly' way to their men and thus, usually quite unconsciously of course, to confirm *their* intrinsic tendency to behave like little boys.

Remaining a boy for life has obvious advantages, the main one of which is having others run around after you like a mother did. That women are prepared all too often to jump into this role clearly shows that to do so answers their needs every bit as much as it does those of their men. In short, such behaviour is usually an unconscious game played out between a couple in a way that suits them both, however temporarily, during their many stages of life together. Sometimes this model works well for the first decade or two of married life then things change in middle age as the woman becomes more assertive and sees that the game, whilst suiting her husband well, does not now do her much good.

There are probably five main stages in a man's life and they all have implications for his sexuality and his relationship with his partner. The first phase of adulthood (other growing-up phases are looked at elsewhere) lasts from about twenty to the mid-thirties. This stage is a big building one with the man marrying, buying or renting a home, settling into a job or career and, usually, starting a family.

The second stage runs from a man's mid-thirties to his mid-forties. At this stage he usually consolidates his achievements in life.

Stage three is the next ten years or so during which a man realises that middle age is upon him. He now looks backwards *and* forwards whereas until this age he had looked only forwards. It can be a make or break stage for many men.

The next stage takes a man up to retirement and can be a good one, provided that he has sorted out his dilemmas of the previous stage.

Lastly comes retirement – a time to relax and reflect and to enjoy grandchildren – or a time to resent what has gone before, to reflect on the disappointments of life and harbour fears about old age and illness.

Let's look at each of these in turn and especially in the light of a man's sexual life with his partner.

Stage one

Most men past middle age say that their lives in Stage One were relatively unhappy or even the unhappiest of their lives. This contrasts with the finding that the early years of marriage are the best for many young couples – though not necessarily sexually. This apparent contradiction can be explained when one sees that Stage One is, for most men, the best *and* the worst time of their lives, depending on which area one looks at.

The best and the worst

Perhaps one of the biggest disappointments for many men is that marriage and sex do not live up to their romantic expectations. This comes about for many reasons but mainly as a result of society's unrealistic portrayal of marriage; and the man's lack of skills in really understanding what people are like. A young man marries with all kinds of false expectations about his one-to-one bond just as most women go into the baby business with unduly romantic and somewhat unrealistic expectations. Both are in for disappointment.

Once the heady sexual attraction wanes and real life sets in most men come to compare their mothers with their wives, however unconsciously. To compare a twenty-three-year-old wife with this paragon of virtue is unrealistic and even cruel. Clearly a young woman just starting out is unlikely to have all the social, housekeeping, mothering and other skills of a much older woman. And it is unreasonable to expect that she should. Personal details of behaviour that are at odds with his views of 'how things should be' also grate. Her tights hanging in the bathroom, the way she eats a particular food, her views on working women, or whatever, all serve to show that he has, indeed, married someone who is a million miles from the other love-bonded female in his life.

Having said all this he still wants her to behave in a somewhat 'motherly' way towards him and the two models of womanhood are, to say the least, confusing.

In today's young marriages the sexes play much more equal roles around the home but even so women still do the majority of the housework and similar domestic chores. This shifting of roles in itself

OVERLEAF: *Many men surprise themselves by being very much better at fathering than they thought. Lessons on intimacy learned here can often enrich their one-to-one bond.*

It can be a rude awakening for the young man who starts to live with a woman – especially if he has had no sisters to prepare him.

comes as something of a shock to many a young man who imagined, however unconsciously, that his wife would run around him and serve him endlessly.

At this stage things are often none too rosy on the sexual front either. Clinical experience shows just how many young couples have problems sexually as they get to know about one another and about sex generally. The early years, whilst often full of genital activity, are also full of traumas and misunderstandings as each feels their way round the other's personality. This all takes time and can be very painful. Sex problems abound at this time, especially early on in Stage One. Many a woman of this age is not orgasmic, either at all (during masturbation) or during intercourse. Men believe that their young, sexy wife will be having multiple orgasms from penis-in-vagina thrusting alone whereas reality is usually very different. This must be one of the commonest problems on which I receive letters in my capacity as an 'Agony Aunt'.

It can take many years for all this to settle out and a great deal of patience and love is called for on the part of both partners if they are to survive and be able to build on this phase in preparation for the next.

During this first stage of a man's adult life he usually also becomes a father. This starts off by his imagining that all he wants is a family and ends up with the stark realisation that for a woman having a child is the most disorganising event, psychosexually speaking, in her life. Things are never the same again and this takes a lot of handling.

For many a young man then the pressures of setting up a career, a home and a deep inter-personal relationship are great. It is all an enormous effort and the rewards may not be anything like what he had hoped. Financial responsibility, buying a home and coping with his wife's loss of earnings on the arrival of their first child all add fuel to the flames and many a young man is almost at breaking point as a result.

It is hardly any surprise that many men look back and ask themselves how they ever got through it. The answer is probably that they only did so by the skin of their teeth because they were young and healthy and because they were driven by their own expectations to 'do what a man has to do'.

Stage two

This stage in a man's life is more settled, more tranquil and more satisfying. Things are now beginning to come right for him. His wife is more at ease with herself, her sexuality, and her children; the worst of the young childhood days are over or nearly so. He is starting to see some results at work for his efforts since he left school; he has at least some time to enjoy his hobbies or other activities that are not work; and so on.

Now he can see what is possible in the world for him as a man, a lover and a father. He has enough maturity to be able to cope with the world and its difficulties and can see where his niche in society is likely to be. His family and friends are a source of pleasure, if hard work, to him and his wife gives him increasing pleasure as she herself comes into her own. Most women find that whatever their starting point sexually they are at their best in their late thirties and early forties as their inhibitions fall away and they build a more mature relationship with their partner. This period from the mid-thirties to the early forties is a good one for many men. This is just as well because the next stage can be the most difficult to negotiate and one that can profoundly influence the pattern of the rest of their lives.

Stage three

As I have already pointed out this is a time for looking in both directions and, as a result, many men become disenchanted both with what they have achieved and what they realise they never will. Just how much of this is the result of a sort of male menopause no one knows.

The male menopause is a much discussed and disputed subject. In women the sex hormones and egg-producing ovaries start to fail in the late forties and this produces profound changes, both physical and emotional. However, in men such gross changes don't occur. In some men, a fall in testosterone can produce fatigue, headaches, loss of confidence, irritability, difficulty with concentration, insomnia, palpitation, and impotence. Hot flushes are rare but chills and attacks of sweating can occur. In some cases psychiatric treatment may be necessary but the symptoms listed here respond to testosterone treatment.

The mid-life crisis

Much more common than any 'true menopause' (or perhaps part of it), is the mid-life crisis. It can occur very suddenly. An individual sexual failure, a sexual or other rejection, or one of many other apparently trivial triggers can make a man feel dissatisfied, inadequate and insecure. He then begins to generalise about his life and soon his self-confidence fades and he begins to dwell on the unattainable hopes of his youth and the futility of his life. Things such as his balding scalp serve only to confirm that he is over the hill, and on the downhill run to the grave.

Physically he is out-performed by younger men, and new ventures, once exciting, now produce anxiety and even horror. Mental functioning may begin to fail and many say that they count time by what is left, rather than by what they have so far achieved. Even the slightest failure in life seems like a tragedy.

In a family where the man is the sole breadwinner he may see himself as undervalued, unimportant and even irrelevant except as a walking wallet, with no one really caring about him. To his children he is simply a source of money, his wife has little interest in him (she runs much of the family's life) and he may feel emasculated by it all. Sex has become a routine bore and his wife stimulates him less and less.

Some men, faced with all this, rebel. They abscond, temporarily or permanently; become hostile to their women; their whole existence, and everything about it becomes a burden; and little meets with their approval. Their women are seen as unloving and unlovable.

Part of this rebellion takes the form of extra-marital sex, usually with a younger woman who, he says, has the warmth and understanding that have for so long been lacking in his relationship. The new woman is interested in him and usually admires him for what he has achieved, partly because of his age. She involves him in the lives of her young friends and he feels invigorated by it all.

Such relationships can be successful but more often this scenario lasts but a short time and the relationship collapses.

It could be argued that on balance an older woman is better for the middle-aged man than is a young one. Many a young woman is still sorting out her own sexuality and may still be inhibited about sex in certain, or indeed many, ways. A more mature woman, on the other hand, has more to offer and is thus better able to massage such a man's flagging ego.

Other men at this stage of life regress to adolescent behaviour. But now they have the money, opportunity and knowledge to be able to indulge their adolescent fantasies with some vigour. Such men easily become promiscuous, partly as a sort of last minute panic attempt to prove that their virility and attractiveness to women really aren't failing. Because if they were it would appear that life itself was slipping by.

'Perverse' fantasies are common and deviant needs may come to light. Homosexual, transvestite, trans-sexual, or paedophiliac yearnings are not altogether uncommon. A latent sadistic trait may show as a sudden interest in bondage and restraint, or even in anal sex. Some of this can be a sign of all too obvious aggression towards a 'failing' spouse but often it is more complex than this.

The mid-life crisis can last for years and the future for such marriages is often bleak. Sometimes, the man goes for a very sudden divorce, which comes as a surprise even to his partner.

All of this seems very depressing, and sometimes it is. Possible solutions include seeking professional help for sexual problems the couple cannot resolve themselves; investing more in the relationship so as to gain a secure base; finding activities from which the satisfaction of success can be gained; and trying to resist bad feeling such as despair, depression and self-pity.

However, against all this it must be remembered that the middle years of marriage can with luck, knowledge, communication and planning, be better than the early years with all the stresses of childcare. Opportunities for friendship and an enriched sex-life are available for all those who are able to see the possibilities and seize them.

Those men who go through these difficult times with the greatest ease turn out to be those who had difficult childhoods, according to a survey of thousands of US men. Such men, it was found, knew very well how bad life could be and were intensely realistic about mid-life crisis-type situations. They had been there before when they were young. They were thus able to tolerate stress and disappointment more easily than those men with enchanted childhoods. *Those who do well*

Men with a strong sense of responsibility for others also seem to do well. Such men look outside themselves and their relationships for advice, and turn their thoughts to the needs of others as a way of dealing with their own troubles. It has also been found that men who have few inhibitions and few worldly achievements do very well at this stage of life. Perhaps some of the worst cases one sees are those men who realise that they will never be able to achieve their childhood ambitions and yet cannot gracefully accept it as a fact. Life, for them, seems to hold little promise and with so little to lose they feel drawn to disruptive behaviour that even in their more immature days would have seemed daft.

An additional burden at this time can, of course, be the man's problems with his wife's menopause. For some quite normal and happy men this can be a burden that drives them to a crisis that has little to do with them themselves.

Once through these storms, perhaps and hopefully with the help of his wife, a man now usually settles down to a calm period leading up to retirement. He is as far up the ladder as he will ever be, he accepts this and enjoys the fruits of his lifetime's labours and starts to enjoy his latter years with his wife.

Stage four

Time for themselves again

The fifties, once the menopause is over, can be a good decade. Most couples now have few or no children at home and have time for themselves again. There is usually no worry about contraception and unwanted pregnancies and most men are tolerably settled in their jobs and realise that a change is fairly unlikely.

Some men of this age are still going through their mid-life crisis and trying to find their lost youth among the young. This is a time when such men have an affair with a girl young enough to be their daughter. Such relationships rarely have a future, except where the girl's psychosexual make-up is such that she continues to need a father figure. The older man fills this role and they can often be happy, at least for a while, until the woman matures.

One of the best things about the fifties is that the couple often now have a combination of time and money – perhaps for the first time in their lives. They can afford the odd meal out, weekend away, holiday abroad together and so on and many couples take the opportunity to embark on a whole new romantic life together. Unfortunately, many women don't see their new freedom in this way at all. They have spent the last twenty years or more devoting themselves to their children and see themselves primarily as mothers, not as independent women. Some such women now do very badly because their whole purpose in life has gone and they can see no other role for themselves.

This is the basis of the 'empty nest syndrome' and such women often become very depressed as the bottom falls out of their lives. Slowly some of them transfer their mothering skills, the only skills and abilities they think they have, to caring for grandchildren, for others, for animals, or even for their husbands.

Increasingly more and more *men* will be affected by this syndrome as they make larger investments of time and emotion in their families.

But as the fifties progress, or even sooner depending on the man's employment, it makes sense to start to plan for retirement. Some look forward to it because they cannot wait to start to do with their lives exactly what they most want. Others begin to mourn the loss of their jobs because they find their work the best thing in their lives. Most men have 'worked' at everything all their lives, including their family, friends and their sex life and when it comes to retirement they simply carry on in the only way they know – 'working' at everything.

All of this makes the pre-retirement years a vital planning time for a couple if they are to enjoy their last years together fruitfully. When researchers have looked around the world at apparently contented and valued old men what they have found is that such men are involved in their community in a meaningful way and that they have active sex lives. This then is a time for a man to start making friends, perhaps for the first time ever, to look to the community around him as a source of interest and support, and to enrich his sex life. These are sure-fire foundations for a happy retirement and can make even poor health (which will be less likely if this path is followed) easier to cope with.

Sexual changes

Perhaps this would be a good place to look at the changes that occur in a man's sexuality when he reaches middle-age.

Sexual decline starts in men at about the age of eighteen but progresses very slowly. For most the decline is not very great by middle-age and things continue much the same as before with a few alterations that affect them in rather different ways. Here are some of the main things a man or his partner will come across in middle-age.

It will take longer to achieve an erection. Most men over forty take longer to get an erection than they used to. The novelty of sex has waned to some extent and hormone levels aren't as high. Most men of this age need quite a lot of direct penile stimulation during foreplay if they are to become erect when they or their partner want them to. Undoubtedly, some men see this as the beginning of the end and worry about it – but they shouldn't – it's perfectly normal. Some women misread this sign and imagine that it has something to do with their loss of attractiveness to the man, or even that he has lost interest in her.

The cure is obvious but the main problem is that some women, as a result of their unconscious, and even conscious, attitudes towards such matters are quite unable to rub or suck the penis. As a result, sex suffers. Such a relationship worked well when the man could be relied upon to erect with little or no genital stimulation from his partner but now intercourse may be impossible. The man may become increasingly anxious about each failure and eventually avoid sex altogether, except in his mind.

Many such men lose their sexual confidence to such an extent that finally erection becomes impossible even in self-masturbation. The partner of such a man then often feels rejected and becomes querulous which makes the problem worse. She'll often refuse to join the man when he seeks treatment, saying that she is willing enough to have sex, in the sense of being penetrated, so if it doesn't happen it must be the fault of the man and not her. As a result, no progress can be made and the man must either give up intercourse or seek another – often younger – partner. In this way the original partner is, thanks to her sexual mis-education in childhood, her own worst enemy. However, such a woman can be in a difficult situation. When she sees the declining capacity of the man to erect as a reflection on her declining attractiveness, she may re-double her efforts to seduce him and put him off by seeming to be over-demanding. The rule to follow in both instances is to take her cue from the man.

Take her cue from the man

Erections may not be so hard. The rock pillar of the twenties is often replaced by a rather less rigid structure in middle age. This need not produce any direct problems and shouldn't be interpreted by the woman as a sign that her man has gone off her or is having sex elsewhere. Either can, of course, be true but it's harmful to jump to such conclusions when the change is perfectly normal.

The way around it is to increase the amount or quality of penile stimulation and to enrich the man's fantasy life so as to supplement psychological as well as physical stimulation. This may involve using some 'perverted' activities in foreplay as most men's fantasies include at least some such pursuits. This is why some men at least, seek anal sex, sex games and so on, more as they get older. They increase their level of arousal and help combat the effects of age.

It takes longer to get an erection and then ejaculate. While the increased time to erection can be a nuisance for some couples, it is usually more than compensated for by the fact that, once erect, the man can last much longer. This is especially pleasant for the woman who needs more time and more vaginal stimulation to achieve orgasm. Some women, as a result of the longer-lasting erection of this age, have better orgasms than ever and some even become orgasmic in intercourse for the first time in their lives. However, as a result of the effects of the menopause, some women can't tolerate such vaginal friction. They should seek treatment if this is a problem.

Once a middle-aged man has had an erection or has ejaculated he will usually be unable to do so again very quickly.

Ejaculation may not be necessary at all. Most younger men are trigger-happy but in middle age things slow down, as we have seen. Not only does it take longer to reach orgasm but many middle-aged men say that they don't mind if they ejaculate or not. Some men see this as a problem, but 'no-come intercourse' has its rewards and is by no means unpleasant for the man or his partner, provided that she knows that he intends not to let himself reach orgasm.

Using this capacity older men can, if they wish, have intercourse several times a day, only permitting themselves to ejaculate on the last occasion. In this way, such a man can maintain rates of intercourse which would be impossible if he ejaculated every time.

Even in self-masturbation, older men tend to ejaculate on fewer occasions, simply enjoying the pleasures of stimulating the penis and the associated fantasies instead. In this respect they parallel younger women, many of whom, due to their upbringing, can enjoy the stimulation that intercourse or masturbation provides but cannot reach a strong, identifiable orgasm.

Ejaculation is less powerful. This is especially noticeable past the age of sixty but the change starts earlier. This doesn't necessarily mean that orgasms are any less pleasurable. Pre-ejaculatory secretion tends to be less and the initial ejaculatory spurt, which can travel several feet in younger men, disappears.

Sex drive falls. Most men past forty want to have intercourse less often than they did in their youth. This is particularly so for men over sixty. Some middle-aged men find that they enjoy sex more and can perform better in the morning rather than in the evenings, after a tiring day at work. There is a generally-held, but erroneous view that sex is

Once erect, the man can last much longer

For the man who has been a 'boy' all his life, retirement can be the final run of boyhood as his wife now looks after him nearly full-time, as she did her own children. For some, of course, this works well as some women never really get over the loss of their children and seek to replace them with others who need mothering.

I hope that this, albeit brief, skirmish with the lifecycle of an average man has given the reader at least some small glimpse of a man's sexual cycles over a lifetime.

It is often said that sex is for the young but there is considerable truth on the reverse of the coin which says that sex is wasted on the young! Today's average couple will have as many years together alone without their children as they did with them. In fact with families getting smaller all the time and most people living together longer than ever I feel that we should spend more time planning our lives together as couples on a long-term basis and this, of course, means taking a much more long-term view of sex. Looked at this way the hard work of learning about one another in the twenties and early thirties, the consolidation of the next ten years and even the strife of the mid-life storms that so many men experience can all be put into some kind of perspective for a happy and durable friendship, with sex, that can last from the fifties well into the seventies and beyond.

x is wasted on the young!

debilitating and many such men refrain from morning sex for fear that they'll be exhausted at work. Because of this unfounded fear and their tiredness in the evenings, they shut down on sex completely. The answer is to perfect no-come intercourse and to make time for it in the morning.

Older men are more tolerant of sexual frustration and this may be one reason why rows begin to decline but, as I pointed out earlier, it is often the woman who experiences frustration and this can make her quarrelsome and depressed.

Sexual function can no longer be taken for granted. As we have seen, the penis no longer springs to either its master's or its mistress's service automatically. This means that if sex is to be enjoyed, or even possible at all, a lot more scene-setting has to be done. The investment usually pays off handsomely, though with a longer-lasting erection that need not necessarily end in orgasm.

Stage five

But to return to our last stage in a man's life. Retirement depends very greatly on the woman being able to adapt to having her husband at home in her domain, perhaps for the majority of the day and night. She may well be adjusting to retirement herself and so has a double problem. Obviously at first she will continue as before as queen of her castle but a well-balanced couple will now start to share the domestic tasks, so that the man has a role in the home that is meaningful to him. In some households there can actually be a role reversal of a kind as the man enjoys his home, perhaps for the first time ever.

For some couples, whatever the state of their sexual lives at this stage of their marriage, the very fact of being together so much can be an intolerable burden. But just because a couple are retired doesn't mean that they have to spend all their time together. It makes sense for each to keep the individual activities and interests that they had before. After all, we owe it to ourselves to retain a sense of autonomy as unique human beings if only because we never know when our partner will die and we will have to go on living our own lives.

For the man who finds the domestic world somewhat strange his wife can take on a totally new role and even a quite assertive man who would not be told anything during his working life can change to become compliant, helpful and ever eager to please. Needless to say this has interesting and often beneficial effects on their sexual life.

In a sense, of course, women do not retire, as many of my patients never cease to tell me. A man may stop his work and the couple's life continue pleasantly because of his pension or their savings, but a woman's work goes on much as before until she is too old or ill to continue with it. In this sense we have come full-circle because given that men tend to die younger their wives often outlive them. So it is that many women see the new generation into the world *and* see their partners out of it.

WORK – THE MOST IMPORTANT THING IN LIFE?

The breadwinners

Of all the areas of a man's life, the one that many women find most difficult to understand is his work. Not only do many women know little in detail of what their partners actually do but men and women view work somewhat differently. This has all kinds of effects on the couple both in and out of the workplace, especially now that women are more active here than ever before. This in itself has altered the balance of men's view on work and such changes are reflected in man-woman relationships, and hence in their sexual lives together.

To men work is a sort of game, even if it is not an entirely enjoyable one. Having said this no one should be fooled into thinking that because it is a game it is not important. On the contrary, to most men work rates as the pastime of highest value to them. While many women, when asked, say that the most important thing to men is sex in fact experience shows that it is not. Work is far more important . . . followed closely by love.

Work – a sort of game

By and large men are still the breadwinners in our culture and are expected to be the major producers of wealth both for the community and for the family. Obviously there are many exceptions to this generalisation but it is true nonetheless.

Women are, of course, increasingly active in the workplace today with over fifty-eight percent of US women working either full or part-time.

However, as a 1987 study of social attitudes found, the vast majority of people think that the traditional domestic system in which the father goes out to work full-time and the mother stays at home to look after children under five, is preferable. In fact only three per cent of those asked thought that in such families both parents should go out to work full-time. Even when the family has teenage children fewer than one in five parents said that they thought both parents should work full-time. Most favoured a father in full-time work and the mother working part-time.

We hear a lot about women working, and of course a book such as this is no place to go into the pros and cons of the subject except inasmuch as it affects couples and their relationships, but overall it is a fact that UK opinion is still very traditional on the matter. According to the above survey, a carefully controlled study that is repeated every year on a sample of more than 3,000 scientifically selected people to represent the whole country's social mix, the ideal family consists of a breadwinner father, a home-maker mother and their two children.

LEFT: *It may well have been 'hell at the office' but how much of that will be taken back home?*

That many women work, even full-time is, of course, a fact but this freedom to work if the couple has children, is often hard-won and the woman often feels torn between her dual roles, each with their expectations, some of which at least are conflicting. That this is hard for many women is borne out by the conflicts it creates within their relationships with their men. The effects of such a lifestyle on a couple's sex life is highly debated with some studies finding that dual-career couples have a better sex life and others that they have a worse one.

Much of what men find themselves having to do on a day-by-day basis is often boring, uninteresting, and unrewarding yet they are compelled to do it, as they see their partners apparently having far more of a choice as to how active they are in the workplace. Many a man has told me with some anger that *he* had no choice about giving up work to become a father – he had to keep on with his job while his wife seemed to have a freedom to select a far more rewarding life having the best of both worlds, working when she wanted and then perhaps taking several years off to have a family.

As increasing numbers of men become more involved with family matters and find that they enjoy it, society's views may have to shift to reduce the pressure on men to work to support their families.

For many men the only reward for their work is the money they are paid. For most this is not sufficient a reward and there is plenty of evidence that men value their job in terms of its worth to them as personalities much more highly than they rate the actual amount of money they receive for it.

Given that working for money alone could so easily end up as a sort of mindless slavery, men have turned the workplace into a clever set of games which make even ordinary tasks appear dangerous, risky, worthwhile, addictive, hazardous to their health, and so on. In a sense this is a continuation of what they did as little boys when running clubs and gangs. There are initiation ceremonies, tests of strength, a sense of belonging, a sense of being different from, and better than, girls, and so on.

Mindless slavery

In other words men, quite unconsciously, create an infrastructure of 'work' that validates their having to do it day-after-day for most of their lives. These tactics make the 'work' bearable and even enjoyable. For some men work becomes so enjoyable that nothing else in life can match up to it.

None of this is necessary for most women because they know, deep down, that they have a meaningful and valuable place in the order of things . . . their reproductive and child custodial roles. There are, of course, some women who work with the same dedication as men do before and even after they have their children or, in some cases, instead of having or looking after their children, but even some of the apparently happy and most dedicated are often not so, as clinical experience shows all too vividly. True, most such women would not want to be full-time housewives and mothers but few find the combination of dedicated work and a family easy.

The attraction of powerful men

Work is about power too of course, not just about making money. Men construct systems, as we have seen, that create power balances even within the smallest of organisations. An ambitious man feels under a lot of pressure to do something in life and much of this often involves the seeking and wielding of power. Men and women are attracted to powerful men yet both are usually wary of powerful women.

By making work their centre of power and time investment many men find that home becomes little more than a servicing area – a sort of physical and possibly emotional pit-stop. Many middle-class men in the Western world see little of their children or indeed of their wives, especially if they commute into large cities every weekday. For some men family life is a weekend affair and, for a few, weekends are so valuable to unwind from the ravages of the week that family life takes a back seat even then.

Such a major investment in a job makes men terribly vulnerable to the loss of it. More men commit suicide in the US after the loss of their job than do so after the loss of a child or a spouse. Men lose very much more than a means of financial support when they lose their job.

A woman's place

All of this is somewhat confusing to many women who, because most of them cannot see work in the same way, find it hard to understand why men should, or even could. Most, even quite successful, career women who have a family, feel an almost constant pull between the conflicting demands of home and work and most of them feel at least somewhat guilty at leaving their 'real job' – that of housewife and mother. This in itself can produce tensions in today's family home because modern women have been brought up to think that they *ought* to be working outside the home. At least some of those who greatly enjoyed working before they had children resent what they perceive to be their husband's 'luck' at being able to continue 'doing his thing'. This can damage even a good marriage. Needless to say such resentments, however unconscious, eat away at the relationship and can have effects that are harmful in the bedroom.

When it comes to women at work men have a pretty dim view of the subject. However men rationalise the matter, it usually doesn't take long to discover that they resent females getting in on the act – except, of course, in that they, the women, service the men. Those working in personnel often say that men find it difficult to relate well to women at work, even if the men are managers. Men tend naturally to take the lead at work, as elsewhere, and this often excludes women on their progression up the career ladder. True, exceptional women get through the minefield to the top but it takes greater effort and skill when compared with a man's. A major US executive dating agency for successful career women over forty finds it extremely difficult to find partners for what would, at first sight, appear to be exciting, high-earning, ambitious, women who are full of personality. Clearly men of this age would rather seek out less intimidating and younger partners.

When women succeed the work they do is sometimes presented as if it were done by the man above them, whereas a similar job done by another man would be praised and valued because the younger man would reflect on the managerial skills or training ability of the older. In this, and indeed in almost all areas of competition at work, younger men are more threatened by women than are older ones. Perhaps the older ones are wiser; perhaps they have given up the rat race; or perhaps they have less to prove than do their younger colleagues.

The low value men place on females at work is naturally reflected in their lower pay and although things are certainly changing for the better there's still a long way to go.

Men and alternative child care

While it is usually taken for granted that it is the woman in a partnership who organises alternative child care if she wants to go out to work this does not mean that her husband is unaffected by the decision.

A book such as this is no place to go into the battle that rages over this subject but suffice it to say that most young men claim that they believe that whatever women in general do *their* woman will stay at home and look after their children, at least until they go to school. When reality dawns things can become very sticky as the man sees his wife let him and his child down. This is just one of the many nettles that has to be grasped by any couple in which the woman with young children intends to work.

Many men whose children end up with minders or even with nannies express at least some concern about it being second best. Shattered images of motherhood They are only too aware that another woman will have her own ideas, set of values, behaviours and so on that their child will start to absorb. This creates more pressure as he tries to balance what he sees as best for his wife's career and their income with the best interests of his child. Understandably, many such men are torn in two as they try to please everybody. All too often, of course, as in so many other similar situations, the man backs out and leaves the whole thing to his wife as he resigns himself to yet another shattered image of the way he thought things would be. Some couples try to organize a lifestyle in which only they look after their children but this is impractical for most. In reality most men decide to settle for second-best care in the hands of someone else.

Sexual opportunity

Many men working with attractive women find that they view almost every meeting as a sexual encounter. Many find it nearly impossible to turn off the hunter-hunted stereotype and as a result end up flirting rather more than they should; using patronising language; or, more commonly, excluding women so that none of this gets in the way of the matters in hand.

This highlights the dilemma many men have with their view of women generally – they find it hard to see a woman as tough and able to make decisions at work *as well* as being soft, warm and feminine. The combination of masculine and feminine characteristics seems to be a difficult or even impossible one for most men to deal with in any individual woman at work. Could it be that such a combination would

Mum's off out to work but is she – or her husband – entirely happy with their child care arrangements?

be too powerful for them, realising, as they do, that women have such a sexual and emotional hold over them in the domestic setting!

Let's look at some of the ways in which men's sexuality affects them at work and then at how all of this affects men's relationships with their partners.

We have seen that work has much to do with power for men and this certainly links in with their sense of masculinity. Work is at the heart of most men's sexual identity and so at work men deal with women as women, not simply as co-workers. Successful men seem to attract women. This means that for many men, and especially those who have any control over their progress along their career path, their promotion at work brings increasing esteem in the eyes of not only their male colleagues but also their female ones.

In any workplace there will be a whole range of 'sexual' activities going on at any one time. Some people will be flirting; some men will be sexually harassing women; other couples will be dating; some men exploiting their positions of power and influence to achieve sexual, if not genital ends; and some men will be indulging in 'sexual' horseplay with other men.

Clearly work is an important place for human sexuality to find an outlet. Most people meet their spouse at work or whilst pursuing their hobbies, so clearly the workplace is a sort of unofficial dating agency. Men will usually tend to maximise the sexual implications of any situation involving women at work and sometimes, of course, this is very welcome. It is exactly what the woman wants. Indeed, when talking with women about going back to work after having their family, many honest ones say that it is mixing with the opposite sex that is one of the things they have missed while at home.

The chances of falling in love with someone you actually work with is far greater than doing so with someone in the next department. Familiarity seems to be a major factor in such romances, according to several studies.

When things go wrong with workplace romances it is the woman who tends to come off worst. She gets the sack or is moved to another department while the man's position and working lifestyle usually remains unchanged.

Sexual harassment of women

Perhaps the most overtly negative facet of sexuality at work is that involving the sexual harassment of women by men. It can destroy workplace morale, often quite insidiously. Harassment occurs at every level of business from the boardroom to the shop floor. It takes the form of suggestive looks; the obtrusive display of pin-ups; making remarks about a woman that are just that bit too personal; talking about a woman's body or parts of it; 'accidentally' touching or brushing past a woman; the telling of sexy jokes; repeated requests for dates; pinching or squeezing; and much more. At least one in ten women have been subjected to some sort of persistent sexual harass-

ment at work, according to one UK study and another found that about half had been harassed at some time or another during their working lives.

Sexual harassment at work has little or nothing to do with forming a relationship with the woman, it is almost certainly more to do with men 'doing what comes naturally', as they see it. To many men all women are fair game and the fact that many are kept corralled in close proximity at work simply makes the task of hunting easier. It is just a part of the boy-like behaviour that many men feel they can indulge in all their lives.

Unfortunately for employers such behaviour is very wasteful of staff. One UK employment agency found that more than half of all women bothered in this way changed jobs because of it. For some of these women not only did they experience such behaviour from managers and colleagues they also had to deal with unwelcome advances from customers. In general, the more men and women work together the more the harassment.

All-male physical games

Perhaps the most baffling boys' games occur between men. In many all-male situations men play silly physical games with one another. These are especially found among young men at colleges, prisons or in military barracks, for example. The horseplay that is characteristic of such behaviour takes the form of physical 'fighting'; games that involve a lot of physical contact; the grabbing of genitals; the pinching of bottoms; and so on.

The main characteristics of this type of workplace sexuality is that women are generally unavailable. It is said that it is a way that men, left to their own and without the 'civilising' influence of women, behave. Without this restraining force many men resort to making degrading comments about women; to telling coarse jokes; to demean marriage and family; and to knocking homosexuality while behaving in a somewhat 'homosexual' way. Much of this common lore takes the place of true friendship but the bond between men who think and behave in the same way can be strong, if short-lived. In this kind of environment men seem to have a need to prove not only that they can be tough and mete out physical or verbal abuse to others but also that they are 'man enough' to take the same treatment from others. The lives of those who do not conform can be made near impossible.

Men 'uncivilised' without women

That at least some of this behaviour is an expression of latent homosexuality cannot be doubted but it is much more likely to be a feature of immature personalities who feel weak as men or who have no opportunity to express their masculinity against the backdrop of femininity. As we have seen throughout the book, men's fears of their own feminine sides are vigorously and even savagely repressed both in themselves and others.

It has been claimed that there is more such horseplay in situations where men are de-skilled by machines, mainly because

RIGHT: *There are few ways in which men have cultural 'permission' to be physically intimate with one another. Horse-play at work and events such as this are just two.*

each man has less personal responsibility. It is also suggested that men who are on permanent shift-work are so separated from the real business of life, families, homes and so on that they are more likely to live in a twilight world of pseudo-homosexuality, even if it is not genitally expressed. It could, in my view, actually all be a cry from the heart to get close to someone when in fact they are feeling intensely alienated from everyone. Many men are excluded from caring for their children, by a combination of factors (not necessarily by their partners) and I have little doubt that this in itself is a de-humanising experience that can lead to odd behaviour such as male horseplay.

Unemployment

This situation has to some extent been worsened by the economic trend in the west in which unemployment is growing and the pressure on those in work mounts as they feel threatened by redundancies.

Then, of course, there is the man who is actually unemployed – his lot is not a happy one. Work and masculinity are so intertwined in our culture that many a man who is out of work really does see himself as less of a man. Impotence is not at all uncommon, albeit temporarily, and some men who are out of work for years become a shadow of their former selves in all dimensions of their lives. Sex is just one area that suffers. If their wife goes out to work the roles are reversed and in certain subsections of Western culture this is tantamount to castration.

That men find this hard to accept is confirmed, I believe, by the statistics that show that even if a woman goes out to work full-time she still does the vast majority of the housework and domestic tasks. Clearly many men take their turn but some, even when unemployed, still see their jobs as something other than taking care of the hearth and home. For many men this is all somehow linked with the 'dignity' of being a man. For many men only work can confer this dignity. This can only be compared, from my clinical experience, with the feelings of a woman who cannot conceive. Both appear to be almost mortally wounded in their views of themselves.

Interchangeable roles

I realise that it will take a generation or two yet but the only answer to many of the problems raised in this section is to bring children up to see male and female roles as much more interchangeable. It will also be vital to start thinking of men as having domestic, caring, loving, family-nurturing skills as well as their competitive, achieving, ambitious ones at work. Similarly, for women the view will have to be broadened so that an achieving woman can be seen also as a caring mother and wife and not as the 'ballsbreaker' she is so often cast as.

As more men have *no* work and more women enter the labour market things are set for even greater changes, many of which will have profound effects on the man-woman relationship.

OVERLEAF: *Whilst it is true that there are many females who are unemployed, a scene such as this will always tend to tear at the heartstrings of a man more than a woman.*

MARRIAGE – AN UNFORTUNATE NECESSITY?

iage suits men

In the Western world about ninety-five per cent of all those who are of marriageable age are, or have been, married. This is undoubtedly too high a percentage and I have no doubt that far fewer people should be married. Clearly, as judged by the failure rate, it is not a state for which everyone is suited. Indeed, marriage at this level is a recent phenomenon. As recently as the 1920s a substantial minority, of women in particular, would never get married and did not expect to. This occurred partly because of so many men being killed in wars and particularly in the first World War but also because so many women worked in service jobs where marriage was positively discouraged.

Today though most people expect to get married and from most of the studies it appears that the majority of men like it. Most men who are married want to stay married and it's easy to see why. Studies of mental and emotional health find that married men fare better than their unmarried counterparts (while the reverse is true for women). Most men quite consciously, let alone unconsciously, see that they have swapped a mother for a wife and some continue to behave little-boy-like in a somewhat dependent role in relation to the new woman in their life. Married men have many valuable (non-sexual) services provided for them by their wives – indeed modern western marriage suits men rather well. It is hardly surprising that they like it.

In a largely hostile world it should come as no surprise to learn that for many men the safety, stability and caring offered by home life comes high on their list of perceived advantages of marriage. Being able to share with someone; companionship and other homely virtues are all rated highly, yet men all too often fail to communicate these feelings to their partners mainly because they find it hard or impossible to communicate anything much about emotions to anyone.

Of course marriage is a convenient forum within which sex can happen but this is usually rated low by men. Could this be linked to the high extra-marital sex figures?

For some men it is the unique individual to whom they are

married that makes marriage what it is for them but it appears that for most this is not so. Many men say that valuable though their woman is, she is not any more uniquely able to fulfil their needs than is any other woman with similar attributes. There is some evidence that younger men are thinking of their partnerships as a source of personal growth and their wives as their help-mates in this quest but it would be foolish to claim that this attitude is common.

It appears that most men get married because it is what society expects of them. It is still the only acceptable way to obtain a culturally-sanctioned sex partner and for many men love and companionship come high on the list, as we have seen.

An uncomfortably common problem in marital therapy is the man who, quite unconsciously, comes to view his wife differently once he is married to her. Given that we live in a culture that still sees sex

She's doing her best to attract his attention but she doesn't stand a chance against baseball.

as a negatively tinged subject, it is hardly surprising that many, if not most, of us think of sex as naughty, dirty, or sinful, however unconsciously.

So it is that a couple who have intercourse before marriage (and that is the vast majority) will have been doing something that is strictly unacceptable however much they might justify the behaviour to themselves or to others. Such a couple then are 'illicit' lovers, even if they are engaged. Many's the girl who, after perhaps years of intercourse with her betrothed will decide to 'lay off sex' for a month or two before the wedding (white of course) so that she can pretend, in however symbolic a way, that she is really still a virgin.

This story can also take another twist. Most couples when first married, spend their sexual lives together as if they were lover and mistress. And then most couples decide to start a family. Now the woman changes her role and becomes a mother.

Pregnancy and the first baby can be a trying time for many men. For more on this see the next chapter on *Family*.

Motherly wives

There is an element in most marriages that reflects the mother-son relationship the man used to have and many men see their wife as a sort of latter-day mother who controls them, stops them misbehaving, and treats them like one of the children. There can be little doubt that some women because of the way *they* were brought up, seek to treat their husbands in a motherly way even to the point of putting them down in front of others. Just how much this is an unconscious game that suits both partners varies from marriage to marriage but in many it is highly destructive as the man is passed from one mother figure to another at the altar rail. Such a man rarely feels able to be himself and anger and resentment simmers just beneath the surface to emerge in the shape of anti-social behaviour, alcoholism, extra-marital sex, or even frank hostility and physical violence. The only hope for such a couple is to seek professional help to sort out their relationship and put it onto a more balanced footing in which both behave as co-equals.

Despite all the bad press that marriage has received, it is still enormously popular, with almost everyone who fails trying again in one way or another. Men are especially keen to try again mainly, in my opinion, because they are such romantics; because they fall in love so easily; and because they don't have a woman's insights into what the problems were that made the first marriage fail. As a result of all this second marriages have higher failure rates than do first ones.

Marriage suits men well, indeed it has been largely designed to do so – by men of course. That many *women* are now questioning much of this is causing a great deal of concern to men everywhere. Perhaps the most glaring example is that of women and work.

When men talk about their own partners working their major concern is that their lives won't be altered in any material way. In other words, however liberated men may appear to be today the vast majority do not want their personal creature comforts disturbed or curtailed by their wives working. A woman's place is still seen to be in the home, even though half of them work, many full-time.

In almost all households women still do the majority of the domestic work even if they work full-time too. A man, when he returns from a day's work is always more tired than a woman is after her day's work because by definition men's work is more arduous and demanding! It is thus only fair, a man argues, that she should look after him and the home too, even if the family need her money to survive.

She's had a hard day at the office but guess who'll be cooking the meal?

All of this ferments quietly in the background of many a marriage and explodes from time to time in rows. Often the subject of the woman's work appears to be the cause of the battle but in fact there is really a cold war hovering in the background and the causes of this are what really need to be dealt with.

I deal with the question of men and work in the chapter on *Work*.

When a woman gets married her life changes dramatically. At a stroke she becomes 'other-centred' and expects to devote most of her life from then on to caring for others. Needless to say the most important 'other' is often her husband – or so he thinks.

When a man marries no such similar transformation occurs, except perhaps to curtail his wandering eye sexually and to become more domestically orientated than before.

Legally a woman still remains 'inferior' to her husband and in most households this position is further reinforced by the man seeing himself as basically superior to his wife. She, he argues, is there to ensure his general wellbeing, and later that of his children. In the pursuit of this lifestyle she sees her world shrink so that she soon comes to describe herself as 'only a housewife' while her husband goes on to create a better world for himself. As a result, more wives than single women are depressed, passive and phobic, according to one major study, which also found that three times as many married women showed severe neurotic symptoms as did the unmarried.

'Only a housewife'

While the average man is growing in his job his wife's skills and abilities receive little recognition from him. His views of what she does are understandably coloured by his male-dominated world and its values with the result that what she does is seen to be of little value. Men, when asked, talk about women's work at home as being low-status, time-consuming, and requiring some of the female qualities that they cannot understand but to call for little in the way of intelligence or initiative.

All of this means that many men see what their wives do as pretty low-grade stuff, not something they'd care to spend much time thinking about and certainly not something to be valued. Obviously such a man cannot view his wife as an equal because he would not demean himself to do such work and so the cycle is perpetuated.

What husbands do know though is that women seem to have the upper hand when it comes to emotions and they seem to be able to make life hell for a man if they want to. We look elsewhere at how men find themselves emotionally blackmailed and how angry this makes them. In many homes the wife in fact runs things from control of the finances to deciding where to send the kids to school, and organising the couple's social life.

Even if she works, in most homes it is the wife who maintains the family's emotional stability yet her husband rarely realises that this is going on and even when he does he doesn't rate the activity highly. Most men keep their emotions away from their wives and when they do open up, often after considerable effort from their wives, they expect the women to deal with them sensitively and not to subject them to too much scrutiny or to criticise them. Most men expect their wives to take their side in any dispute or argument at work, or elsewhere, often at the expense of their wives' opinions. Once more then men seek reassurance from their wives in a little boy-like way.

But though men expect all this from their wives they do not return the emotional support they receive. Women are generally more open about emotional matters so their husbands don't have to work away at prising out the truth and given their uneasiness with emotions, they don't feel they have to make much of an effort to

For too many couples this is seen as the pinnacle of their life rather than as the first step into the unknown together.

understand what is going on anyway. Most husbands are confused or even immobilised by their wives' emotional distress and many find the best way to deal with such matters is to remain uninvolved and, if possible, to deny the realities of the event.

It is probably this area more than any other that is the biggest problem zone for most men and their wives. Most men's masculine image of themselves contrasts harshly with their sulky dependence on their wives to deal with their own difficult emotions and their almost complete inability and passivity when it comes to helping their wives deal with theirs. So it is that in the vastly important areas of emotions most women are deeply disappointed in their men and see them as a sort of overgrown child who has to be dealt with gently and from whom they can expect little in return.

All this is tied in very deeply to men's inability, or near inability, to deal with intimacy. Men come to adulthood after years of training not to show feelings and certainly not to show weakness. That we all have to know our own weakness if we are to be strong is a bitter pill for many men to swallow. Alas, by never really knowing their weaknesses many men never truly understand themselves because they are living their lives on a superficial plane that denies so much that is real. By denying the pains and hurts of others, men also deny their own and in doing so they remain unable to become vulnerable.

When a man's wife makes emotional demands on him he can feel somewhat betrayed. He will often claim that he is working for her and the family and that he needs endless support rather than being upset or challenged in his intimate relationships. Many men say that given the tough world they operate in their women owe them loyalty rather than criticism so that they can compete successfully against other men. The wife who seeks to put emotional matters on the agenda is treated as a nuisance and many men sincerely hope that if they escape for long enough the subject will go away, hopefully for ever. This, of course, leads to terrible frustrations among women who are 'going mad' trying to get a matter off their chest.

Emotional matters a nuisance

The sadness of all this is that most men discount their own emotional needs and thus the need of others, yet to confront all this honestly renders the average man powerless because so much in the realm of the emotions cannot be changed by dint of hard work, money, effort, better organisation, or even rational thinking. Because the average husband feels so unskilled in this area he either absconds from the business entirely or sustains a pretence of being able to cope with emotions that he really doesn't begin to understand.

Being intimate with someone means being able to be truly vulnerable, to let one's defences down, and to remove one's mask. This is hard enough for anyone to do but is near impossible for many men except within the boundaries of a trusted loving and caring relationship. This is usually only to be found within marriage and is why for most men their partners are so important. It is in this trusted relationship that most men feel able, however inadequately, to become at least a little vulnerable.

Unfortunately, even in a good marriage some men still think that the woman might use this lowering of the mask against them as indeed some women do much to their discredit and to the detriment of their relationship. In an ideal world a married couple should be able to feel totally free to share with one another all their feelings without fear of loss of face or future recrimination.

For many men the only time that they really let the mask down and are themselves is in the context of sex. This is why, in my view, sex is seen as so central by many men. Women obtain the same end-point by other means, often with their friends. It is also why things seem so disastrous to men when sex goes wrong. One of the reasons men turn to pornography is that it offers excitement without responsibility and they do not have to become vulnerable. It is a way of being sexual without being intimate.

All of this is exceptionally sad in the context of marriage because here, if nowhere else, a man should feel able to be himself. We look on page 178 at how a woman can help her man express his emotions better and how to encourage him to be more vulnerable.

It was Nietzsche who said that in marriage a woman gives herself but the man adds to himself by taking her. There is little doubt that this is substantially true for many marriages. That so many fail when founded on such a basis is hardly any surprise. Successful marriages have no such implied master-servant relationship – the couple really believe that they are equal and help one another to reveal their deepest secrets and concerns in the knowledge that their love for one another will enable them to cope with what is shared.

Sex outside marriage

Of those men who have affairs, probably about eighty per cent, even if they don't end in intercourse, about one in six have one within the first year of marriage and about one in four do so within the first two years. Clearly there isn't much time for these men to have become bored, they have simply carried on behaving as if they were still single – at least in this respect. The early stages of married life are often very stressful for a couple as they learn to come to terms with being monogamous and living alongside another human being in so intimate a setting. It is well known that many of those who get divorced claim to have known that the relationship wouldn't work within the first year of marriage. Indeed clinical experience shows that a minority knew things were doomed well before the wedding yet they still went ahead with it. Such a couple clearly don't have a large investment in the partnership and either or both will be open to extra-marital activities.

Most men, when asked, do not feel regret or guilt about their affairs, especially if their wife doesn't know about them. Most men claim that their affairs have nothing to do with their marriage, or any problems or shortcomings within it. Few of us who work in the marital field would agree with this view. Most men understandably draw a distinction between affairs that are known about by their partner and those that are not.

Many men who have had secret affairs say that they think it did them good. They talk about the boost to their ego; how much more independent it made them feel; how it released them from the trap of marriage; and so on. For some who are sexually inexperienced before marriage an affair widens their knowledge and skills of both women in general and sex in particular and this could be said to be an advantage to the marriage. Indeed many such men say that it is. However, and far more commonly in my view, the 'other woman' serves to create dissatisfaction and longings most of which are quite unrealistic (if typically male), if only because it is unreasonable and unfair to

No guilt about affairs

Constant watchfulness and secrecy are both the life-blood and the horror of the clandestine affair.

compare a clandestine extra-marital affair with what is on offer at home. Forbidden fruit always tastes better.

Most men, when asked, say that they are not on the lookout for extra-marital sex but that if it presented itself they wouldn't fight off the woman too hard. This means that men *are* open to offers outside their marriage because there are many women who are sexually available and see almost all men, married or not, as fair game. Indeed to a certain type of female predator married men are *more* attractive not *less* so. In this sense it is other women who are the married woman's worst enemies not their 'weak' husbands. Clinical experience shows that most men would *like* to be monogamous (just as they are in favour of motherhood) but find it difficult, or even impossible, not to go in for a 'touch of' adultery from time to time.

Those men who feel guilty, and studies show that they are few, don't remain afflicted for long, even if their partner knows about the affair. This isn't too surprising given that in our culture males are supposed to 'put it about' before they are married. Clearly this attitude carries over into married life and men forgive themselves very quickly for affairs because they see them as a perfectly reasonable expression of 'the way real men behave'.

If a wife *knows* then clearly the story is somewhat different if only because the man now has to cope with her response to the affair. For some women the discovery that her man is having sex with another woman is seen as the end of the world, or at the very least the end of the marriage. While this usually says a lot about the woman and her personality there must also be at least some humbug here given that women are only half as likely as men to have an affair – statistically speaking.

On the contrary, it could be argued that because women fall in love with more difficulty than men and still by and large have sex only in the context of at least some love and affection, their affairs could be said to be much more serious and threatening to a marriage than a man's. Men, by and large, are not looking for a change of spouse when embarking on an affair. In fact, when men are asked about the matter, they usually say that there is no question of leaving their wife. That this is a simplistic and somewhat naïve view all too often becomes apparent as the man realises that the woman is not an inanimate object but has her feelings and needs too.

Women's affairs are more threatening

It is interesting that almost all men who have had an affair say that they liked it whatever the upheaval if they were found out. Only a very few men would not do the same again and most of these would probably shy away from a repeat performance only because of the adverse effects it had on their marriage. Having said this, a minority of men have affairs for exactly this reason. They know deep down that the marriage is a failure, or not what they perceive they want, and so quite unconsciously provoke an ending by behaving in a sexually disruptive way.

If a man does not tell his wife there is usually no adverse effect on the marriage. As we have seen, some men will be better (or less contented) lovers as a result but overall the effects are minimal. For some the affair enables them to continue with what, to them, appears to be an unworkable relationship. By having the occasional fling they keep the marriage ticking over. This, for many reasons, seems to them to be the most practical and sensible way to handle things, especially if there are children. Those men who find that their sexual and intimate lives have become boring, say that the injection of excitement and the ego boost makes them better with their wives all round, not just in bed and that this alone was a worthwhile outcome of the affair.

The effects on the relationship when the wife *does* know are unpredictable. For some women it is the last straw and they throw in the towel and go for a divorce. Others go out and have an 'I'll get even with you' affair themselves. For others their husband's affair is seen as a sort of sexual blackmail because they feel they now have to be more sexually active with him or he'll go off with someone else. Some see it as a spur to improvement – and indeed it might be. Certainly it is a foolish woman – or indeed man – who doesn't use a partner's affair seriously to take stock of the state of the relationship. This response is especially likely in the older woman for whom an alternative part-nership is not too likely should she be abandoned. Some women use their husband's affair to blackmail him into behaving better to them in other ways. This can take the form of threatening to leave with the children or withholding sexual favours within the marriage. At least some men end up paying dearly for their affairs as their women punish them financially and in other ways. Some marriages take years to heal after an affair.

A few women are actually pleased, however unconsciously, if their man has an affair, because they are, perhaps, not all that interested in sex and are glad that their husband will look elsewhere for physical relief yet return to the family nest for love, affection and to perform his other marital and family duties. It has to be remembered that not all women (or indeed men, for that matter) enjoy sex and in some such households the woman overlooks tell-tale signs that something is going on on the unconscious understanding with herself that she doesn't want to scupper the ship.

Having said this, men claim that even if their wife did know or was told about the affair the dishonesty did nothing to harm the relationship. Women, when asked, tend to think differently about this and say that the loss of trust is a major blow to the whole relationship. It is not for nothing that the term 'cheating' is so widely used.

Loss of trust

Surprisingly only a few marriages actually break up over an affair. Those that do were probably doomed anyway. This contrasts with the finding that most people put fidelity at the top of the list of their requirements of their spouse.

As we have seen throughout the book, men look to their wives as their main source of love in their life. When a man has an affair it is not usually love that he is seeking, or at least not consciously so. On the contrary, most men *say* that they deliberately try to keep love and sex separate. Unfortunately this is something of a vain hope because men fall in love so easily.

Although it is probably too glib to be the general rule I believe most men in having an affair think they want sex and find love; and most women think they want love and find sex. This isn't too surprising given our cultural stereotypes.

Most men do not, however, usually describe affairs as times when they are in love and almost all say that their love for their wife is greater than that for the other woman even at the height of the affair. Of course a man who, however unconsciously, is on the verge of leaving his wife or who is looking for another partner so that he can divorce her will be more likely than other men to be looking for, and finding, love in an extra-marital affair.

It is the belief of many men that since they need more sex than their partner can supply, and given that most men are having affairs, they are simply being normal by having more than one sex partner, if only from time to time.

Many men think that sex with the same woman over many years almost by definition becomes boring and lack-lustre. Of course for a few men things improve over the years and I do not believe that boredom need be a feature of long-term sexual relationships.

But boredom within marriage *is* common and could be due to the fact that most men, when asked, claim not to have married the woman who most excited them sexually. Most men say that one or other of their girlfriends was more sexually exciting or desirable but that they married the woman they did because she'd make a better wife. They settled for practicality rather than passion. Just how much of this is wishful thinking, is impossible to know but it could be that given men's perpetual dissatisfaction with their sexual lot they could simply be remembering an old flame as being more sexually interesting than was in fact the case.

Unfortunately, looking outside the one-to-one relationship is usually not an effective way of overcoming sexual boredom. Boredom *can* be overcome, as we shall see, but for most of us it is within our main relationship that this is best achieved.

Some men believe that monogamy is 'unnatural' and that it's quite unreasonable for their wives to expect them to be sexually faithful. Affairs to such men are the way that men behave if not artificially constrained by marriage.

Although a lot of wives also have affairs, most men find it difficult to believe. When they are faced with the fact as a stark reality they are often very negative and even hostile. While, they argue, it is 'natural' for a man to 'put it about' this is certainly not true for women in general and especially not for their wife, who is, after all, their 'property'. The implied criticism; the age-old dual standard; the social stigma of being cuckolded; the belief that because women don't just 'screw around' she must be in love; the threat to his love bond; and much more all make the discovery of a wife's infidelity threatening and even terrifying for many a man. He has invested all his love in her – how could she do this to him?

Such a response is understandable, if unfair. After all, we bring up youngsters to believe that girls and women have less of a sex drive than men and that women only have sex with a man if they are in love with him, so it is hardly surprising that men imagine that if their wife has an affair it must mean that she has fallen out of love with him and in love with another man. This, given that the average man looks to his wife as his main or sole supplier of love, can be pretty devastating.

Perhaps before leaving the subject of affairs we should consider casual sex for a moment. One-night stands and similar casual encoun- One-night stands ters contain no emotional component and certainly no friendship – they are seen as sex for its own sake. The vast majority of men do not like the idea of casual sex – and didn't even before the AIDS threat. This goes right against the old myth that a 'real man' should be ready for sex at any time and with any woman. But most men are not that easily interested in purely physical sex; and most say that promiscuity is unpleasant.

While, as we have seen, most men having affairs do not claim to be 'in love' with the woman involved they nevertheless want some sort of feelings and many are unconsciously on the lookout for love. Younger men who are still batchelors, whether in reality or at heart, are more likely to think positively about casual sex but most older men think it crude and unsophisticated and steer away from it. However the AIDS scare has reduced the incidence of casual sex dramatically.

FAMILY – A STAKE IN THE FUTURE

I t has been said that men want a family but that women want babies. Clearly the two are somewhat different. While it is dangerous to generalise it is probably fair to say that women seek babies and children as other human beings with whom they can create and nurture a relationship, whereas men tend to see them in dynastic terms – as a way of continuing the family line.

There can be little doubt that, for a woman, the commitment involved in conceiving, bearing and raising children is vastly greater than that for a man. His reproductive job is over in a few seconds, yet a woman's job as a mother starts at the moment of conception and ends when she, or the child, dies.

However society is changing and whatever the modern role of women the vast majority still say that they want children. World Health Organisation statistics show that about one in ten couples choose not to have children but it is difficult, or near impossible, to know how many of these take this path because the man doesn't want a family. I suspect that many, if not most, such couples decide not to have a family because of the man's feelings on the matter. It is still the cultural norm for most women to have children and many feel an almost irresistible urge to do so at some stage in their reproductive lives.

Choosing to be childfree

So for women, having babies answers many more of their needs than are immediately apparent. The hidden agenda is a lengthy and complex one. We shall not go into detail on this here because this is a book about men but suffice it to say that women's power mainly resides in their control over the procreation and nurturing of the next generation and they are understandably reluctant to relinquish it. After all, in what is still largely a man's world this is something exclusive to women. Procreation also gives a woman even more of a hold over men in the sexual and emotional arenas and this is vital for women if they are to retain their central role as moral restrainers of society.

In short, whether a woman likes it or not, and whether or not she ends up exercising her 'rights' she is born with the potential for a very different approach to family than is her partner. This is all too apparent when I am working with infertile couples. It is almost always the woman who is the more devastated by her inability to conceive. Of course many men are terribly upset about their infertility but often this is in the context of not being able to give the wife what *she* so wants.

To most men having a family is more about continuation of the family line than about the creation of unique, individual human beings. Or at least this is the starting point in their minds. Of course, as men come to know their children their views can change but however it comes about in our culture it appears that, by and large, a male's world tends to be focused away from hearth and home so babies and children will always tend to be more tangential to the average man's life than to the average woman's.

There are many other reasons why men want to have a family apart from the desire to 'promote their line'. Historically, and one cannot overlook such a motive even today, fatherhood has conferred power and respect, especially among other men. And just as with women, though I believe to a lesser extent, fatherhood justifies men's sexual desires. This ability to 'sire' children is deep-seated in most cultures and is usually seen as a sign of real manhood. In many ways this still persists today in western cultures where men even now see children as an affirmation of their virility. Without children it could be thought, horror of horrors, that they 'didn't know how to do it'. This is something that infertile men have been saying to me for years. A baby confirms that he is a 'real man' – after all there is no more concrete proof of his sexual potency than his pregnant partner.

A baby confirms a man's virility

However valid all these psychological overviews and historical perspectives are, at the personal level men also want children, although they often do not consciously realise it, because children offer perhaps the only opportunity that most of them will have to experience culturally sanctioned intimacy with another human being. In a monogamous culture this cannot, or rather should not, be sought outside the marriage with another adult female yet a man can quite happily be seen to gain emotionally from his children without any loss of masculinity.

Perhaps one of the more heartening signs of masculinity becoming softened in our culture is that more young men are involved with their children than ever in the very recent past. Clearly at least some of this is the result of pressure from their partners but many men find that the rewards are far greater than they would ever have predicted.

This in itself raises fascinating questions because some fathers in this situation find themselves seen as second-class parents when compared with their wives. After all, their critics argue, women are really meant to parent children and a man who devotes more than a tiny amount of his time to it must be somewhat odd and possibly not even a 'real man'. Men's liberation movements are now exercising their muscles on matters such as a father's custody over his children in cases of break-up or divorce and I suspect that we shall see a growing movement for men to assert their rights as parents within the family as they continue to lose roles that were traditionally theirs elsewhere.

Pregnancy

Pregnancy is a confusing time for many men. On the one hand they have done their reproductive duty and are proud to have done so because it confirms their potency to other men but on the other hand they are ambivalent about pregnant women. Many men say that they find all pregnant women unattractive though as judged on neutral grounds the opposite should be the case as women become rounder, have glossy hair, better skin, larger breasts and increased vaginal lubrication, as if they were permanently sexually aroused, when they are pregnant.

Off sex during pregnancy

A few men go off sex altogether when their partner becomes pregnant. This is often the result of the unconscious belief that their job has been done and that further sex is unnecessary or even wrong. Some men rationalise this by expressing concern about the safety of the mother or the baby, while the wife climbs the wall with sexual desire and the unfulfilled need to be cuddled, wanted and loved. To many men another man's pregnant wife is unattractive because she is so clearly 'his' property. Many men deny the sexuality of pregnant women, a fact that is to be seen every day in any ante-natal clinic or labour ward. As an extension of this many men say that however much they normally enjoy a woman's breasts, when they are being used for breast-feeding they are out-of-bounds. This is one of the reasons men have for encouraging their wife to cut short breast-feeding.

To many men the coming of pregnancy forces them to acknowledge that their woman has changed her role. She is no longer a mistress but a sort of generic 'mother'. This change of view comes about because all women who are pregnant or have children are seen as the same by such a man. They are all part of the clan of mothers – a clan which, of course, includes his own mother. The main feature of mothers in our culture is that they are sexless and it is a very short step from this unconscious assertion to finding any pregnant woman, or even in some cases, any woman who *has* been pregnant, sexually unattractive. To a man who, however unconsciously, sees his wife as a sort of mother *to him* the fact that she is pregnant confirms this reality and on the grounds that one cannot have intercourse with one's mother, he goes off her.

Although many women have health problems during the first third of pregnancy, in the middle twelve weeks most feel more sexy than usual and as pregnancy progresses many women say that they want more closeness and cuddling, if not more actual intercourse.

A first pregnancy can be a time when a man starts to look around for sex. Indeed, it is not at all uncommon for this to occur. Some such men feel quite consciously shut out sexually if their partner goes off sex in the early months; others feel that she is pre-occupied with the pregnancy and the impending baby; and yet others, quite consciously, see it as the end of an era and the start of competing for his wife's time and affection once the baby takes over their lives.

At least some men in this situation, however, are simply unconsciously acting out old scripts from their own childhood, fearing a loss

of love, or perhaps a sharing of it as happened long ago when another baby was added to the family. Such a man can become distraught at the thought of losing his beloved to sleepless nights, endless feeds, tiredness, or post-natal depression. Sometimes such bleak thoughts are worse than the reality turns out to be but for some men their worst fears are well-founded, especially in a culture that provides so little support for women who have just had babies.

Seeing his partner, who was until recently a busy career woman, become a laid-back nest builder can baffle many men.

All of this makes at least some men exceptionally susceptible to the attractions of other women even if the *sexual* relationship with their wife is good at the time. It is love and reassurance they are unconsciously searching for, not sex, though both partners think that sex is at the heart of the affair.

But whatever happens at the depths of any individual relationship, there is a much bigger emotion just beneath the surface of all men – the envy they have of women's ability to be pregnant. When a woman is pregnant she is the centre of the stage in a way that he can never be. She is valued by society, and by other women especially, not because she is his sex-object but because of something that is intrinsically hers rather than his. Many women have, until recently in historical terms, seen themselves as of value only in relation to their husband. In pregnancy and childbirth, however, *they* become the stars of a drama that no man can control. Men quickly find themselves excluded from this women's world of pregnancy and birth and this is often an unsettling experience for the man who is used to being in control. He finds himself being upstaged – and in a way that he cannot combat.

All of this makes a man feel, however temporarily, irrelevant.

These events hit men harder than they would women if the situation were reversed because men, as we have seen time and again, have made such an emotional investment in one person, their partner. When she becomes unavailable, otherwise absorbed, and perhaps even 'lost' into the mystical world of pregnancy and birthing many a man feels excluded in a way that he rarely has before. This exclusion can lead to disruptive behaviour that is at least in part a form of attention-seeking like a little boy who is demoted in his mother's life on the arrival of a new baby.

Yet even though a man is substantially shut out of pregnancy and birth, however symbolically, the heart of the matter is still *his* baby, the product of his masculinity. And this makes the exclusion all the harder to bear. Once a woman becomes pregnant the focus of her world becomes rather different and many a man, especially if he has a weak self-esteem generally, not to mention sexually, feels that from now on he could be relegated to the role of a sort of fertilising machine.

How men change

But things are changing for him too – not just for his wife. From now on he is a father, a rather different sort of person from a lover of his mistress. Now he too is bound by the needs of the child and many men say that for the first time they feel truly responsible for someone else's life. For the man who is none too sure about the relationship with his wife, the added responsibility of a child can make it even more difficult for him to leave her. He may now feel more trapped than ever in the marriage and so start to de-love his wife in preparation for leaving. This is especially likely if the man feels, however justifiably, that his sexuality has been rejected by the woman since she became pregnant.

All of this makes it vital, in my view, that we as a culture do all we can to make pregnancy a time of normal or even enhanced sexual activity for both men and women. The medical profession has played its part in treating pregnancy as a disease during which women should abstain from intercourse at the slightest excuse but thankfully today this notion is no longer so commonplace. It still holds sway in many bedrooms though, as clinical experience shows. Indeed, for some men the fear that their only sex partner will be removed from their grasp at the slightest medical excuse blights the entire pregnancy and the weeks immediately following it. Those women who, for whatever reasons, are inhibited about or do not enjoy sex, seize this excuse and refuse their partner sex on all kinds of 'health' grounds.

The temptation to run away from what he does not understand, appears to be excluded from, and cannot hope to equal, is great and some men do so into the arms of another woman, into their work, or into hobbies or other pursuits.

Birth

It is currently fashionable for men to be present at the birth of their babies, but this is not usual when looked at in the worldwide perspective where birthing is considered to be 'women's work'. This male presence at birthing comes about mainly because in our culture most women have no other important person on whom they can depend in such a major life crisis. Today's young woman doesn't look to her mother to support her in labour and few women call upon their

Sharing the 'chores' of baby care opens up endless opportunities for communication.

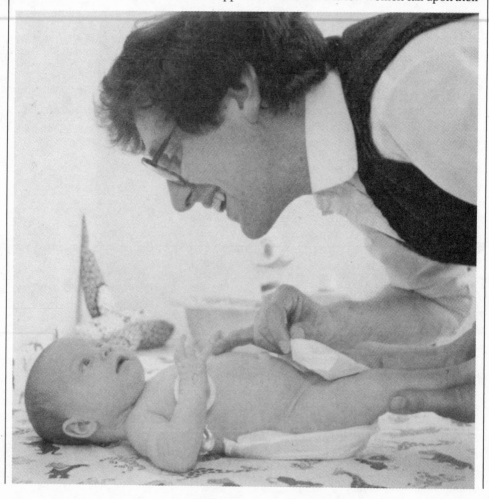

sisters to do so. The medical profession has taken over the birthing process and has graciously allowed men to come in on the act often under sufferance.

That many men do not want to be there is obvious to those of us who have a professional experience of birthing. And they are probably right. Were it not for the fact that so many women want someone who is emotionally close to them to be with them while they give birth, it would be easy to make a case for excluding men from the birthing room unless they particularly wanted to be there. This would only be acceptable today though if the woman could be supported physically and emotionally by someone of equal value to her. At the moment this seems unlikely.

Certainly some men greatly enjoy their wife's birthing experience but many do not and I have no doubt that negative memories can adversely affect a man's relationship not only with his wife but with his child too. To the woman who wants, however unconsciously, to present her husband with a baby as a gift, the fact that he has seen all the gory details including the mutilation of her genitals, somewhat takes away from the joy of the giving. Some men are so affected by the unpleasantness of the medicalised birth process that they are put off sex for some time in an unconscious bid to protect their wife from further horrors. This is especially likely to occur if there was surgical intervention such as a Caesarean section; difficult forceps; or a particularly large episiotomy.

Caring for small children

In many cultures men have little to do with children until they are about seven. And then it's the boys who are removed from the women and who go to live with the men. In the West though women have so little support from their friends and relatives that their partner is thrown into the baby business whether he likes it or not. And many do not.

What this does to men is almost impossible to say but at least some retreat from being available to be recruited to 'mothering' by working more, by disappearing with the 'lads', or into their hobbies. Escape from 'mothering' The effect that this has on their partners obviously differs from couple to couple but some women at least are glad that their partner is out of the way to leave them to establish a relationship with their baby. It is easy to forget that for many women this relationship is the most special that they have ever had. For the first time now they experience unconditional love and some women are jealous of their baby sharing this love with their partner. Such a woman argues that she has gone through many months of pregnancy and the trials of birth and that she's loath to give up this relationship to someone who turns up now and again to do a 'touch of parenting'.

Of course many women are delighted with their partner's help and interest and some would be unable to survive without it, especially if they have older children who need love, care and attention.

Caring for older children

As children grow up the subject of the mother returning to work is often raised. This is a vexed subject for most men. We have looked at men's attitudes to women at work generally but their attitudes to their own wives' working is even more complicated and tortuous. When a wife expresses the desire to work outside the home, and most eventually do, it is hard for a man to be openly antagonistic because so many other women work and because the family needs the money. But even when they agree in theory, most men are disparaging about their wife's work in practice.

Some men resent the competition that her earnings represent; others see it as an opportunity for sexual contacts and others acknowledge that once the woman is out to work they lose at least some of the power they had over her. Many men also realise that if their wife is out at work there'll be less of her time and energy available for them and that this will leave them feeling undervalued or even unloved. However most men appear to be reasonable on the subject of their wife returning to work but when it comes to the crunch they are only really happy about any new arrangement if it does not have adverse effects on their own lives.

Still a rare sight even among helpful, liberated men.

High on the list of problems that have to be dealt with when a woman expresses a desire to work is what will happen to the children. We believe in our culture that the mother is the best person to care for her children and that they will somehow suffer if she does not devote herself wholeheartedly to them. Men encourage this view but in truth it is often used to mask their terror of being expected to take over any of the child-care themselves. A woman who has a serious full-time job is still expected, by most men, to take time off if the children are ill, for example. A man certainly does not expect to be asked to do so himself.

All but the most 'liberated' of men still find it embarrassing to wheel a baby around in a pram or buggy, except when out with his wife as a family. 'Real work' for a man, is a full-time, exclusive affair that doesn't include washing, dressing, caring for, comforting, or playing with children. At least not on a day-to-day basis.

Some of this attitude comes about because men are ill-prepared for caring for children and it is also further encouraged because many women, however unconsciously, dissuade their men from having a meaningful part to play with the children because it is the only role they, the wives, have that is of value to *them*. Such women put their men down as fathers, perhaps even telling others how inept they are, often as a joke, but the damage is done and the man feels inadequate as a father. Given that for many men any display of caring and nurturing puts their masculinity on the line, it is unwise of a woman who might ever need her husband's help with the children, to do anything but encourage him.

Don't discourage men

Fathering

Until quite recently Mother and Baby books and magazines were just that – books about women looking after children. Now there is a rash of books about fathering and they are long overdue. These books are at last beginning to acknowledge the role of fathers.

Could it be though that many, or indeed all, men are in fact not as good at looking after children as are women? Certainly at first sight it appears that the majority of the skills called for are not very 'masculine'. Young babies and children do not respond to reason and don't behave rationally much of the time. They have to be dealt with on an intuitive level rather than an intellectual one.

Given that men are taught that it is not manly to show tender emotions, unless they are linked to sex, many do not know how to be loving to their children and end up 'fighting', playing rough games, or being sarcastic to older children, especially boys. Men find it easier to be loving and affectionate with their daughters, but with the onset of puberty many find it impossible to deal lovingly with their daughters without feeling threatened by their own, or other's, thoughts of incest.

Because so many fathers are emotionally unable to deal with their children at the level they, the children, need they understandably try to make up for the deficit by doing things they *are* good at. This can mean working harder to provide material goods and services which the children value. Many youngsters have told me that they wish they had seen more of their fathers and less of their wallets – or words to that effect.

Dad's home from a trip. He brings the presents but Mum has managed alone while he was away.

Because so many men are product-centred rather than process-centred, and because the vast majority of caring for children is a process rather than a product, men tend to make their presence felt by creating goals and events rather than contributing to the everyday process of parenting. So it is that they seek to organise outings, surprises, the buying of presents, and so on. They see such sporadic activity as being their most appropriate or practical contribution, whereas the mother often sees it as a way of buying love, much to her annoyance. She services the children in a somewhat unglamorous way day after day, year in, year out, yet her husband can, at a stroke, come in and play the fairy godmother with goodies paid for with money over which he usually has personal control.

Bringing up children is a strangely longterm affair and the rewards are hard to define. To most men this is a difficult pill to swallow because everything else in their life is geared to producing results on a day-by-day or month-by-month basis. This kind of achievement-centred life is hard to apply to children especially when they are young. This leads many fathers to express an interest in their children's achievements rather than their feelings or their lives in general. When their children 'achieve', they are functioning in a way that their fathers can understand and value, and as a result the children are rewarded for it.

Rewards are hard to define

Of course this goal-centred approach to life is not all bad. It teaches children about the masculine side of the world and this is vital for both boys and girls. Fathers also bring back the outside world into the home and this can enrich both wife and children. But to achieve anything of value in this regard the father has to share his experiences with his wife and children.

Having said this, it is a sad fact that most fathers hardly talk to their children. One study found that fathers actually spoke directly to their children for only seven minutes a day!

One US expert in this field claims that the commonest complaint he hears from children is that they cannot talk to their fathers and Shere Hite found that 'almost no men said they were or had been close to their fathers'.

The sad thing is that most fathers say that they'd like to be closer to their children. Yet ironically they are unable to be because their fathers were so distant from them. They have no model to follow.

The only way to break this downward spiral of disappointment and loss for both father and child is to encourage little boys to deal with and express their feelings; to show them the pleasures of being understanding to others; and to help them to value the caring and nurturing sides of their personalities. Such boys will, with luck, grow up to be better able to cope with their children. This could be a considerable advantage in a world in which work, as we currently define it for men, becomes more scarce and women seek more help from them with the day-to-day care and management of children.

To those readers who feel that this might emasculate men to the detriment of their women, I must strongly protest that the opposite is most likely to occur. Perhaps women's greatest single complaint about their men is that they don't understand emotions and feelings. By bringing up boys to be more in touch with their feelings, we not only enhance their likelihood of being better fathers but also of being better partners for their women.

THE FEAR AND HATRED OF WOMEN

Although most men say that their partner is their best friend and that they are happy with their man-woman relationship, men as a group fear and sometimes even hate women.

Early fears

The seeds of the problem are sown early in life. Most pre-pubertal boys see girls as unacceptable, silly, not worth bothering with, and frankly, somewhat irrelevant. One of the worst things that a young boy can call another as a form of abuse is 'a girl'.

There is little doubt, as any parent will confirm, that by about the age of four or five most little boys know very well what is male and what is female behaviour. They also know which they should be exhibiting. Boys of this age already restrict themselves to activities and interests that they perceive to be boyish or masculine. Boys who do not fall into line are called 'sissies' and can even be excluded from other boys' games.

Stereotypes set by the age of ten

By the age of ten or eleven most boys have strong views about the difference between themselves and girls. One study, and it is typical of many, found that boys of this age expected girls to be unadventurous; to play quietly; to be gentle; to be afraid; not to be rough; to be cleaner than boys; to cry at the slightest provocation; to play with silly things; to have to learn how to take care of children (hence the play with dolls); and not to have to think too much about maths and spelling – certainly not as much as boys.

This stereotype then is ingrained very early in life. A more recent study found that what boys say in response to questionnaires on the subject is often at odds with their own experiences. One researcher asked a group of eleven and twelve year old boys about domestic life. In discussions most said that shopping, cooking and cleaning were women's jobs yet in subsequent interviews it transpired that this was not what happened in their homes and that many of them had

experienced washing up, cooking and cleaning. The researcher concluded that they seemed to see their own experience as an aberration:
it had no effect on their stereotypical picture of reality.

In another study things were no more uplifting. In this, fourteen
year old English boys were found to think that girls were bitchy
gossips obsessed with their hair and clothes. Women were already
seen to be second-class citizens who lived boring lives tied to the
kitchen sink. The results came as part of an exercise set by a school in
which the children were asked to describe a day in the life of someone
of the opposite sex. The teacher who set the exercise found it intensely
depressing reading the children's essays.

This study mirrored others in the US. In one of these, girls
enthusiastically wrote about going out at night, staying out all
night, coming home and dropping their clothes all over the place for
someone else to clear up, and leaving the dishes in the sink for *Girls look on while boys*
someone else to wash up. The boys, on the other hand, responded *create the 'action'.*

with little enthusiasm and with hardly any curiosity about women's lives. They stayed at home and did their chores or went out, watched TV and went to sleep.

In the UK study the English boys showed hardly any more enthusiasm for the life of a woman and many of them went on at length about women's vanity. Time and again they spent hours in the bathroom, and most of the boys thought that women did a great deal of talking. Activity, such as it was, was taken up with gossiping with girlfriends, chatting up boys, avoiding fattening foods, and going into town occasionally to shop. They felt that, overall, girls led pretty boring lives.

Paid work for women was hardly mentioned but much of the time the boys describing themselves as women said how they would

be scampering around looking after the needs of their men. Time and again in the girls' essays it became clear that they deeply resented men's freedom from domestic chores.

Although there can be no doubt that girls are being treated more equally in many ways the current trend towards mixed-sex schooling may not be helping them to be better understood or less feared by boys. A UK study in 1985 found that boys 'battered' girls in co-educational classrooms. An enormous amount of energy and time was spent by boys in what amounted to the 'social control of girls' the researcher concluded. This doesn't prepare girls for life, she claimed, and discourages them from thinking aloud. In this study the boys dominated the classroom physically and verbally. They did not notice the physical presence of girls and didn't see it as important to do so. When diagrams were drawn of classroom seating it was discovered that the boys dominated the teacher's lines of vision reducing girls to marginal positions. Teachers frequently encouraged the girls to keep their comments short in case the boys started to fidget and play up.

In the playgrounds the boys monopolised things too with the girls frequently watching the boys from afar.

It was clear from this study that the function of the girls was to 'service' the boys. They helped them with homework, went for sweets and crisps and supplied them with school equipment such as rubbers, pencils and so on. Sexual harassment was also very frequent. Boys grabbed their breasts, dropped things down their blouses, pinged their bra straps and put their hands up their skirts. They used highly graphic language in front of them to shock them and one group of girls was able to list eighty obscene words the boys used in front of them, or about them.

The author concluded that co-educational schools are 'highly undesirable' for girls.

But perhaps even more disturbing are those interviews carried out with young teenage boys that have found that their views of women are so negative as to be distressing. Such boys see women as 'slags', almost sub-human, and already think it permissible to hit them and abuse them verbally in any way that seems appropriate at the time. Hopefully this is a minority perspective but I fear that it is not.

A survey of thirty commonly used US children's textbooks showed that females were described more often than males as lazy and incapable of direct action as well as being more likely to give up easily, to collapse in tears, to betray secrets, and to act on petty or selfish motives. Nearly all the adult females were seen as assistants to men.

Given all of this, it is hardly surprising that boys in another study said that they should be: able to fight off bullies; athletic; able to run fast; able to play rough games; able to play many games; able to take care of themselves; able to carry things; more generally able than girls; able to stay out of trouble; and more able at spelling and arithmetic than girls.

The way boys describe themselves in all such exercises is always at the other pole from girls. This leads, according to one leading

Which of these boys is likely to grow up with the more balanced view of females?

researcher in the field, to 'an overstraining to be masculine, a virtual panic at being caught doing anything traditionally defined as feminine and hostility towards anything even hinting at femininity, including females themselves'.

This type of behaviour might seem strange at first to the reader who has not come across it before but it is characteristic of the way most men behave much of the time. It is an example of the unconscious psychological process known as projection. In this we attribute to others facets of ourselves that we cannot come to terms with and do not like. So for example, I, knowing unconsciously that I am mean, accuse a friend of being so. He and I know he is not but it suits my unconscious to accuse him of this failing rather than facing it in myself.

So it is that any behaviour that appears to bring boys closer to that of girls is seen as threatening and rather than appear at all girl-like such a boy then attacks the girls who provoke the feelings in him.

All of this is made easier for boys, but almost more sad for society as a whole, because boys 'know' that they are intrinsically superior to girls. Most studies that have asked girls and boys about which they would rather be found that few, if any, boys want to be girls but that lots of girls would like to have been boys.

Boys 'know' they are superior

If a boy really believes that being a girl, or a woman, is so inferior it is hardly surprising that he doesn't want to be anything like them. Comments such as 'women haven't enough strength in the head or in the body to do most jobs'; 'their work is regular drudgery'; 'women do all the household things like cooking and sewing because that's all they can do'; are common in interviews with boys on both sides of the Atlantic. It seems hardly credible that in the eighties this should still be so but it is and it lies at the heart of male fears of being like women.

Feminine feelings

To some extent at least this rather depressing behaviour in men can be explained by another type of defensive psychological behaviour known as denial. There is little doubt that all men have at least some feminine characteristics in their personality. When these surface, however unconsciously, many men find it easier to cope if they deny the feelings, emotions, or behaviour characteristics. To any analytically trained therapist it is always an important pointer when someone stresses a matter with great force or repeatedly speaks of it. To the analyst it is clear that whatever the individual says consciously his unconscious is hitting him very hard with the subject he keeps on denying. In other words, such an expenditure of psychic energy in denying the matter must have a purpose. And indeed it does, the purpose is to protect the individual's unconscious from the pains of reality. In this case the man in question has feminine feelings and emotions which he would rather deny.

An example of this is the man who strenuously talks about his inability to get on with his children when they are babies. 'Once they become *"people"*' he says, 'all is well' and he becomes a real father to

women, even at work, acting as if they were scolding mothers. It is an indisputable fact that many, and some would say all, men continue to act as if they were little boys all their lives. In this regard they need mothering and many wives or other women step in and fill the role. Because so many men feel dependent on their partners for emotional support and sexual fulfilment this puts them in a vulnerable position. Because the average woman fills so many roles, especially in a service capacity, she becomes very valuable to her man on a practical day-to-day basis irrespective of her value to him socially, emotionally and sexually. Whatever the sexual politics behind this arrangement the fact is that many men realise only too well that they are vulnerable to their partner withdrawing her services be they in or out of bed.

All of this gives women considerable power, especially when it comes to emotional matters because here most men have no alternative confidant(e). This system of relying so heavily on a woman works well for many couples until something upsets the equilibrium. This might be the arrival of a first baby; the woman going back to work; the burden of an elderly relative to care for; or whatever. Now the man realises that he is less likely to receive the service he has become used to and starts to act more obviously like a little boy who has been done out of something that was his.

Women have the emotional power

Anger now hits the scene and harsh exchanges occur during which his longterm hurts and dependency needs are aired, albeit obliquely.

Once this cycle sets in, the tolerated and even valued 'little boy' becomes a damned nuisance and the woman retreats emotionally. Her husband now feeling 'unloved' sees himself free to find someone who will love him and the scene is set for an affair.

Reproductive power

This is all heady stuff and the very meat of marital problems up and down any country in the Western world. But this in itself is tied into another basic fear that men have – a fear of women and their reproductive power.

To most men, the working of a woman's reproductive system is something far too mysterious to fathom. Given that this is perceived to be so it is easy to understand why it is that men prefer to leave contraception to women. However they might justify it intellectually, most men find this lets them off the hook of taking responsibility for reproductive sex.

By and large women see sex, however unconsciously, as being about reproduction (mainly because they are far more aware of their reproductive capacity than are men of theirs). Men, on the other hand, see it as more about the appropriation of their woman; a source of recreation; or as a reaffirmation that they are loved. So the average intercourse episode is being played out by two actors working from somewhat different, if overlapping, scripts.

So many women feel guilty about non-procreative sex that

they try to thwart it as frequently as they can, albeit unconsciously. This is undoubtedly why there are so many unwanted pregnancies – currently running at about two hundred thousand per year in the UK alone. There are also a quarter as many abortions as there are live births. Very few of these babies are truly unwanted by the woman's unconscious – to her sex *is* babies and contraception an intellectual nicety that gets in the way of her having the babies she sees as the penalty she should pay for the pleasures of sex.

So it is that even in some very well-balanced marriages the woman's drive and need to have more babies (even if she knows intellectually that it is unrealistic) is in constant tension with her husband's drive not to. This puts the pressure on such men – a pressure that some cannot stand. True, many modern women say that they'd rather be at work and that they want only one or two babies but most of this is true at the intellectual level only as their contraceptive 'failures' prove. Only in their late thirties when we see women being sterilised in large numbers, can we believe that they truly do not want to have more babies and even this could be an erroneous assumption because in my experience a significant proportion of these women would rather not be sterilised. They'd rather, in truth, be out there gambling that they might get pregnant again – just for the last time! Expediency has won out but deep in their hearts they have lost.

Given that in our culture men are still supposed to maintain their families and given that however great the advances in equality for women most men still bear the major financial burden within the family, it is hardly surprising that for many the reproductive roulette their wives play is less than amusing and one which leads them to avoid sex more often than they'd like to admit. Indeed many men have told me how threatened they feel if their wife does not wholeheartedly share their views about more, or any children. Men everywhere know that women are infinitely wily when it comes to sex and that they'll go to extreme lengths to fulfil their, often unconscious, wishes. And they are right. A woman who really wants to get pregnant is hard to stop.

Of course some men are desperate for babies and some women are dead against them but overall the position I have outlined seems to hold true in most households.

Reproductive roulette

Letting go

Against this background of a general fear of women and of being like them we can now look at some specific things that men fear when it comes to sex.

Perhaps one of men's greatest sexual fears is of letting go. A 'real man' it is said, is in charge all the time, knows exactly what is going on, and is usually responsible for making it happen. How then can this conductor of the sexual orchestra relax for long enough really to enjoy himself or lose himself in the 'performance'? It is probably true that most men don't allow themselves to be sufficiently vulnerable during intercourse, they remain spectators at their own love-making – keeping a managerial eye on everything. This is one of the reasons why men want more sex than they currently have. That which they are 'getting' is poor quality because they don't relax and really let themselves go.

Clearly this is tied in with what they perceive to be feminine. After all, men are supposed to be in control not only of others but also of themselves and any loss of vigilance could mean that they are behaving, horror of horrors, like a woman! To many women this male inability to be vulnerable when making love seems unloving and demeaning to them, the women, and it is hardly any surprise that so many women say that they feel 'used' by such a man. She is expected to get carried away like a girlie magazine sex goddess while he remains firmly 'in control'.

Closely linked to this fear of being vulnerable is the fear that he might express some untidy emotion. Whilst it is probably true that women are more affected by this particular bedroom fear it is also very common in men. Many men fear showing their true animal selves. What the average man *does* know though is that he mustn't look silly or effeminate.

Physical fear

Physical fears are not uncommon in men. Some fear that they aren't sufficiently muscular or hairy, for example, but all of these pall into insignificance compared with the fear that his penis will be thought of The penis falls short again as too small or that it won't work properly. Because men see their own penis from on top they always see it as smaller than it is because of the fore-shortening effect but try as they might to understand it this simple optical fact often eludes them. We look at this more on page 137. Impotence is considered in more detail on page 219.

Overweight is another concern for many men. Today we stress the importance of a slim, fit body and for many men their beer belly induces fears of rejection or sexual refusal. Men by and large tend to blame physical things for almost any sexual failure or problem and their looks are much easier to blame than their lack of consideration or sexual skills when a woman refuses them.

Fear of performance

Fear of failure is high on the list of many a man's bedroom fears. Impotence is a subject of its own but well short of this is the odd occasion on which a man fails to have an erection or has a very poor one that doesn't last the course. Many a young man especially fears that he'll be disappointing to his partner and given that men, and indeed most women, make the assumption that the man should make things happen, if he isn't a good 'doer' he'll be viewed poorly by both of them. People today have often had several previous partners and this alone makes at least some men fearful. 'Will I be as good as Jim was?';

'Am I as inventive as her first husband?'; 'Is this really what she'd like best?' These sort of fears plague many a man entering into a new relationship.

This concern with quality of performance is all a part of a man's desire to make each love-making episode into an event comparable with a sales presentation at work. But sex is a far more precarious adventure than most of men's other pursuits. And the reality is that for most successful couples, sex is magic about twice out of ten times and good the rest of the time with the odd failure thrown in. This fear of poor performance then dogs many a bedroom and keeps many men unnecessarily over-tuned, over-vigilant and under-rewarded.

A part of this and a natural follow-on is the fear of not performing well for the *woman*. 'Will I last long enough for her to orgasm?'; 'Will she have an orgasm at all?' 'How will I cope if she starts to take the lead?'; 'What will happen if she asks me to do something I can't cope with?' These are just some of the commonly expressed fears one hears in clinical work. Some men are terrified of really getting to know their partner's sexuality too intimately in case it places burdens on them that they cannot deal with. This can happen when a couple start to share fantasies. Many a woman today wants her man to share her fantasies and even to act them out but even, or perhaps especially, the bar-room bragster falls short on such occasions as soon as it becomes clear that he'll no longer be in charge. Men who want to act out *their* fantasies often have considerable fears too just in case their woman throws them out along with the request.

Masturbation

Not what a 'real' man does   Masturbation fears are also common. A 'real man' doesn't masturbate, he fucks. Of course this isn't true and never has been, even of happily married men. Some men fear that they might become hooked on masturbation given that it is so pleasant and that then they'll not want intercourse again. In some relationships this is undoubtedly wishful thinking if the man has fallen out of love with his partner or is unconsciously de-loving her for someone else.

Whereas in women frequent masturbation seems to increase their interest in and desire for intercourse the reverse is true of men and especially for those over about forty. So there is some sense in saving oneself for intercourse if one is male and into middle age. This is just one more way in which Nature is unfair to men.

Words of love

Some men are afraid of what to say when they make love. Protestations of love seem to be expected yet most men say that they feel silly saying such things. Some men want to use crude language to turn themselves on but fear putting the woman off or even driving her away. It is certainly a great turn-on for the average man if his partner uses such

Anglo-Saxon crudities. Ironically the need to talk all the time can be a sign of an inhibited man, not a sexy lothario. Such a man talks so as to keep in control and to prevent himself from becoming too carried away with it all. Such men are a real nuisance to their partners who often complain that they want to get on with their own fantasy and that his talking gets in the way of their enjoyment.

Experimentation

Although men are supposed to know what to do sexually and are supposed to be open to anything, the truth is rather different. Many even quite normally sexed men are unable to cope with experimentation and such expectations can be crippling for less confident ones. A request by the woman for anything that is out of the ordinary, and such requests are coming thick and fast these days, raises all kinds of questions and fears for many men. Is it natural? Is it harmful? Will it hurt? Is it illegal? What would my friends know if they thought I did this? Will the children hear? and many others are common male fears.

Men know what to do

If women called men's bluff more over their sexual suggestions they'd probably find that the men backed out of the arena far more often than they, the women, did. After all, men have more to lose by falling short of their own expectations.

This section has, I hope, put men and their fears of women into some sort of perspective. It is not intended to be a litany of horrors that illicits the response 'poor little things' but if women are to understand men better it is a vital area that has to be dealt with. Many women go through a whole married lifetime imagining that their man is fearless, in control and on top of everything (literally and metaphorically) yet all too often the truth is quite otherwise. An openness and sharing of men's fears is, I believe, the basis for a truly valuable relationship between a man and a woman. As long as the man is playing Tarzan to his wife's Jane real communication is impossible and they both lose out.

MEN'S LOVE FOR
– AND FEAR OF –
OTHER MEN

It is impossible to write a book about men and sex and not devote at least some space to those men who love and have sexual contact with members of their own sex.

The word homosexual has nothing to do with the Latin word *homo* (a man) but comes from the Greek and Latin combination word *homo* (Greek) meaning same and *sex* (Latin). So homosexual simply means sexual activity between two people of the same sex.

Whilst it is difficult to be sure how common homosexuality is among men current figures suggest that there are about two million male homosexuals in the UK. There are probably more than this if one were to take those men who are bisexual (enjoy sex with either men or women) into account.

In the Western world most people think of homosexuality as unacceptable and this was true long before AIDS. In the UK and several other countries, sexual acts between consenting adults carried out in private are now legal but this does little, if anything, to make most people feel *happy* about the practice.

Why homosexuality is badly thought of

There are probably three major reasons why homosexuality is so badly thought of by so many people. First, in a culture in which sex is still, however unconsciously, seen to be a largely procreative matter (even if most of us thwart Nature's efforts much of the time) homosexual men are seen as 'unnatural' because they indulge in a form of sexual activity that cannot result in a baby.

The second thing that goes against the grain for many is that men, by obtaining sexual satisfaction without women, appear to undermine the institution of marriage and thus the value and position of women.

The last reason that so many find homosexuality unacceptable is that they see it as 'unnatural' and 'disgusting'.

Of course it is not only men who indulge in same-sex activities. Women too have homosexual relationships but for many reasons they are not so abhorrent to most westerners and so are not as condemned. This being a book about men and sex is no place to discuss female homosexuality.

There are two types of homosexuality. The first is that practised by young people as they mature sexually. Most boys and quite a few girls go through a stage of experimentation with the same sex. For boys this occurs in the early teens when groups of young lads compare penis size, how far they can ejaculate, the numbers of pubic hairs, and so on. All this is quite normal as part of male psychosexual develop-ment. The vast majority of boys who discover things about other boys in this way do not end up becoming homosexual – it simply appears to be a way young males have of learning about other males, and thus about themselves.

The second group of homosexual males are adult men who decide to run their lives in a way that includes same-sex partners. Some such men have sexual and loving relationships exclusively with other men and others have sexual intercourse with both men and women. Many homosexuals are married or have been married. Some homosexual men are still married, appear to the outside world to have 'normal' marriages and often even their wives do not know about their homosexuality.

Why do some men become homosexual?

The short answer is that no one knows. Given that so many boys go
through a 'homosexual' learning phase it is tempting to think that at least some homosexual adults have simply stopped at this stage of their psychosexual development. Most adult homosexuals find this an unattractive hypothesis in that it makes them appear immature.

Theories abound

The biological explanation is a fertile area for dispute. It appears from recent research that the hypothalamus (a specialised area of the brain) is 'cycled' in the earliest stages of fetal development. In male fetuses this becomes 'uncycled' but in some homosexuals it appears to remain cycled. It has been suggested that something in pregnancy prevents the male fetus developing normally into a typical male.

Work with rats in Germany suggests that extreme stress in a pregnant female rat produces greater than expected numbers of homosexual offspring. This has led some scientists to claim that stress during a woman's pregnancy might be the 'cause' of homosexuality. Evidence for this is not yet available in humans.

We all tend to have at least an element of what psychologists call narcissism: that is we are attracted to those who are like ourselves. This is perfectly plain in everyday life in the way we choose our friends and even our spouses. Some experts argue that homosexual males are so narcissistic that they can find pleasure and a sense of ease only with those who are like them.

I have no doubt that at least some homosexual men have had bad experiences with women and there is no doubt that some men turn away from women in their teens and come to see men as more like them and thus easier to understand and to deal with.

Of course some men become temporarily homosexual if de-prived of the opposite sex, as in prison or in other confined single-sex situations. Such 'homosexuals' return to heterosexual activity once normal life resumes.

Some men are frankly unable to deal with women and so run away from them. Their sexual drives, however, still crave an outlet and they turn to other men.

During the teens years, and especially during the late teens, some boys are in an experimental mood and try lots of things. Homosexuality can be one such activity. Most such young men never go on to become homosexual but a few do, perhaps being recruited to the homosexual scene by an older man. Such a youth then becomes caught up in a sub-culture that precludes further heterosexual development and he can easily get stuck as a homosexual forever. This is arguably more likely for the lad who is scared of girls or of getting them pregnant.

Many individuals are what is called 'latently' homosexual – they could quite easily experiment or even go further with the homosexual life but choose not to do so. Such people will, however, demonstrate their homosexual side at the slightest provocation.

Latent homosexuality

A complication in this matter is that some of those who express the most vehement anti-homosexual tirades are often unconsciously homosexual in their leanings but have built up formidable internal and unconscious defences against their 'disgusting' and 'unnatural' unconscious desires.

What do homosexuals do?

Homosexual males kiss and cuddle one another just as heterosexuals do. They find pleasure in being close to one another, caring for one another and sharing their concerns and joys in life. When it comes to more explicit sexual pursuits male homosexuals usually use one or more of the following when making love; they rub their bodies against one another to reach orgasm; they masturbate one another; they suck one another's penis; they stimulate their partner's anus with their fingers; and perform or receive anal penetration. According to one study almost all homosexuals will have indulged in five of these practices within any one year and a quarter will have done them all.

What so many, even very tolerant heterosexuals, find difficult to come to terms with is the fact that many homosexuals are highly promiscuous. It is not unusual for a homosexual to have had many hundreds of partners during his sexual lifetime.

Of course AIDS has had an effect on the gay community and there are signs that homosexual promiscuity is falling all over the western world.

Why worry about whether men are gay or not?

Very few women can cope with the thought that their man is gay or even bisexual and this is without any consideration of the AIDS problem. Few couples can sort out the emotional earthquakes that result from such a revelation and professional help is almost essential. It is arguable that more men today will tell their partners about their bisexuality because of the dangers associated with AIDS. But such knowledge is hard to deal with even with specialist help. Most women, especially those who have never had homosexual feelings or experiences themselves, will find it near impossible to understand why a man should prefer another man to them and the man himself may have problems understanding this himself.

Homophobia – the fear of being homosexual

Women often have many friends, indeed for lots of women their friends are the most important people in their lives after their immediate family. Men, on the other hand, tend to find it difficult to make or sustain close friendships with other men. This comes about because of the greatest fear men have – that of being thought homosexual.

To suggest to a heterosexual man that he is homosexual is to chip away at the very foundations of his masculine identity. And a man can be seen as being homosexual if he doesn't fit in with the cultural stereotype of what a 'real man' ought to be. So, for example, a man who touches another man, hugs him, puts his arm around his shoulders, cries or 'cracks up' under emotional stress, is seen by some men and not a few women as 'homosexual'.

But the fear of homosexuality doesn't just affect the emotions men show to one another, it affects how and if they actually get together in the first place. When a man phones another man to ask him to come around to his house the other man immediately asks what the reason is for the invitation. Men are so goal-centred and so driven in their behaviour that it seems inconceivable that the caller should want him to see him simply to share something or just to be together. There has to be a reason for the meeting. So it is that men tend to construct all kinds of excuses for getting together. They drink, fish, play sports, do business, or whatever but all too often these activities are a front for the real business of being with one another – something women do all the time but more openly and honestly.

Excuses for meeting

Being together like this is also safe for men because most such activities take place in groups. Most men are happiest with other men if they are in groups. This reduces the likelihood of their having to interact personally with any one man. Men are brought up from early in life to see group activity as of great value and safety. The concept of 'the boys' is a powerful one and has many functions apart from allowing men to be together without having to be closely involved with one another.

In historical terms all this is nonsense, of course. Until recently, even in Northern European cultures, men could express tender emotions and have close friendships without being thought of as homosexual lovers. Survey evidence suggests that this fear of being thought homosexual is no more than about sixty years old.

This could have something to do with the changing role of women over this time. As women become more liberated, doing the same jobs and even behaving socially like men in many ways, men have to work hard at retaining their gender identity in a confusing and confused world.

For many men the thought of being the 'active' homosexual partner is not too distressing because this is the role model he has of himself in his heterosexual life. But homosexuality involves a passive partner too, the one who receives. Dominating other men is a sign of virility in many spheres of life and is thus acceptable but *being* dominated is certainly not. In ancient Persia and Greece triumphant warriors used to rape their male victims to complete the degradation and humiliation.

Most men feel ill at ease when in the company of homosexuals. They cannot readily cope with the distortions of social regulation and can all too easily be pushed into a situation in which they abuse the homosexual physically or verbally. This is, of course, a form of self-abuse, a type of punishment for the man who finds himself, however unconsciously, revolted by the thought of what such a man could make him be – a passive sexual victim.

If the homosexual man he sees is the active, virile type of homosexual, knowing that men tend to get what they want sexually, he fears that he might become the hunted rather than the hunter. This fills him with considerable fear because he has no training to play the role. To some extent this feeling is even more cruel than is the same feeling experienced by women for much of their lives because men in our culture are not reared to think of themselves in this way and so find it

The purpose, however unconscious, for this get together is much the same as a women's coffee-morning but few, if any, of these men would acknowledge it.

more difficult. This is not to say that women find it easy because many do not and greatly resent being 'hunted' all their lives.

LEFT: Here, man is once more pitted against man yet with some degree of social companionship – albeit at a discreet distance.

Clearly the subject of homophobia is a fascinating one yet it is hardly talked about and most women have no idea that their men are affected in this way. To be fair most men don't realise it consciously either but this doesn't make it any the less real. It is interesting to someone like myself, who deals mainly with the unconscious, to watch current attitudes to the AIDS crisis because many of the men who are so vehemently on the side of the wrath of God in this context are also frantically homophobic. At last in AIDS they have the ammunition they have longed for. That this is a pathetic perversion of any sort of natural law is all too obvious when one looks at the relationships between men around the world today and in cultures throughout history. AIDS has, in this sense, done men far more harm than most people have so far realised if only because in a society in which men find it difficult or impossible to be friendly on anything other than a very superficial level, anything that further fuels the fires of homophobia will do us all harm as men have just another reason for shying away from one another.

It appears that we have arrived at a perverted situation in the West today in which men come to see friendship as necessarily going hand in hand with sex. This is true for the man-woman relationship and seems to be increasingly so. In fact it has been said that the AIDS epidemic will drive men and women closer together in their loving relationships. If this means that they are less promiscuous sexually I am all for it but if it means that men will continue to look to women, or more particularly their individual partner, to answer all their emotional and friendship needs then I'm not so happy because for many marriages this is too great a strain.

What many men need today are real, close friendships with men with whom they can share serious issues that matter in their lives. But as long as they erroneously link such friendship with sexual intercourse they'll miss out. Sadly, so will their spouses.

PORNOGRAPHY – SLAVERY OR SALVATION?

Pornography is a subject that cannot be ignored when thinking about the sexuality of men. It is often a matter of some confusion to women, who by and large, don't share male interest in the bodies of others, or at least not in this context. The average woman, finding that her partner reads girlie magazines, is baffled as to why he should need them, and feels at least somewhat threatened by the fare on offer within their covers. All of this makes pornography a fascinating subject for both men and women.

Pornography is vast business

Just in case any reader imagines that I am making a mountain out of a molehill and that pornography is a sort of aberration indulged in by a few odd-balls they should think again. In the USA pornography is a vast business estimated to turn over the same amount of money per annum as the legitimate film and music businesses put together.

So clearly, porn in all its forms is gigantic business and there is no sign of its growth slowing down. Obviously in a book such as this we can only skim the surface of the subject, one to which whole books and learned studies have been devoted. What I want to do here is to look at the individual men and the effect of porn on them and on their partners.

Soft-core or hard-core

There are basically two types of porn. Soft-core porn is widely available over the counter in newsagents and bookstalls in most Western countries. The usual style is the girlie magazine in which there are features of interest to men (usually about cars, erotica, travel and so on) liberally interspaced with high-quality photographic spreads of young girls desporting themselves in various stages of undress, often in exotic locations.

The second type of porn is so-called hard-core porn in which the entire matter is erotic or pornographic and whose level of explicitness leaves little or nothing to the imagination of the reader. By and large this type of material is not readily available in the UK but anyone who really wants to get hold of it can do so. It often involves matters such as lesbian sex acts, men engaged in sexual activities with women (including full intercourse), and at the more extreme ends of the market people performing sexual acts with children or animals.

The distinction between hard and soft porn is a blurred one with many examples of current soft-core porn being 'harder' than some so-called hard-core material of the past. As well as these historical variations there are also, of course, vast personal differences in what people would accept as hard or soft porn.

Today sex is increasingly being used to sell everything from cars to shoes and many advertisements are verging on soft-core porn. Indeed many a man finds the ads for women's underwear in the women's press every bit as arousing as the girlie magazines he reads.

Sex sells everything

Escapism

But whatever porn shows and however explicit or subtle it is the vast majority of it is used by men as an aid to masturbation. To understand why this should be it is important to remember that men are, by and large, visually aroused by women and their naked bodies whereas women are, on balance, more interested in men in the context of their personalities, who they are and how attractive they are. So it is that the porn of women is the romantic novel and the porn of men the girlie magazine, video or pin-up.

This escapist element of porn is a vital part of its attraction. Indeed it could probably be said that most men would not be much aroused by their own partner appearing in a girlie magazine – it is the fact that the woman is someone else's that is part of the attraction.

How harmless is it?

But is soft-porn really totally harmless and innocuous? Does it have any untoward effects on men or on their relationships? Answers are hard to come by but some thoughts are worth consideration.

When looking at the place of porn in men's lives we have to bear in mind what their views, however unconscious, of women are. Men are brought up to see themselves as in control, unafraid, self-sufficient and independent. They are 'in charge' sexually and make things happen.

Porn, be it hard or soft, furthers this image that a man has of himself. There on the page is a woman who is posed to offer herself to him. He is in control, she is complying with his needs and appetites and reassures himself that all is well with the male-dominated world. As women have become more assertive in the real world, men have less social and economic power to wield or to trade in return for a woman's understanding and emotional support. As a result a man's sense of insecurity is greater and his dependency needs more. A way out of this dilemma is to look to the fantasy world of the girlie magazine where things seem to be 'as they should be' with eager women wanting him unashamedly with no strings attached. After all, many men say, their one-to-one relationship is highly conditional, or so it appears. He has to be a good father, breadwinner, do-it-yourselfer, lover, or whatever and in return he'll be loved, sexually serviced, and supported emotionally. The women in the girlie magazine make no such demands, they simply offer themselves like sacrificial lambs. This is heady medicine to any man and especially so to the one whose one-in-one bond is neither strong nor fulfilling.

Sacrificial lambs

But the story is even more complex. As women make more demands on their men both in and out of bed and men become more concerned about sexual performance, seeing themselves as having to have sex even if they don't want it, it is hardly surprising that for many the soft porn picture spread is a blessed relief, and not just emotionally.

Women often ask why it is that men can 'use' the women in girlie magazines as pure masturbation fantasy figures but if the subject is looked at in this light I hope things become clearer. In a very real way the girls in the centrefolds are using the men who buy the magazines. In this respect I think many of the more vociferous of the women's movements have got it wrong. Men are far more trapped by their needs in this area than are the women who parade their bodies for the photographer and the reader.

What all men do

But there's yet more to the attraction of porn for men. By using soft porn men somehow bind themselves together with other men, who they know are doing exactly the same. Not only does this make the whole thing appear more acceptable but it reassures him that he is normal, has a healthy sexual appetite and is in control of it. Many of the messages he receives from society and from his partner in particular give him quite the opposite impression, so it is understandable that he should want to 'put things to rights' in this way. Any 'normal' man, he argues, would be attracted to this available, sexy, woman so he is not odd in wanting her. On the contrary, he'd be less than a man if he didn't.

However, what results from the porn business is not intercourse but masturbation. True, some couples use porn as a feature of their sexual lives and it can be highly arousing to some women, but the vast majority of users are solitary men (even if they have partners) who use porn as a source of arousal to masturbate by. Masturbation is always likely to be highly attractive to men. Of course, this is true of women too but this is not a book about them. When masturbating a man can control his arousal and to a great extent his pleasure without having to take a partner into account. Emotional and practical hindrances do not feature, as they do in real life. All that really matters is his desire and its satisfaction. This can be a delightful change for those men, and they are many, who have all kinds of hindrances to sexual pleasure in their day-to-day lives.

Indeed, masturbating with the aid of pornography is somewhat like a holiday, however brief. As on a holiday the man has choices not normally available to him and the option to relax into that choice and make it real.

Young and willing

The women in soft porn are interesting. They are always young – about eighteen to twenty-five – they expose their bodies easily and 'shamelessly' and they return the reader's gaze by looking directly at the camera. In this respect they are dealing one-to-one with the reader making him feel that they are offering themselves directly to him. Such a woman is thus on offer in a way that other women, perhaps even his partner, rarely, if ever, is. This often contrasts tragically with the real world because women are not this available, ready for action and open sexually – not to mention the exotic locations. Normal sex is full of anxieties for many men, indeed I believe this is more true than most women realise. Masturbation in the presence of such an accepting, even encouraging 'partner' thus takes on far greater meaning than is generally assumed. With no fear of failure and no one to monitor his performance or criticise him, many a man who is quite incapable of doing well with a real woman can at least do so with his soft-porn partner.

All this is made more easy for the man to believe and to act upon because so many of the photographs in soft porn today show the woman's genitals so clearly. As I know from clinical experience this Fantasy vaginas can be off-putting to some men but to the majority it is powerful stuff. Not only is the woman in such a picture offering herself but she is implicitly saying 'my vagina is yours too'. The man by now has an erection and expects to use it. The obvious place to do so is in her vagina in his fantasy.

Alongside the pictorial matter in mass market soft porn is the editorial. Almost none of it is concerned with emotional matters, it nearly all deals with ways in which men can enhance their view of themselves as men. This helps bolster the 'value' of the picture spreads by association. In the fiction in such magazines the women are always eager, highly orgasmic, and most important of all very responsive to what men do to them. Simultaneous orgasms are an everyday event; the women are physically perfect; never have a period; are contraceptively safe; have no unwanted body hair; are never fat; do not suffer from pre-menstrual tension; and so it goes on. Their only role is to be delighted with what the man does to them. Such a woman revels in the size of his (enormous) penis, which is often so large that she fears that she'll choke on it as it mounts from her vagina through her entire body; she moans and screams with pleasure as he thrusts into her and generally behaves like a 'real woman' should. All of this implies to the reader that he, because he is a man too, could just be the

subject of such rapture – and for the moments of his masturbation fantasy, he is.

Central to all of this is that the women involved love it. They cannot get enough of it and want more and more, bigger and bigger, time after time. In short they are insatiable. This is good news for most men and especially those who like to think that women experience sexual pleasure only in the hands of men. The sense of power that this gives the reader is enormous and it is, I believe, this sense of power that makes such fiction so compelling.

Damaging aspects

But could all this be actually damaging men, or indeed their women? There are certainly those who think it could.

Perhaps the first effect is the blatant unreality of it all. True, a James Bond film is pure escapist fiction but it is such a pantomime that few, if any, believe it to be anything else. Misleading men sexually is far more dangerous because there are few women who could hope to match up to the fantasy as portrayed in men's fiction and this must contribute, however insidiously, to men's dissatisfaction with real women and be harmful to man-woman relationships in general. In my view it is more harmful than the female equivalent, romantic fiction heroes who are equally unrealistic in the average woman's life, because men are more simplistic and gullible on the subject of sex than women are about romance.

So in that such fiction distorts reality grossly and perverts the average man's expectations, however unconsciously, I think even soft porn *can* be harmful. This is not to say that it *is* harmful because clearly many a healthy, psychosexually balanced man can read it and take it for what it is, a piece of escapist romping that bears no relationship to his real world. His partner too might enjoy sharing such reading with him and if this pleases them both who is to say that they are wrong?

Perhaps of more concern are the young and the single whose ideas are open to be moulded and who can seriously mis-learn about women by reading soft-porn. To the shy, inadequate man it may act as a prop which sustains him but at the same time it can actually hamper the growth of his sexuality because he becomes terrified just in case a sexual encounter actually did turn out to be like the fiction. If it did, he simply wouldn't be able to cope. This, in fact, applies to many more men than would care to admit to it and is yet another reason why such adventurous and abandoned sex is popular in soft-porn – it would be much too threatening in real life.

Dangers for the young

So in that such porn leads to mis-learning I think it can harm some people. However, it is not just the men who read it that can be hurt. Many women see their partner's interest in even quite innocuous soft porn to be a sign that he has gone off them or has stopped loving them. This can, of course, sometimes be the case but usually it is not. Men, as we have seen, have just as insatiable a desire to see women's bodies as women have to be a party to romantic adventures. Most men, whilst understanding perfectly well, and even enjoying, their partner's interest in romance cannot for the life of them see why they should want to read such similar repeats of the same scenarios time and again. Yet this is exactly what women accuse men of when looking at women's bodies. Perhaps if the sexes understood that they both craved such interests but that their interests are different (if overlapping) then soft porn and romantic fiction would cease to be the bones of contention they are today in many relationships.

Some women, of course, feel directly threatened by the lovely young bodies in the magazines because it 'proves' to them that they are not as desirable, at least not physically so.

Women generally are all too easily made to feel physically inadequate in our culture and they don't need any more evidence, however spurious, that this is so.

The irony is that most men, when asked, say that they are quite pleased with their partner's bodies and that they wouldn't change anything about them. Women focus on their varicose veins, their stretch marks and their fat tummies but men tend to see beyond these things to the woman herself – at least when it is their own partner. Such imperfections in a film star or girlie magazine spread would, of course, be unacceptable.

Men's projected fears

So men in practice appear to be much more easily pleased than women think or fear but this is largely caused by the insecurity we breed among women in subtle ways as in advertising. The implication is always that if you are less than perfect or attractive you might get dumped. This, as with so many things about men and sex, is exactly the reverse of the true picture. What is a far bigger problem is men's fears that *they* might get dumped – a fear they project onto their women by making them feel disposable.

Do-it-yourself porn

Perhaps then the best sort of 'porn' is the do-it-yourself kind. Some couples experiment with taking their own erotic photographs, even perhaps in exotic settings on holidays. They create their own centre-spreads, perhaps with them both in. By doing this a couple have the pleasure of knowing that they are the stars. Some couples include such games in their fantasy life and thus build up the pleasure in advance. Few men can resist a story about their lover being their personal sexy model for the day.

Whether or not such a couple actually make their fantasy come true is almost beside the point but, if they do, that too can give them hours of fun.

Some couples like to have erotic literature, videos, films, books and magazines around them much of the time to keep up their level of arousal and interest. To such a couple true porn holds few attractions because they'd rather revel in one another's *real* sexuality than retreat to the fantasy world of solitary sex and true porn. For some men, of course, this is not an option, porn is all they have. Just as for those women for whom romantic fiction is their safety valve. Some at least of these men and women are 'happily married'.

Feminists and moralists will, no doubt, continue to put their points of view but whatever they say pornography is likely to remain a major industry, even if it were to be driven under the counter. Men will, if anything, need more reassurance on and more outlets for their sexuality as women become even more dominant in what was until recently a 'man's world'. Mankind has used erotic art and what would today be called pornography since recorded time and there is little *Porn is here to stay* sign that things will change dramatically. Indeed, it could be argued that with the scare over AIDS men, and women for that matter, might turn to non-intercourse sex and possibly even more to masturbation than they have in the past, if only because it is the ultimate in safe sex. Ironically then, pornography could become widely accepted and even possibly valued as a socially responsible answer to people's needs that they'll fear to satisfy elsewhere.

VIOLENCE AND AGGRESSION – THE WEAK MALE

Arguably one of the most commonly-held beliefs about the differences between men and women is that men are more aggressive and violent. Men's natural aggression is, it is said, the reason why they are the dominant sex all over the world both today and throughout most of history. Of course there have been notable exceptions and there still are but in public life (what happens at home can be rather different) men are seen as dominant almost everywhere. This dominance has come about, it is claimed, because women are too busy having children and breast-feeding them for long periods in most countries of the world. This, coupled with the fact that men are intrinsically 'more aggressive', means that they end up with the best of what is on offer.

Are men more aggressive?

There are many theories as to why men appear to be more aggressive and we shall touch on some of them in this section. Some scientists think that men are biologically more aggressive; some people think it is simply a matter of social conditioning; radical feminists think men cannot and will not even think very much about the problem because the power it gives them is too valuable to relinquish; and there are other views on the subject.

Not necessarily so

It is always said that given that men start and fight wars, they must be more aggressive than women. Unfortunately, this doesn't appear to hold true in the real world. Soldiers, when asked, do not seem to be exceptionally aggressive, except, understandably, when being attacked. Wars are not primarily about aggression they are the result of political manoeuvring which is, on occasions, protective rather than aggressive.

The fact that the vast majority of prisoners in jails in the western world are men is also seen as evidence that men are more violent or aggressive than women. But it is probably true to say that economic motives are behind most crimes, especially as men are still the main breadwinners in the West.

If certain anthropologists are to be believed all human beings are naturally aggressive. However the vast majority of adults of either sex are exceptionally unaggressive. Most of us never have a physical fight with another adult and only a few are truly aggressive verbally at all frequently.

It does appear that boys are brought up from the very earliest days to be more physically active but studies of boys and girls show that boys in general are given a bad name for being rough or violent by a small, rough group. However it is rare to find one that shows that girls, in however small a percentage, are generally more aggressive than boys.

When it comes to adults, over half of all the laboratory experi- Research is equivocal
ments carried out by research psychologists have failed to prove that men are more aggressive than women, but most of the rest have found that men *are* the more aggressive sex. As is found with children the differences are much greater when judged by responses to questionnaires than when actual behaviour is studied. Men *see* themselves as more aggressive but when it comes to test situations the differences between the sexes are not nearly so great. What appears to happen in many tests of aggression is that women hold themselves back from behaving aggressively because of what they think others will feel about them.

When men become aggressive it is often because someone has made them so but studies show that women become aggressive when there is a matter of principle at stake or if they see someone being unfairly treated.

Biological arguments on the sources of aggression are many and complex and cannot be entered into here in any detail. It is interesting in the context of this book that there is possibly a link between aggression and the male sex hormone testosterone. It is claimed that the area of the brain that is involved with aggression and rage is primed by male hormones to be more susceptible to being activated in men than in women. Animal research certainly supports this argument. There probably is a connection between male sex hormones and aggression but it is certainly not a simple one because hormones affect behaviour and are, in turn, affected by it. It is also fascinating that some women have levels of testosterone that are as high, or higher, than those of some men.

How do children learn to be aggressive?

Almost all parents discourage their children from being aggressive, or at least from showing signs of aggression. Mothers are especially found to do this. Fathers, however, behave somewhat differently. When fathers are studied playing with their sons and daughters, they usually favour more physically aggressive play with boys than they do with girls. Studies have also found that when boys are naughty they are twice as likely to be punished physically as are girls. Girls are usually punished verbally, often by threatening a loss of love.

So it is that boys quite quickly become used to being hit and to hitting others and to see physical violence as a part of being masculine. This pattern appears to linger into adult life where males tend, on average, to express anger more physically and females more verbally.

However violence or aggression are not valued by children. Children and adolescents say that cleverness, physical attraction and prowess at games are the reason that people get on in a group of their peers. Aggression is seen as counter-productive and most groups of children studied actually avoid violent or aggressive children. I think this dispels the often-made claim that men are at the top of the pile in most cultures because of their male aggression. In the vast majority of life-settings aggression is shunned and avoided by almost anyone and those who behave in such a way are not valued.

Aggression in marriage

Some aggression is helpful

In marriage power is a major issue, albeit an unspoken one for much of the time. Most couples who get on well together have an unconscious power-sharing arrangement with a pattern of what has been called shifting dominance. In certain areas of life, or at certain times, one is in charge and this is recognised by the other. Actual physical violence is rather rare in man-woman relationships though we understandably hear a lot about it when it occurs. Of course some women will allow their man to get his own way more than they would like for fear of physical violence or his greater strength but no one knows how commonplace this is.

Wife battering is a vexed subject that we can only skim the surface of here. It used to be said that some women are destined to become victims of this crime by virtue of their previous experiences of violence. A study in Sydney, however, found that this was not so with fewer than one in ten of the women in refuges having experienced violence previously. Alcohol did not cause their husband's violence either. The only conclusion the researchers came to was that women with children and without jobs were more susceptible to battering. A Welsh study, on the other hand, found that more than half of the women questioned felt that their husbands had a right to hit them. Obviously the old messages about male physical domination are still alive, even if they are not universal.

Loss of power

In our culture men are seen by most people, even today, as somewhat dominant or even superior. As we see time and again throughout the book men are in fact probably less superior today than they have ever been. Men today need women's emotional support more than ever before and when it is withheld or rationed they become angry. Clinical experience shows that men today are *less* sure of their 'superiority' and are, in fact, suffering from a *loss* of self-esteem. The confusion and unhappiness that this loss of power has produced has made men realise that their 'power' was rather fragile.

Animal urges

Male sexuality is usually said to be linked to innate aggression and men claim that because it is they who have to make something happen during intercourse, they have to be at the least assertive and possibly even somewhat 'aggressive', however positively this aggression is manifested.

Darwin's studies convinced him that woman's evolutionary role Darwin's theories was to restrain the animal urges of men and direct them into the positive advantages of family life. This gave scientific approval to the notion of women being chaste while men did the chasing – a model that still holds today, however unconsciously, in most of us. In this model men are said to have urgent and aggressive sexual needs which crave an outlet and women to have only, or mainly, the need to receive the penis. This sort of thinking is at the heart of much rape and other sexual assaults on women and girls.

Much male pornography, or even fantasy, deals with aggression against women in various forms. Just why this should be is complex and ill-understood. Some men are undoubtedly too ineffectual as lovers, or even have a generally poor self-esteem, to make anything assertive happen in bed with a partner and so resort to porn or fantasy to make good the deficit. Some young men, or even boys, are influenced by stories in fiction or even in the newspapers that depict women being abused physically by men. A few will have direct experience of such behaviour domestically in their parents' behaviour and some at least will continue to do likewise to their own partners.

In all of this at least some women themselves encourage their men to be aggressive sexually towards them even to the point of violence. Some women are so guilty about sex that they need to be 'punished' in advance if it is to be enjoyable, or even in some extreme cases, possible. Gentle sado-masochistic games are not at all un-common among quite normal couples and are particularly liked by women who need their men to make all the running and thus absolve them from any responsibility for the sexual events that follow. Much of this kind of play is hardly true aggression or violence but having said this it is impossible for the very passive man because he cannot summon up enough aggression to do such things even in play.

Many men gain sexual pleasure from taking a woman roughly or even quite violently. There is something in the western sexual stereotype that encourages such behaviour in both sexes and on occasions, the dividing line between what is acceptable and what is not can be a fine one.

Many of us who work in sexual and marital therapy are aware of the woman who, quite unconsciously, baits her man into violence so

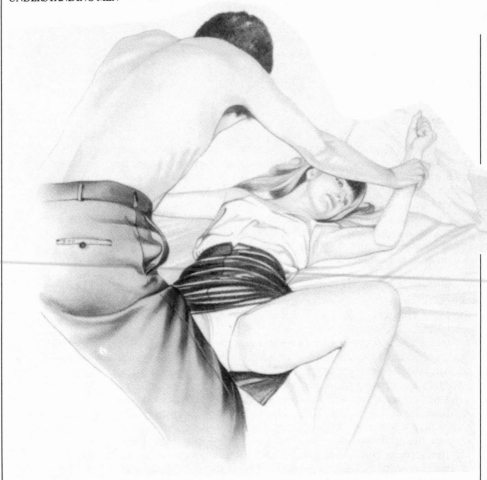

This couple always start off a love-making session with a wrestling match which she knows she will 'lose'. As he tears her clothes off she can deny any sense of responsibility for what follows.

that he will take her, hit her or overpower her sexually. This is, for a number of complex reasons, the only way that she can really enjoy sex. Many wives have told me how exciting near-rape is if they are in the mood for it and here again the line of acceptability can be fine and it is impossible to draw up rules that apply widely. Each couple has to find out for themselves what level of sexual aggression suits them and this itself will change as the years go by.

Certainly there is no need to imagine that sex should be neat, sanitised, and gently loving all the time. Most couples enjoy some degree of sexual aggression . . . it is simply a matter of agreeing on how much and when.

Natural sex drive

I think the whole subject of male aggression and sex has, to a large extent, been mis-read, however understandably. Men, like women, have a sex drive. But the need for sex is not necessarily, or even at all on many occasions, linked to aggression or the 'superiority' of men. Sex is a way that men express many emotional as well as sexual needs but most of these are absolutely *not* aggressive. Men use sex to re-affirm their relationship with their partner; to show her that she is cherished; to relax after a busy day's work; to make babies; to obtain intimacy at a level that isn't available elsewhere; to say 'sorry' for a real or supposed misdemeanour; to celebrate a special occasion; and so on. Many of these reasons for having sex have nothing whatever to do with being aggressive or violent. In fact quite the opposite is often the case. Many men, in fact, retreat into sexual activity when they feel vulnerable.

So, unfortunately many men, because they are so emotionally crippled, find themselves using sex to say things that should be expressed in other ways. This makes women think that their men are more interested in sex than is, in fact, the case. It also leads to men asserting their so-called sexual needs more often than some women would like. What the man often really needs is some other sort of outlet for his feelings but our culture has conditioned him into believing that real men don't have or need such outlets, they fuck.

Another mis-use for sex

Outlet for anger

Against this background then it is hardly surprising that intercourse ends up carrying burdens that it was never designed to carry and one of these is anger. Many a man, unable to express his anger with the world in general or with his partner in particular, (mis)-uses sex to vent it. This comes over as being aggressive and it often is. But as with so many such problems one sees in clinical practice it is a matter of appropriateness. No one denies that men should feel angry from time to time, or even frequently, but what women find difficult to cope with is that they so often channel their anger into sexual activities. In other words, sex is not a suitable occasion on which to deal with anger and frustration – at least not repeatedly. To use it in this way is to demean the woman and harm the man. It also reduces what should be loving intercourse to an activity little better than animal copulation and few would favour this shift.

Of course none of this means that men should not, from time to time, use intercourse to express their conscious or unconscious needs to be aggressive or assertive. This would be a great loss to many a relationship in which the woman enjoys her man's ardour and sexual aggression. Rather I am concerned with those men who use their partner as a vent for their generalised aggression and anger, usually to the detriment of the relationship.

Most men do not hit their partners physically, even under quite severe provocation. They do, however, 'hit' them in other ways, some of which are sexual. Some men punish their wives by keeping them little girl-like and dependent to shield themselves from their own dependence; others punish them financially; some retreat from the sexual arena so that their partner has no sex life; and so on. Almost all of this happens unconsciously, of course, but the effects of such veiled hostility and aggression are every bit as real as throwing a plate at the wall.

Clinical experience suggests that men are not aware of these psychological mechanisms and are likely to become violent or aggressive when their traditional roles or 'true masculinity' are threatened for whatever reason. It is the man who is least in touch with his feelings and most committed to traditional notions of masculinity that is the most dangerous in or out of bed. Marital rape is a consequence of such a gap between the real world and such a man's perception of it. Unfortunately, without being unduly depressing, there are millions of such men around today.

But this unhappy spiral doesn't have to continue for ever. Men, once they come to accept themselves as people with feelings, and once they can express their feelings in ways that do not involve sex, all too quickly find that aggression and violence become things of the past. And this is exactly what happens with such men in therapy. In fact it is strangely sad to see how many such men are eternally grateful to be let off the hook and released from the tyranny under which they had laboured for so many years. The psychic energies that had for so long been channelled into maintaining this absurd position of power and aggression now find expression in creative outlets that benefit not only the man himself but also his whole family.

An end to tyranny

To far too many women today it appears that a violent man is a strong man. Exactly the opposite is usually the case. Violent and aggressive men are almost always weak and insecure and many need help to make them stronger. Seeking such help is of inestimable value because only the strong can afford to be weak.

LOVE – THE ULTIMATE FOUR LETTER WORD

Love is an almost impossible subject to write about and even more difficult to research. Perhaps we should look, albeit briefly, at how love develops and how a man learns to love because it is by understanding the background that we can see how so many men come to have such trouble with love. And trouble they certainly have.

Research in the US has found that men fall in love more easily and more often than women. This Boston study followed 231 couples between 1972 and 1974 and the results mirrored a similar UK study in the Fifties. The studies also found that when men fall out of love or are abandoned by their lovers they come off worse.

First love bond

A baby boy's first love is, of course, his mother. She answers his daily Early lessons remain needs for love, shelter, warmth, cuddling, food and cleanliness. A mother who provides all these essentials fairly reliably and quickly after the need is expressed is seen by the little boy to be a 'good' mother. On occasions, however, she cannot come at once and he starts to panic just in case she won't come at all. Will he ever eat again? Has he been abandoned? These and many other thoughts no doubt run through his tiny mind. Such behaviour repeated many times probably makes him angry and frustrated that she won't answer his needs when he wants and such a boy can all too easily come to see his mother as 'bad'. Surely she cannot really love him if she behaves like this? Of course all of this can, and does, happen with girls too.

So it is that a baby boy can see his mother as both 'good' or 'bad' inasmuch as she looks after him well or not. But things aren't this simple because when he feels angry at his mother because she is 'bad' he cannot express too much fury or she might *really* abandon him. As a result he turns at least some anger inwards and thinks that it is he who is bad for her not coming when he wants her. It is thought that some of this bad feeling can give rise to later depression.

Love and hate

An added complication that all babies and young children experience, and it is one that lasts with us all until the end of our lives, is that of ambivalence. It is surprisingly confusing to many adults, let alone to little babies, that we can love *and* hate somebody, even possibly at the same time.

Indeed it has been said that someone who has never really loved cannot really hate. Most of us like to love and feel loved but are less able to handle hate. If we bear in mind that both are simply different sides of the coin struck in infancy it can help us deal with such apparently conflicting feelings towards the person we love as adults.

Around the age of about three months a boy recognises his mother and has an extra special smile for her. He now cries if she leaves him or if a stranger approaches. He is now said to be 'attached' to her and clearly likes her better than anyone else. They have a 'love affair' with each smiling at the other and living to some extent in their own private world of mutual pleasuring.

All this behaviour forms a bond between mother and baby that we call love. They both want to be with one another, are unhappy when apart, share private gestures, have their own private language, and feel inseparable. She looks after his physical needs and he, in turn, gives her warm, emotional feedback as a reward for her efforts.

It is through this first love bond with his mother that a little boy learns to give love to others later. The more wholeheartedly and adequately his emotional and physical needs are met the better he'll be able to do likewise to others later. Although it is impossible to be sure what the effects of poor mother-baby love bonds are on later life it makes sense, from clinical experience, to suggest that a really close loving relationship is the best possible way to start life.

One way that we can recognise love, even if we cannot define it, is to look at what people do with the things or people they love. First of all they care for them. It matters what happens to the love-object. They are prepared to make sacrifices for it. They jealously guard it in the face of threats and want the best for it. Mothers, of course, know all about this and so do little babies even though they cannot articulate it.

Few people have trouble with such concepts of baby-mother love, which is just as well because every love experience in life to some extent takes us back to our first childhood experience. In every loving adult relationship there is the seed of child-like love. Indeed those of us working with love and sex problems see the living proof of this every day.

Mummy fixation

But love doesn't stand still at the baby-mother stage – like everything else about a child, it grows. The earliest type of love in babies has to be mutual or they would not be cared for for such a long time and would probably not survive. But at around the age of three or four many parents find that their little boy now starts to have a crush on Mummy. He now de-loves his Daddy, feels jealous of him, wishes he were out of the way and wants his Mummy to himself. Some little boys at this stage even talk about marrying their Mummies. Slowly as the early school years advance this Mummy fixation goes and the boy becomes male-centred, entering the world of men.

Seeking another love-object

In early adolescence his mother is completely de-loved and the boy starts to invest his love in himself. He now becomes increasingly aware of his needs for a sex-object.

In late adolescence a teenage boy seeks out someone of the opposite sex to be his love-object, usually at the same time as his sexual life starts to flourish. For the first time he starts to link his need for a sex-object with that for a love-object. Now his masturbating, self-centred love gives way to other-centred love and he invests his caring and loving in his partner.

But sometimes these stages do not go well and all kinds of disorders occur so that a man has trouble with loving anyone, perhaps even himself.

Some men, for example, cannot have a meaningful sexual Holy sex relationship with a woman they love (their wife for instance) because she is seen as untouchable. Such men can enjoy sex only outside marriage – they see their wife as too special (somewhat like a Holy Virgin Mary) to sully her with their 'filthy needs'. Most of this attitude is, of course, in the man's unconscious, as are almost all disorders of love. The other side of the coin is the man who sees his partner as only a sex-object – he has little or no loving relationship with her. Such a couple can enjoy loving other things in their lives but relate to one another mainly as sex-objects.

The ideal man-woman relationship has a satisfying blend of love and sex but this lays the way open to all kinds of different definitions of what love is. Many's the man who says in therapy 'if she really loved me she'd do X', whereas his wife doesn't think that X has anything to do with loving at all. This makes communication vital within a loving relationship because we all get our 'strokes' in life in such different ways and there is no telepathic way of finding out which works best for our partner.

Falling in love

'Being in love' and 'falling in love' are strange experiences. The person who is 'in love' is, in fact, somewhat ill. The signs of the 'illness' are restlessness, agitation, raised blood pressure and high pulse rate, clammy palms, sudden flushes, a loss of appetite, poor sleep, an inability to make good decisions, extreme mood swings, and even hallucinations. Small wonder that the newly-in-love feel so strange.

Although women tend to fall in love earlier and to have more attacks before the age of twenty, once past this age women tend to

become immune to the 'illness' whilst men go on to be affected repeatedly. The most vulnerable time for falling in love is during adolescence and those teenagers whose parents are divorced, those at odds with their parents or authority in general, and those with a poor self-esteem are most at risk. Later in life adverse events tend to make people profess love for one another, perhaps as a bid for biological survival or reassurance.

LEFT: To lose oneself totally in the presence of a partner, to be vulnerable and totally intimate, are just a few signs of love.

Men fall in love more during the mid-life crisis (see page 46), just as do some women in the few years leading up to the menopause.

No one knows why we fall in love, chemical theories vie with brain-centre theories but, whatever the cause of the feelings (and some people cease to have them after certain sorts of brain oper-ations), a man usually becomes affected by the condition well before his love-object does. Men seem to be more easily pleased than women. Men are first usually most attracted by a woman's looks because they are visually orientated. A man makes this decision within seconds of first meeting a woman. He then decides whether or not he wants to get to know her better. Some men at least, fall in love at this very early stage.

Women are not nearly so fool-hardy about it all. They tend to look at men much more deeply and very much with the future in mind. A woman will talk about what sort of father the man will make, how reliable he seems, what his personality is, and so on. One study found, for example, that how much money a man earned was a crucial factor for a woman. This is just one facet of the decision for a woman who is making the choice not just for herself but for her children who are not yet born.

Women are also more in touch with their feelings and are less likely to confuse those two four letter words, love and lust. In the early days a woman tends to be more cautious about the man than he is about her. All this can change, of course, once the woman is 'sure' the man is right. Now she enters into the romance and emotion business with a vengeance and everyone knows that she is in love. This kind of 'illness' cannot last for long though – it is too intense, too exhausting and too unrealistic.

But whatever the historical background to love we in the West seem to think we must experience it if we are to make a good choice of partner for a lifetime. It is my view that people should *not* be allowed to make such important choices at this stage of the 'illness'. There should have to be a cooling-off period during which the couple get back to normal and then see how they feel.

Don't choose while you are 'ill'

When love ends

Just how long this sort of heady love lasts in any one couple is anybody's guess but it is usually gone by two years after marriage. For those couples who have substituted true unconditional love for the infatuation of being 'in love' a stable and happy marriage is a distinct possibility. But some couples do not survive the loss of what they perceived the partnership to be about. Now the man becomes depressed thinking that the bottom has fallen out of his world. He becomes lonely and some actually die of broken hearts. A study in Israel found that men with unhappy love lives were more likely to have heart attacks in middle age than were other men. Men are also three times as likely to commit suicide over an unhappy love affair than are women.

Men fare badly then when love ends but many of their friends and relatives do not realise it and thus can be of no help because they bottle up their feelings, often until it is too late. Much of this pain and unhappiness could be avoided if only men would talk.

A new deeper love

Private language

For those that survive the initial stages of infatuated love, and the majority do, there follows a stage of growth of love which takes the couple into a more mature, caring and loving relationship. This sort of love comes from shared experiences, losses, joys, sorrows and pains of life together. Now the couple become true friends, care for one another through thick and thin, are loyal, understand each other, perhaps communicate without speaking, have their own private language, form a 'therapy group' of two, fight the world together, share their unique needs for child-like love, rear children together, and find a joy in putting the other first in life.

Such a couple are formidable as a partnership, they work and play together well and are immune to sexual temptation by members of the opposite sex.

When love falters

Unfortunately, even in the best of relationships, upsets in the shape of an unwanted pregnancy, an ill child, a serious business setback, financial disaster, or redundancy, can rock the ship and even threaten the love bond that seemed strong.

At such times men appear to fare less well than women because for most their one-to-one love bond is the only really deep emotional relationship they have, thus making them more vulnerable to its withdrawal. If something threatens this, either from within or without, a man can be left deeply wounded and, without the infrastructure of friends that his partner has, he can all too easily seek solace or oblivion elsewhere.

Some men throw themselves into work as a sort of anaesthetic but this may well not answer their needs and they start to falter. If this happens around the time of the mid-life crisis or when his wife is having troubles with the menopause things can escalate and get out of hand.

Now the previously loving couple can find their emotional and romantic bank account running low and some falter even after many years of happy marriage to be divorced in middle age as the children leave home.

Very often such couples split unnecessarily. All they need is a professional to help them set their path straight again or to cope with their run of bad luck. Perhaps one of them has grown faster or in a different direction. We all grow and mature at different rates and it is a lucky couple who find that their lives progress exactly in parallel for forty years or more.

The Chinese have a delightful saying that helps in such circumstances; they tell the one who is 'advanced' to 'take his/her tiger to the mountain' while the other catches up. This can call for all the power of love that the one who waits can muster and some people become disenchanted with the waiting and leave both the mountain and the marriage.

Love and sex

But however much a man may see love as a part of a total relationship it is impossible to study men's views of love for women without coming to the conclusion that they link love very closely with sex, however unconsciously. Most men, even if they are closer to their partner than to anyone else still see women in general in a rather limited way. Most men, when asked, find it difficult even to consider a 'loving' relationship with a woman they are not having sex with and most say that any true relationship with a woman would inevitably lead to sex at some stage.

Some men, of course, relate to women easily, indeed there are those who do so more easily than they do to men but as a generalisation most men see any deep relationship with a woman as likely to involve sex at some stage.

Relating to women

Perhaps this is linked to men's views about what they most admire about women. When the subject is discussed with men most start off by talking about something to do with women's bodies.

While it is, of course, an over-simplification a man tends to see his love bond with a woman as intrinsically tied up with sex whereas a woman is less likely to do so. This could be why it is that a man falls in love more easily than a woman does.

Such a close linking of love with sex has its advantages and hazards. A man who is in love with a woman or who really loves her will greatly enjoy sex with her and will also want her to be his emotional support and friend. However, given that men appear to be more fickle about their love bonds than are women such a man, should things go badly in the relationship for any reason, appears to be able to de-love his partner fairly easily so as to be ready to re-invest his love elsewhere when he finds another woman he is attracted to sexually. Women tend, by and large, to see their one-to-one bond as a serious commitment for life (rather like mothering) whereas men still have the tendency to be love-hungry even if they are well suited and happy at home.

Love hungry male

This yearning for more love partly comes about because of men's desires for more of everything in our western culture; partly because of the old messages that tell him that real men can 'pull the birds' at any time, and he has to prove that he is still able to do so; partly because, like all other boys, he knows that he once de-loved his mother, his most cherished female love-object and was able successfully to re-place her with another female; and lastly because there is often the sneaking suspicion that there could just be a better deal around the corner. On this last point women are much more realistic about the partner they have.

All this striving for love, and indeed for everything else, is not easy to explain but it could be partly due to men's needs to be compensated for their perceived inferiority in life. At first this might appear a laughable concept but it is my belief that most men are so insecure at the deepest levels of life that they constantly have to reassure themselves that they are valid, manly, worthwhile, and lovable.

Given that the love of a woman and the needs to appropriate her sexually are such powerful validations of maleness it is hardly surprising that many men seek to act out this drama more than once in a lifetime even in a so-called monogamous culture. Many women see this simply as a penis itchy for sex but I fear it is much more profound than this. I say 'fear' because an itchy penis can easily be scratched but the man who does the scratching is in danger of throwing up his one-to-one bond in the search for more evidence that he is lovable. In this sense mature men are more love-hungry than are mature women and as such represent more of a threat to the stability of society – at least in terms of bonded one-to-one relationships.

The 'itchy' penis

Differing views

Obviously, from what has been said in this section the subject of love is a complex one, though few people ever really examine it in the context of their relationship. I have only scratched at the surface here and have not dealt with matters of closeness and intimacy but many other parts of the book take various facets of the subject further in other contexts.

The message on the matter of love is, in my view, that men and women often see love rather differently. All too often the partners are acting in the same play but from a rather different script. But this is not the first time that we have seen this problem in this book and it will not be the last.

UNDERSTANDING MALE SEXUALITY

M uch has been written and said about men and their genitality yet new discoveries about its physical make-up are still being made each year and there are still women who have only the most fleeting knowledge of male sexual functioning. Even those who are well informed and experienced in such matters often find that they don't really understand the attitudes of their men, or indeed men in general when it comes to genital matters.

Partly because our culture would have us believe that all men do is 'fuck', both sexes tend to underestimate the hidden agenda that is present in almost any genital encounter between a man and a woman. Quite clearly much of this agenda results from the man's views, be they conscious or unconscious, about his genitality.

Now that we have put male *sexuality* into perspective, however briefly, in Part One, we can look at how men think and function in more genital terms – in other words what most couples mean when they talk about men and sex.

MAN AND HIS PENIS

Phallic symbols

W hen either a man or a woman thinks of a man's body they focus, quite understandably, perhaps, on the most noticeable difference between men and women . . . the penis. Not only does this little organ differentiate men from women but it has, over the centuries, become a symbol of masculine power and domination.

Until fairly recently, in terms of human history, it was thought that women simply 'became' pregnant by some mystical process. Once it was clear that men played a vital role in the matter, males in general started to recognise the power this gave them. For a minimal expenditure of time and effort they could create a new life and change the whole future of the woman whom they had inseminated.

Because Man found his penis so amazing an object he started to 'erect' landmarks everywhere as symbols of his power. Egyptian obelisks and modern skyscrapers are much of a muchness when it comes to phallic symbolism and most of them are an all-too-visible reminder of man's relationship with his penis. In a sense these are simply more subtle ways of expressing man's fascination with his penis – ways that have been expressed throughout most of history in a much more blatant acknowledgement of the phallus.

In the ancient world men were highly involved with other men, both emotionally and sexually. In ancient Greece, for example, love between men was considered to be of the highest order and that between men and women something of an irrelevance. That intercourse had to occur with women in order to procreate was, of course, acknowledged but it came a poor second to homosexual love.

With the coming of Christianity and the suppression of public displays of the phallus masculine phallic power was turned inward, especially at the time of the Renaissance, to become more of a spiritual power and male homosexual desire was sublimated into other more socially acceptable pastimes. This sublimation is generally held by psychoanalysts to be a sign of civilisation as men transform unacceptable or inappropriate sexual drives into more socially purposeful activities. Be this as it may, it is certainly possible that the desexualisation of the relationship between men enabled them better to work *together* and *for* each other.

But just because Man's penis is no longer seen in public or revered in the way that it was in ancient times doesn't for a moment mean that it has lost its influence. Unfortunately, for much of its life the penis is a little flabby bit of skin that doesn't inspire much confidence, let alone a sense of power. It couldn't be more helpless or unthreatening if it tried yet men persistently refer to it in harsh terms such as being a 'tool', or 'weapon'; and represent it as being cold, hard and blade-like.

Over the centuries the penis has had many names and metaphors applied to it. Even in Roman times there were many which mirror today's words. The Romans used terms such as rod, lance, rake, poker, boundary marker, plough, and tiller all of which are little different from the 'prick' we use so widely today.

By retaining this kind of imagery man tries to keep a hold on the power that thousands of years of experience have taught him are consequent on his having a penis. Most men would rather think of their penis as a phallus, even if most of the time it is not one.

It doesn't take much knowledge of psychology to understand that this dichotomy is a persistent unconscious headache for men because their symbol of power and their organ of reproduction is so vulnerable to attack, be it physical or emotional.

Circumcision is a form of genital mutilation practised through- out the world for thousands of years. Although it has different functions in different cultures there is no doubt that it is a ritual that establishes the fact that the boy will become a man who will, in turn, assert his power and authority over society. Circumcision used to be a pre-marriage ritual among the ancient Jews but the Old Testament transformed it into a sign of the covenant with God and made it mandatory almost immediately after birth. So it was that in ancient Judeo-Christianity a man passed his power and authority onto his sons. In today's largely Christian-influenced western world people still circumcise their boys in their millions on the grounds of cleanliness or for other 'medical' reasons but deep down the motives are still the same, ancient ones of making the penis look more effective as a phallus and drawing the baby male into the masculine world of power and control.

Most men are somewhat ambivalent about the penis. It is so vulnerable and, in its un-erect state, so insignificant, that it is hardly surprising that men only truly appreciate it when it is erect. In this condition it is, at least to some extent, conceptually like a muscle in that it is hard and powerful and concepts such as these are acceptably 'manly' in our culture.

Many a man is ashamed of his penis or bashful about it being seen by men or women. They are worried that it isn't big enough! Most men are extraordinarily interested in the size of their penis and are easily made to feel inadequate. It is often a surprise to women that their man keeps his underpants on right until the very last moment in a love-making session and not a few realise that this is because he wants

Reasons for circumcision

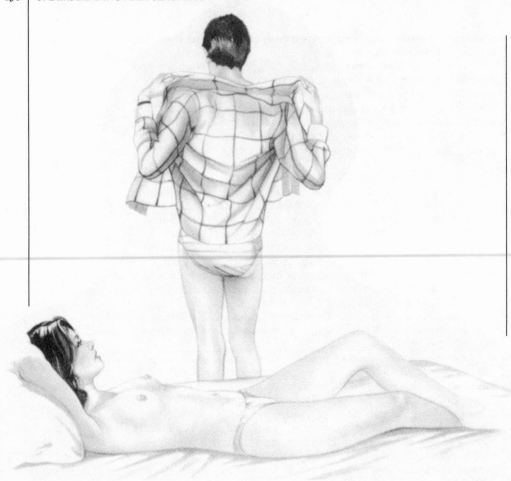

He's bashful about undressing. What will happen when he takes his pants off?

to cover his penis up until it is in its erect, and thus 'acceptable', state. Only now can he advance on the woman with confidence and use his 'weapon' for its real purpose.

A woman need only give a man the wrong kind of look let alone make a thoughtless – or well-placed – remark in order to render the most threatening 'weapon' harmless. And most men are only too aware of this. One expert when teaching women how to deal with flashers instructs them to make a suitably denigrating remark to the unwelcome advance if they want to be sure to defuse the situation. Phrases such as 'Is that the best you can manage?' seem to do the trick.

There are all kinds of myths about the size of a man's penis being linked to race, his amount of sexual activity, and the size of his body, to mention only a few, but careful research has shown that all such theories are nonsense. There is no direct correlation between a man's body size and his penis size; black men do not have larger penises; and there is no evidence, if interviews with prostitutes and other highly experienced women are anything to go by, that women generally like a large penis anyway. Some women say that they greatly enjoy a *thick* penis because it stretches their vaginal opening which is very arousing but an over long organ can, in fact, be a source of discomfort to many women as it produces pain on deep penetration.

Men, on the other hand, seeing their penis as some sort of biceps muscle that can be trained to be stronger and bigger believe, however unconsciously, that the bigger it is the better it will be for the woman. Presumably this reflects his unconscious views that a bigger penis makes him more powerful or potent in some way. Many men, because they are so concerned about the size of their organ, ask women with whom they have sexual relationships how it compares with that of other men. Ironically, most men rarely, if ever, see another man's erect penis and so have to rely on women as their source of information on the subject.

It appears, from quite meticulous research, that whatever the size of a man's limp penis, it'll end up being much the same length when erect. The problem with penis size for men is that they always look down on their own organ and so obtain a fore-shortened view of it. This gives the impression that it is shorter than those of other men whom they view head-on.

This pre-occupation with penis size is not new. One of Noah's sons, Ham, was cursed through his descendants for ever because he took advantage of his father's drunken sleep to satisfy his curiosity about his father's 'nakedness'.

As we have seen, this fear of being found too small alters the way that men behave in front of women. It can also very much affect how they behave in front of men. A man standing next to another in a public urinal will often shield his penis with the fingers of his hand that holds it so that other men cannot see the size of it.

Given men's predisposition to competition in almost every sphere of life it is hardly surprising that they also compete over penis size. This starts consciously at around the age of twelve when young boys, going through their homosexual development stage, compare everything about their genitals from how big they are to how many pubic hairs they have and how far each in the group can urinate or ejaculate. Needless to say biggest or furthest is always considered to be best. This sort of competitiveness continues throughout life in many guises and there are those who assert that all male competition, and there's a lot of it about, comes down to a sort of primitive, if unconscious, contest of penis size.

Competition is rife

So if, by his other achievements in life, a man can, by implication, make a woman assume that his penis is as powerful and substantial as his other activities then he has won a primeval battle for power and domination over the woman.

Much erotic literature is near-obsessed with penis size, as is some erotic art but one of man's greatest problems is that however much he may huff and puff over the matter he cannot enlarge his penis. Manufacturers of penis enlargers have made fortunes from those who disbelieve this simple fact but it remains true nevertheless. Some of the vacuum-type gadgets enlarge the penis very temporarily and there is a possibility that a man who is highly excited by using such a piece of equipment might have a better quality and thus larger erection, but this is all that can be said.

A man's penis is central to his life in a way that a woman's vagina is not. How much this reflects the implied power and domination of a patriarchal system is open to debate but there are undoubtedly other matters involved too. Perhaps the greatest of these is performance. Intercourse, or even copulation (for a discussion of the difference see page 155) requires that the man have an erection. A woman need not be sexually aroused to be impregnated yet a man cannot be successful as a father if he cannot obtain and sustain an erection at least long enough to penetrate and ejaculate.

This puts considerable performance pressures on men and we shall look at them elsewhere but here suffice it to say that a man's concern about success or failure dominates his sexual life, however unconsciously, much of the time. The fact that by its very nature his organ is so publicly on view also makes for problems. No one much worries about the size of a woman's uterus in the sexual arena though, of course, breast size can attain equally problematical proportions in women as does penis size in men. Here again though the problem is usually *men's* concern over size and what is 'ideal'. Few women in isolation from men would worry much about their breast size.

What women like best

Women often say how much they like their partners' penises and indeed some say that it is the size that they enjoy. Most, however, look to other features of their man and 'firm buttocks' and 'broad shoulders' come much higher on the list of physical attributes that women seek. From time to time I hear a woman describe her partner's penis as 'sweet' or use other words of affection or diminution. Such notions, to the average man, are quite irrelevant. What really matters is how effective it is at inflicting his masculinity on his partner. This is reflected in literature at all levels of excellence – or otherwise. Many a men's magazine regales the reader with stories of men who are so enormous that the woman nearly chokes to death as the monster ascends her vagina to tear through her whole body. While it is true that some women say that they like deep penetration and some men assert that they want to virtually 'get inside' the woman during very passionate love-making, the reality of such a beast of a penis hardly bears thinking about, except to the lone masturbator reading the story who can, by association, imagine for a moment that it is his gigantic weapon that is ravaging the woman in the fiction.

Now that we have looked, albeit briefly, at man and his penis in general terms, let's see how the penis is made and how it works.

UNDERSTANDING THE BASICS

Because almost all of a male's sex organs lie outside the body many people imagine that they are simpler than those of the female. This isn't so. In fact there is still a lot that isn't known about the male sex organs and only a very few years ago a totally new nervous system was discovered in the penis.

The penis is a structure which is made up of three tubes. As you look down on the penis from on top there are two visible tubular masses of tissues beneath the skin called the *corpora cavernosa*. They are called cavernous because they swell up to fill with blood. The third cylinder lies underneath the other two and is called the *corpus spongiosum*. It ends in a bulbous swelling at the end of the organ called the *glans penis*.

All three cylindrical parts swell when a man has an orgasm because the outflow of blood from the penis is partially shut off so damming up the blood that continues to come into it. This hardening is vital if a man is to fulfil his function in procreative terms . . . that is to enable him to place sperms near the cervix of his partner.

The urinary passage, or urethra, runs the length of the penis. This narrow channel carries urine from the bladder in the pelvis to the outside. Semen too comes down this tube, so the urethra has a dual excretory and reproductive function in men. Because the urethra runs through the spongy tube it becomes compressed when a man has an erection which is why he cannot urinate when sexually aroused and for a few moments afterwards. Urine is held back but semen is allowed through by a clever arrangement of the shut-off point. Certain medical disorders and some medications can so affect this control that the man ejaculates into his bladder instead of down the urethra.

Clever design

The shaft of the penis is covered with darkened, loose skin with hairs on it at the base where it continues to cover the scrotum. Here the skin is much more wrinkly and there is a lot more hair. At the other end the skin hangs over the tip of the penis in a loose fold to form the *foreskin*. It is this that is removed when a boy or man is circumcised. A tiny band of very sensitive skin connects the under-surface of the glans with the foreskin. This, if stimulated, makes a man become aroused very quickly. Indeed, for many men it is the most sensitive part of the penis.

The *scrotum* is a bag of skin covered with hairs, inside which lie the two glands that produce sperms – the *testes*. The height of the testes is controlled by small muscles called the cremasters and these, together with the muscles in the wall of the scrotum itself, can alter the position of the testes quite a lot. So it is that on occasions they are low down in a floppy scrotum and on others high up in a tight one. Changes in position of the testes occur according to a man's level of sexual arousal, the temperature of his scrotum, his emotions, and several other factors. People sometimes say how surprising it is that a man's sperm-producing equipment is outside the body and so vulnerable but the fact is that the testes have to be kept at a temperature of about two to three degrees lower than that of the rest of the body if sperms are to develop normally.

The nine week cycle

The formation of sperms in the testes takes about nine weeks. After passing through lengthy tubules in the testes they are collected in the *epididymes*, little structures that sit on top of the testes. Here they mature and become able to move under their own power. They then enter the *vas deferens* on each side and proceed to the *ampullae* where they are stored. It is the vasa that are cut when a man has a vasectomy. Sperms are still produced but are reabsorbed by the body. Beyond the ampullae are two blind sacs that produce fructose – a sugar that nourishes the sperms in their journey to fertilise an egg. These blind sacs are called the *seminal vesicles*.

The *prostate gland* lies at the base of the bladder in the pelvis and surrounds the first part of the urethra. It produces substances that lubricate the sperms and buffer them from attack by acid vaginal secretions. Beyond the prostate is a small pair of glands called *Cowper's glands* which also add lubricant to the seminal fluid just before ejaculation. Only about ten per cent of the volume of any ejaculate comes from the testes, the rest comes from the prostate and other reproductive glands.

Sperms, unlike a woman's eggs, are being produced all the time. They migrate into the various parts of the male reproductive system mentioned and are ready to be ejaculated at a moment's notice. Most men can ejaculate several times a day when young and even a middle-aged man can do so two or three times ... the supplies of semen seem to be plentiful. In old age though things appear to dry up a little and semen volume falls.

There is no point in holding back on any sexual activity for fear of running out of sperms. The only time that this could be sensible is in the sub-fertile man whose sperm count is low when he wants to impregnate a woman. For him it makes sense to refrain from ejaculating more than once every other day so as to allow sperm numbers to build up to optimal levels and so make a pregnancy more likely.

In the average man there are more sperms in the first few spurts of any ejaculation than in later ones. This is sometimes used in the so-called split-ejaculate technique in which the first few spurts are collected and used to inseminate the woman artificially. Many a woman has been able to become pregnant using this method.

Male sexual arousal

Male sexual arousal, like that in women, starts in the mind. Messages then travel from the brain to the spinal cord and thence to the genitals. These impulses shut off the outflow of blood from the penis whilst the inflow remains much the same. This changes the limp, downward-hanging organ into a rigid, upwardly-pointing, throbbing blue/reddy purple one with its veins standing out. This is called an erection.

It is impossible for a man to will an erection. He might, by thinking sexy thoughts, be able to set the action in motion but if he isn't in business to become aroused no amount of goodwill will make anything happen. Many, even quite sophisticated and experienced, women don't realise that a man cannot make himself have an erection and so become frustrated or offended when their partner doesn't have one. Such is the power of mental processes though that the slightest encouragement, be it visual or verbal, can set the erection-producing system in motion in seconds. But this works both ways and, although it is less true of teenagers and young men, the slightest negative input can cause a man to lose his erection. This can take the form of a baby crying in the next room; an unco-operative or thoughtless partner; a sudden thought about work; worry about the woman getting unwantedly pregnant; and much much more.

This finely-tuned mechanism puts men at a considerable bio- Biological disadvantage logical disadvantage compared with women and makes it likely that they will, if only from time to time, fail to set the erection mechanism in action when they or their partner wants. A woman can fake willingness or readiness but a man cannot.

Alongside the changes in the penis other things are occurring in the man's body too. His pulse rate goes up, his nostrils flare, his breathing rate increases, he becomes flushed in the face, his muscles tense, his pupils enlarge, and he feels sexual tension mounting inside him. At the same time his scrotum thickens and the testes are drawn in closer to the body. About one in four men have a sex flush over their upper chest and neck when aroused.

If stimulation stops now the man can return to normal over a few seconds and, apart from feeling let down, will soon be as he was before the excitement started. Most men though go on to the next stage of arousal.

In this the penis swells even more, its tip becomes darker in colour and the content of the scrotum increase in size. From now on it is increasingly difficult to return to the resting state until after he has had an orgasm.

At orgasm the man has no choice but to ejaculate. His pelvic muscles contract, as do all the muscles associated with his genitals, and semen spurts out of the urethra, often for some distance, especially in young men. This produces very particular types of sensation as the engorged reproductive glands discharge their contents into the part of the urethra that runs through the prostate. As the spurts of semen hit and expand this tube, the sensations produced are exquisitely pleasant for the man and he obtains the thrill of his orgasm. A series of four or five contractions at a rate of one every 0.8 seconds follows as the man ejaculates the semen in store. Each spurt produces less and less semen and a man who had recently ejaculated will have less overall volume than one who has not done so for, say, two or three days.

Eventually, the man relaxes his previously tensed muscles, his penis returns to its normal size and he may feel sleepy. Unless he is very young or very aroused a man needs several hours to regain the ability to ejaculate again. By and large this 'refractory time' increases with age.

It is possible for a man to ejaculate without having an erection. This is usually only achieved if his prostate is massaged by his partner. For some men this kind of stimulation gives them their best orgasm.

Some practical tips

The hardness of a man's penis is usually a good sign of how aroused he is but he can have many of the other signs and yet have a poor erection because he is tired, not ready for sex, or impotent. Inserting the penis in this state can often save the love-making session because many a man can be taken on from here with the right encouragement and enthusiasm on behalf of the woman. Almost all penises respond well to oral sex in this half-aroused state and once fully erect can be transferred to the vagina if that is what the couple want.

Far too many women think that if their partner cannot obtain a full erection he doesn't want to have sex. This is often simply not so and many a potentially good session is lost because of this mis-apprehension. True, it will often mean the woman taking a more active part than she otherwise might but if she is unable or unwilling to do this then she cannot, in all honesty, blame the man.

Some women, and especially those who like to time their orgasms to coincide with that of their partner (though I never recommend this as particularly desirable), like to know how to tell when he is about to climax. This is also useful to know if you have a man's penis in your mouth but don't want him to ejaculate inside you. Knowing when your particular partner is about to ejaculate has to be learned by careful and meticulous observation but in general most penises undergo a final enlargement just before ejaculation and the man becomes totally carried away with the events and seems to be in another world. Some women find that when their man's testes are tight up against the body he is ready to come.

Although it is undoubtedly a fact that for most men their most arousable areas are those covered by their underpants, it is also true that far too many women ignore other areas that can greatly contribute

to male sexual arousal. For example, many a man likes his nipples stimulated, the scrotum and testes themselves are very arousable and some men like their testes squeezed quite hard as they become highly aroused. Massaging the 'root' of the man's penis can be very pleasant and the area between the penis and the anus is a source of pleasure for some. Almost any area of the body can be sensitive in a man but only trial and error will prove what is pleasant and what is not. Stroking and teasing a man's body with lips, breasts, or hair can drive him wild with desire and naturally kissing and cuddling will have the same effect. We look at these latter pursuits in more detail later.

Many men, thinking it unmanly, fail to ask their partner to do things that they best enjoy. Sometimes this is because they are shy but on other occasions, as many men say in therapy, it is because they are afraid that the woman will think them silly, dirty, too demanding or will refuse to do what they want, or even call an end to the love-making session altogether. It is often said that women are sexually inhibited and unable to seek what they want in bed but there are many men who have exactly the same problems.

Although we shall look at the concept of impotence in more detail elsewhere it might be interesting to consider some provocative notions about it here while we are looking at male sexual arousal generally.

Frigid men

Men are said to be impotent when they cannot obtain an erection and women frigid if they cannot become aroused. But this is too simple a viewpoint because frigidity is arguably just as common in men and impotence in women yet they are both largely unrecognised.

Frigidity is, by definition, the absence of sexual pleasure and impotence the inability to gratify one's desires but both of these are common in both sexes.

A woman's reproductive system works very much like that of a man and she can be physiologically every bit as impotent as he. A man's erection is parallel to a woman's vagina becoming aroused, swollen with blood and wet with natural lubrication and she will fail to do this if she is impotent. No woman is ready to make love at a moment's notice and neither is a man yet her impotence is usually ignored. Even Masters and Johnson, the renowned sex therapists, claim that 'it could be provocatively said that there has never been an impotent woman' yet it is quite clear to anyone with the most rudimentary knowledge of women that they do not become sexually aroused the minute they open their legs.

Men spend so much time thinking about performance that they often completely miss out on their pleasure. This phenomenon, when applied to a woman, is called frigidity. Many a man has pretty joyless and pleasureless orgasms yet no one accuses him of being frigid; if he cannot perform he will be called impotent but this same label is denied women with exactly the same problem.

Wilhelm Reich studied this at some length and wrote that '. . . this was especially true of those men who bragged most about their sexual conquests and about how many times a night they could "do it" . . . There was no doubt; they were erectively very potent but ejaculation was accompanied by little or no pleasure, or even the opposite, by disgust and unpleasant sensations.' Certainly many a man will echo these sentiments because they know that ejaculating doesn't necessarily mean having an orgasm.

Just why this should be is a matter of some complexity but has a lot to do with many a man's inability to let himself go and become totally abandoned during sex. Most men restrict their pleasure to penile sensations and spend a great deal of time concentrating on their woman's body and its responses. In this way many men experience a genital climax but not a whole body orgasm.

It is also probably true that most men are so determined to follow a kind of pre-set path to sexual pleasure that they become too goal-centred and so concentrate on the end point rather than the process of intercourse. As a result, as with so many other areas of life, they miss out on much of the pleasure, especially if the 'goal', once achieved, is less enjoyable than they hoped it would be.

Too goal-centred

Having looked, albeit quite briefly, at the basis of Man and his penis let's now consider more of the areas of sexual activity that men have important views on and see what a woman can learn from them.

MEN AND FOREPLAY

Foreplay for men

W hile there is no doubt that many men greatly enjoy giving and receiving pleasure before actual intercourse there is still a large core of the male population that perceives that all such behaviour is mamby-pamby nonsense. Every well-read, middle-class *Cosmo* reader knows what is expected of him yet often feels that it is something of a chore actually to do anything about it. A 'real woman' should be able to have an orgasm as soon as he puts his penis inside her without all this 'fiddling about'. Surely if she doesn't there must be something wrong with him . . . or more likely, with her. All the women in the girlie magazines have multiple climaxes on penetration – so what on earth is going on?

Of course, real women don't usually behave or respond in this way and if they are to enjoy orgasms will need quite a lot of foreplay.

What many women don't realise is that most men like foreplay done *to them* and that they think they don't get enough. Even that which they do get is poorly done. Men are loathe to say what they want, especially if it is something other than penetrative sex and so go without the sorts of stimulation they'd best like during foreplay. It is an amazing paradox that men, usually so in charge of things both in and out of bed, make so few demands on their lovers during foreplay. This is, in my view, an extension of the cultural lie that a man wants only sex (penetration) and that everything else is a kind of poor second best that leads up to the 'real thing'.

Because women are used, by and large, to men saying what they want in life . . . indeed the complaint is usually that they demand too much and need looking after like little boys – they assume that they need nothing other than penetrative sex. But this is not so and is at the heart of many an unnecessary affair. The man knowing yet not wanting to ask for what he wants, lets the matter go by default until he gets bored or annoyed and seeks another partner who will somehow 'know' how to please him.

Many men say that foreplay is a vital and enjoyable part of making love and that it shows that they are accepted by their partners and worth some effort to arouse and delight. Alas, many men reject foreplay, or even a hint of it on the basis that they might ejaculate 'too soon' and thus ruin the 'real event' . . . penetration of the woman. Clearly this is an understandable fear for the man who ejaculates prematurely but for most this is a cop-out and serves only to further the myth that sex *is* intercourse.

But even when women do take time and trouble to indulge their men in foreplay many men say that they do not like what they do. Over the last twenty years almost every women's magazine has regaled its readers with details of how to stimulate a woman to orgasm. There can hardly be a liberated male of sexually active age who doesn't know what to do, even if he never does it. Most men, on the other hand, complain that their partners have never taken the time to learn how to masturbate them properly, for example, and that they haven't ever really explored their genitals, or indeed their other erogenous zones. We shall see on page 192 how these problems can be overcome.

When it comes to making love to a woman and performing foreplay 'on her' most men are adamant that they have to do too much and that all the running is left up to them. So, although many men feel that they are unmanly if they are on the receiving end of foreplay, they still feel that they put too much into any particular sex encounter and that women should do a lot more than they do. For some men at least the chore of having to worry about yet more performance-centred behaviour is too much. However, for others, *their* best foreplay is to arouse their partner.

A common complaint is that women give too little feedback during foreplay so that the man feels insufficiently encouraged or, indeed, valued for what he does. This is, of course, in keeping with our cultural teaching that women who say what they best enjoy are tarty. As a result, most women keep quiet and endure foreplay that turns them on very little or positively irritates them. No wonder that the man thinks he's wasting his time and tries to get onto the 'real thing' as quickly as possible.

Too little feedback

It is generally said that a man can be quickly aroused and wants to climax immediately. This is not so. Most men greatly enjoy a long time from the start of stimulation to climax, just as most women do. True, both sexes enjoy a 'quickie' from time to time but on most occasions it is much more pleasurable to take plenty of time. Some men say that after a very long period of stimulation without orgasm they become tense and uncomfortable in the pelvic area and others say that they are afraid of losing their erection but most men like arousal to last for some time. Most men claim that the longer the arousal period the better the quality of the eventual orgasm, even if they gain an erection, lose it, and then have another one.

Kissing and cuddling

Although some men say that they think kissing and cuddling are not manly and a few actually refuse to be petted at all, the vast majority greatly enjoy these activities as a part of everyday life and especially of love-making. When the matter is discussed with men most say that some of the best things about intercourse are the physical closeness, body contact and all the other non-genital embraces. In the Hite Report only three per cent of men asked why they liked intercourse mentioned orgasm at all! For many men the main pleasures of intercourse are emotional and sensual. Many say that it is one of the rare occasions on which they can honestly and openly express their feelings and others say that they are rarely allowed to lose control and that this is the magical element of intercourse. For others it is the only time that they feel (rightly or wrongly) that they are receiving love from anyone.

For many, of course, it is the ability or at least the opportunity to express their love *for* their partner that is the nicest thing about intercourse. Just how this is interpreted is, however, something of a problem. Could this mean that men like to experience the physical and other sensations associated with intercourse and that they simply feel well-disposed towards the person who helps it all happen? Could it be that in true male fashion it gives them a sense of power to be able to give her so much love and that this fuels his self-esteem? Or could it be a mixture of self- and partner-centred motives and emotions?

Women often say that men seem to be more physically-centred in their love-making while they themselves are more emotionally fired up. I think this is a harmful distinction because a deep knowledge of what really goes on in people's bedrooms shows that many women are every bit as physically urgent in their sexual needs as are many men and that many a man is emotionally committed and involved in a way that some women never are.

Kissing and cuddling only

Of course kissing and cuddling *can* be an end in itself. If you are a woman, that is. Few men consider this a meaningful option. They want, or have been conditioned to expect, penetration and ejaculation. Kissing and cuddling however pleasant, must therefore be put into its true perspective, as a watering hole on the journey to the 'real thing'.

Kissing and cuddling are, however, important to men, probably more so when not in the context of intercourse. Most men say that they like to be cuddled and petted during the day, even if it doesn't lead on to intercourse but as most women know a man who is petted too enthusiastically sees it as the first step towards intercourse and cannot easily stop what he sees as inevitable. Here again we come back to the biological argument that sex is simply 'what a man does' as a sort of reflex response to being touched, or even looked at by a woman.

Oral sex

Of all the sexual practices that men say they enjoy and that they would most like more of, oral sex comes at the top of the list. Fellatio, sucking a man's penis with or without ejaculation, is almost universally enjoyed by men. Most men who have not experienced it say that they would like to and many of those who have experienced it say that their partner doesn't do it very well. Most men feel that women don't like to bring a man to a climax in their mouth, and in this they are probably right. However, for many men this is seen as a rejection of their sexuality, their semen, and even sometimes of themselves as men.

Oral stimulation is almost always more powerful at arousing a man than any other kind of petting or caressing and even the most reluctant or tired penis can usually be aroused or re-aroused by oral caresses. For details of how best to achieve this, see page 213.

Many men are very keen on cunnilingus (oral caresses of the woman's vulva). They see it as a very personal form of service to a woman they really love and some say that they cannot get their tongue or face deep enough into the woman, so excited and delighted are they by it. About half are none too keen on it though and do it to please their partners, to appear 'with it', or because it is such a powerful way of giving her an orgasm. Many such men enjoy the sense of control and mastery this gives them.

For those men who like it, cunnilingus is so intensely intimate that it makes them think that the woman must really love them. Why A sign of love else would she allow a man such intimate access to her most 'private parts'? Just as with a woman kissing and sucking a man's penis, cunnilingus demands a level of trust between the couple that is rarely found elsewhere in love-making. The tissues are tender and soft and pain can easily be inflicted if care isn't taken. The odour too is unique to each individual and in the case of a woman there may be a plentiful flow of vaginal 'juices' to add to the mix. It is this extraordinary combination of factors that makes oral sex so powerful an arousal agent for both sexes but perhaps especially so for men. Women are, it is said, traditionally more reticent whereas men are so 'sex mad' that they'll let anyone suck their penis if they do it well. Women who allow their partner to perform oral sex on them are thus highly prized because it proves to the man that he is really valued because, they argue, no woman would do such a thing with a man she didn't value. For many women oral sex is far more intimate and personal than is penis-in-vagina sex, so perhaps these men are right.

MEN AND INTERCOURSE

Although there is a lot of talk about men becoming more sexually considerate and interested in pleasing their women in bed there is little doubt that to the vast majority of men sex *is* intercourse. When the subject is discussed with men in a clinical setting they have great difficulty in thinking of sex without intercourse. To most men sex follows a predictable pattern of foreplay, the man penetrating the woman and then having an orgasm in her vagina. This is what sex means to most men.

With recent and growing pressure from women to be satisfied sexually many more men are now stimulating their partner first so that she has an orgasm before he enters her and has his. But many men find this a nuisance and say quite openly that it is a sort of courtesy that they could well do without.

Some men, on the other hand, enjoy caressing their partner before intercourse either manually or orally, perhaps to orgasm, knowing that she'll probably have another on penetration.

What men do

Men do not consider themselves to be true men if they don't want to have intercourse. It is widely held to be 'what men do'. So it is that most men think that to be 'real men' they must have intercourse, even if they don't particularly want to at any given time. This understandably puts them under some pressure because not to want sex seems less than manly and might even give the woman the impression that he has gone off her/has another woman/or is gay. The sober truth is that some women at least *do* think just these sorts of things so perhaps men's fears are not totally unfounded.

How much this expectation bears on the consistent finding that men say that they want more sex, however much they currently have it, is difficult to know. In almost every survey carried out the majority of men say that one thing they can be sure about sex is that they want more of it. Given that intercourse is seen as being so central a feature of 'being a man' in our culture could it be that men are expressing a desire for more sex as a way of obtaining ongoing confirmation that they are in fact men? It is argued by many that this has, at least to some extent, come about because men are under siege sexually and in many other ways.

Unfortunately, for some at least, this concentration on perform-ance rather than pleasure kills such eroticism as there is and reduces the average love-making session to a poor shadow of what it could be. Some men, worried about losing their erection, and thus unable to 'perform', cut short foreplay to the detriment of both themselves and their partner. With such a pre-occupation with genital function it is hardly surprising that many men become cut off from what their bodies really could feel. That most men don't realise this is sad enough but that so few women do either is a tragedy because in our culture women have so much more to do with emotions within relationships. If *they* are unaware of what's going on they can do little or nothing about it.

One of the most widely-held beliefs of both men and women is that sex comes naturally to a man . . . that sex is somehow the essence of men in a way that is not true of women. Undoubtedly there is considerable cultural pressure for men to have intercourse but this is probably all that can be reasonably claimed. This starts early in life and comes to a head in the teen years when sexual competition is rife. Obviously any individual man will have personal reasons for wanting to have a sexual relationship with his partner but there can be no real need to have intercourse as often as he does . . . not, that is, if procreation is what it is all about. The belief that men and women have intrinsically different 'needs' for sex seems, in fact, to be totally erroneous, as anyone working in sexual medicine knows. That men tend to be pushed culturally into too much genital activity and women into too little is probably a feature of western civilisation but this is all that can safely be said.

What does seem to be true is that intercourse has taken on a massive burden of importance in human sexuality to the extent that, as we have seen, a man doesn't consider sex as being anything else. Many, if not most, men would, however, be a great deal happier if they weren't made to feel that intercourse was compulsory in some way. Of course they'd have to be 'taught' what else they might do. Studies and clinical experience show that they wouldn't have much of a clue unless they *were* taught.

Some feminists, and indeed an increasing number of sensitive men, point out that intercourse with the man ejaculating in the woman is the ultimate exploitation of women. It is symbolic, they claim, of man's ownership of women, the central pillar of patriarchy and the very heart of the way that men appropriate women. The confusion has been that a man has to ejaculate if he is to impregnate his partner yet a woman can lie there and do nothing yet contribute to the procreative process. This has undoubtedly made a man's orgasm *appear* to be more valuable than that of a woman, in pure biological terms if nothing else.

However this ignores the fact that sex is *not* simply a matter of reproductive biology. The vast majority of sexual intercourse episodes have little or nothing whatever to do with producing babies. As such it

Sex comes naturally to a man

is a cop-out of enormous dimensions for men to behave, however they justify it, as if they were somehow governed by a biological imperative that excludes the feelings and experiences of their partners.

Because of this 'biological sex' myth both sexes have expected women to minister to the man's orgasm and to his pleasure generally whilst at the same time putting the sexuality of women firmly down as worthy of little consideration. This has continued, however unconsciously, to make both sexes see men as superior and stronger in the sexual arena than women. Ironically, the reverse is almost certainly the case.

Men on top

Even in these liberated times most women still prefer the missionary position. There is nothing intrinsically wrong with this of course but it seems to me to perpetuate a continuing male-dominated pattern of intercourse. That most women say that this position is 'more romantic' proves my point. They would rather accept the *status quo* in this regard yet are only too quick to complain when the self-same dominating, superior (on top) man treats them in everyday life as if he *were* these things.

That women take longer than the average man to have a climax 'proves' yet further in the eyes of many men how inferior women are when it comes to sex. I have had male patients say to me that they agree with Rex Harrison in My Fair Lady when he asked, 'Why can't a woman be more like a man?' The trouble is that although we have moved on apace culturally we simply haven't biologically. Ancient man probably ejaculated very quickly with little or no concern for the pleasure of his mate. To play around for long periods of time during intercourse would have been disadvantageous because at such times the male would have been at risk from predators or his enemies. Perhaps then 'premature ejaculation' was normal millions of years ago and that what we are aiming for today is a perversion of our biology as our cultural expectations take the upper hand.

Today though intercourse has changed into a form of inter-personal behaviour that has more to do with pair bonding and long term love bonds than reproduction. As a result the very nature of intercourse has changed – at least in its style and intent. Alas for many men – and especially their partners – caveman sex is still the norm. Like all anachronisms though it has a faint charm and can even be wheeled out as a method of choice from time to time but for most people most of the time it is as out of date and inappropriate as the stone-headed axe.

There can be no doubt that most men like intercourse but there is also little doubt that most have problems at least some of the time; that most think they aren't getting enough of it; that almost all are sensitive about their performance; and that there is generally far too much of an emphasis on the matter in human sexuality.

I am not making a plea for men to stop enjoying intercourse but rather to 'allow' them to see that there are other things that are just as fulfilling; less goal-centred and possibly even nicer for their partners, if only on occasions. By taking the spotlight off intercourse we would also help men who, under pressure that sex is no longer for babies (which they could easily enough justify and come to terms with) unconsciously want to back away from the arena without actually leaving it.

At the moment most men have no choice in the matter. Either they have sex (intercourse) or they cease to be a 'real man' in their eyes and possibly in those of their partner. That so many men are dissatisfied with this state of affairs is hardly surprising and will ensure that marriages continue to collapse as both sexes battle to understand the dilemma they find themselves in.

Copulation or intercourse?

While on the subject of intercourse it would be helpful to look at what most people consider intercourse to be. At the simplest most basic, level it is, of course, the process in which a man puts his penis into a woman's vagina.

To define intercourse in this mechanistic way though is to do it an injustice because for many people it means much more than this. Perhaps what we should be looking at is the difference between true intercourse and what many men mean when they talk about 'sex' which is, all too often, copulation. In other words, we need to look at the difference between 'making love' and 'fucking'.

Let's start by looking at 'fucking' or copulation. This is a biologi- *What is copulation?* cal event that can be undertaken with anyone. All that is necessary is a man with an erect penis and a woman who will open her legs. It is often self-centred and involves little other than genital activity. There is little or no commitment between the people involved and is a sort of end in itself. The woman need not be interested or willing for it to be 'successful' and her preferences, or those of her partner, are imma- terial. Whether or not she is satisfied by the event is beside the point and because the whole business is so unimaginative and uninsightful the pleasure gained is small and the whole thing becomes boring after a short time. Behaviour tends to be somewhat stereotyped with very restricted horizons. Failure of the mechanics to work is a tragedy because the whole process is largely mechanical. Few, if any, emotions are revealed or even involved and as a result all that happens is that one or both partners are sexually relieved at the end of it. The gains and rewards from copulation are short-lived.

Many women reading this list will be only too aware that this is what they experience week after week, year in and year out with their partner. And this is one reason why so many men fail to satisfy either themselves or their partners sexually. Of course there is no harm whatsoever in a couple copulating from time to time and 'quickie' sex is undoubtedly a form of such enjoyable copulation. However, be- cause it so depersonalises and takes account of so few human needs, it can never be truly satisfying as a sexual way of life and leaves many men saying that they want more *sex* when what they really *need* is to start having intercourse and to stop copulating.

Intercourse is totally different. It is intensely partner-centred and is thus the most intimate form of inter-personal communication and supposes a level of commitment that is quite unnecessary for the copulating couple. Certainly intercourse involves the genitals but it also involves the personalities of the couple. It is an integral part of a couple's life together rather than an isolated event that is an end in itself. True intercourse requires full cooperation between the couple and the partner's needs are central. While making the occasion pleasant for one's self it is also vital to take that of one's partner into account. This calls for insight and imagination and means that, unlike copulation, intercourse improves with time.

Rather than being stereotyped intercourse varies from time to time and from occasion to occasion to take into account the moods and feelings of the partner and, as a result, the horizons are limitless. Because the physical 'plumbing' side is so relatively unimportant failures can be easily coped with, particularly if they are only occasional, as the emotional commitment makes up for any lost physical sensations.

Communication is vital

Communication is every bit as important as is the relief of physical tension and this involves revealing more and more about oneself to one's partner in such a way as to create a unique, caring relationship based on one another's secret desires. Such a policy leads to continuous improvement, the banishing of boredom, and opens up limitless possibilities for the future. In short, it becomes a life-time investment that yields interest daily.

There is little doubt that many couples copulate much of the time and, as a result, find little joy in their sex lives. Men, being mechanistic at the best of times, finding themselves wary of or unable to express emotions, and looking to short-term gains in a goal-centred way, tend to go for copulation more readily than do women. They then understandably feel dissatisfied and want *more* copulation to remedy the dissatisfaction or look elsewhere for *better* copulation. Neither path yields anything other than more frustration because more of something second-rate rarely matches up to a smaller helping of something really good.

Unfortunately, too many of us dignify our copulation with the term 'love-making' and wonder why it is that we aren't satisfied or are positively dissatisfied. We look on page 192 at how to transform copulation into love-making. It is a transformation well worth making.

Anal stimulation

In our culture anal matters are often considered to be dirty, sinful, or otherwise unwholesome and the subject goes largely unmentioned. The facts, however, are that for many people of both sexes the anus and the area around it is very sensitive sexually. For some men it is their best and most erogenous zone yet they go through their whole lives without ever obtaining the pleasure they could.

Detailed discussions with men, and the few surveys that have addressed the subject, (such as the Hite Report on men) find that men

are more anally-centred than most women realise. Most people think of anal stimulation and penetration in particular as being a homosexual pursuit. Certainly anal penetration is one sexual activity that most homosexuals enjoy but it is also pleasurable to many men whose main or only sexual alignment is heterosexual. In fact receiving anal penetration by a finger is a source of pleasure for some men.

Many men enjoy anal stimulation but few declare it to their partner for fear of rejection, ridicule or being accused of being homosexual.

To many men, and indeed their partners, the notion of receptivity goes hand in hand with passivity. Women have always 'received' a penis into their bodies and have been thought of as passive as a result. This requires some rethinking in a modern relationship. After all, who is to say that receiving or being penetrated are passive activities? Many women would strongly disagree. Once this confusion can be settled the desire that some men have to receive in this way can be seen as part of a loving exchange and not a sign of passivity or homosexuality.

Of all those who have tried it the vast majority say they like it and most say that it gives deep feelings of sexual pleasure that are not obtainable in other ways. The act of being penetrated is probably a feature of femininity in both sexes and there is little doubt in my mind that some men enjoy the act of being penetrated just as much as many women do. Certainly men who enjoy being penetrated say that they have a deep sense of fulfilment and satisfaction afterwards. Such men also say that any orgasm that occurs along with anal penetration is exceptionally exquisite. Indeed, for some their best ever orgasms are obtained when some sort of penetration takes place at the same time.

Two or three inches inside a man's anus on the front wall of the back passage lies the prostate gland. Stimulating this produces highly arousing sensations in most men and in some it can produce an erection very quickly. This area has been called the male G-spot but perhaps this is an unnecessarily complex way of looking at the fact that the prostate yields similar pleasures to a man when stimulated as does the front wall of the vagina in a woman. After the initial apprehension that some men have about such stimulation few fail to be delighted by the intense sensations prostatic massage produces.

Shere Hite found in her study that about one third of men who were heterosexual had tried anal penetration with a finger (either during masturbation or love-making) and that another twelve per cent had tried being penetrated by a penis or penis-sized object. Given the considerable shame involved in anything to do with the anus I am sure that these are both underestimates of the true position.

Anal penetration

Most of those men who had been penetrated by a finger liked it, as had those penetrated by a penis-sized object. A few men like anal penetration only when they do it themselves, probably because of the guilt attached to the practice. Many more like the idea, or indeed the practice, during masturbation but cannot bring themselves to ask their partner to do it for fear of having her think they are homosexuals or perverts. Some men, incidentally, fear that any form of anal play or stimulation could turn them into homosexuals and there are few things that men fear more. This is especially likely after being penetrated by a penis-shaped object such as a vibrator or dildo.

The sensations involved with anal stimulation can be so great that some men have an orgasm without any other activity. For the majority though the penis has to be stimulated too. A few men, when stimulated around the prostate, ejaculate without an erection yet have all the exquisite sensations associated with ejaculation. The majority of men who have experienced prostatic orgasms say that they are different from normally-produced ones and that for most they are far better. The orgasm seems to engulf the entire body, rather in the way that women describe when the front wall of their vagina is caressed. Of course, simply penetrating a man with a finger or indeed anything else is highly unlikely to produce an orgasm in itself. Just as in a woman there is no reason to suppose that penetration alone will do the trick.

Today, perhaps more than ever, people are concerned about the safety of any anal activity during sex. First, let it be said that unless the individual or his partner has AIDS or is HIV positive there is no risk at all. However, anal stimulation can cause tiny breaks in the surface of the lining of the anal canal and so can, if the woman has the HIV virus in her body, lay the man open to contracting the disease. For the couple who are sure of one another though this should be no problem and a gentle, well-lubricated finger or two will do the man no harm. Naturally, it makes sense not to go in for any kind of anal stimulation if you have an infection on your fingers; to be sure that your fingernails are kept short and clean; to go gently at first while the activity is unfamiliar to the man; and so on.

The only precaution in the AIDS-free couple is to be sure to keep any finger that has been inside a man's anus away from the vagina. If this simple precaution isn't observed it is possible for the woman to get a vaginal or urinary infection (cystitis).

Of course some women are suspicious that their man might want some sort of anal stimulation because of his interest in playing with *her* anus, or even in having anal sex with her. Anal sex is a very ancient sexual activity and has been used as a form of contraception for countless centuries. It has received a bad press recently because of AIDS but for those who are sure of one another's faithfulness and health there is no danger from it. This being a book about men and their sexual needs and desires, is no place to look at why women enjoy anal sex, but some do.

I believe that many a man who really wants anal penetration for himself projects this need, quite unconsciously, on to his partner and so tries to interest her in anal sex.

Also men like anal sex because it is forbidden. 'Naughty sex' is all the more enjoyable to most people.

Naughty sex

Other men see anal sex as something of an unusual activity that only the most loving of women are likely to be interested in. They then, quite unconsciously of course, make demands for anal sex on their otherwise quite conventional partner, to test the relationship. 'If she *really* loved me she'd do it' is the sort of unconscious thinking going on here. When she then says she'd rather not he begins to question the relationship.

Some such men use demands for anal sex as a make-or-break in the relationship knowing full well that their partner will not tolerate it. A few such men quite consciously want to get out of the relationship and use anal sex, or some other unusual pursuit, as the passport to doing so.

Some men introduce the matter by way of extending their love-life with their partner and of course a proportion of these will be rewarded with interest from their woman. For the woman who has had several children the tightness of the anus is pleasant not only for her but for her partner and this is (along with the contraceptive safety) a considerable bonus to such couples. Provided that the woman is well lubricated (perhaps with the man using a condom too) anal sex will continue to be a pleasure for many a couple who are sure that they are not at risk from AIDS and there is no reason why it should not be. Men and women like to be penetrated – it is an exceptionally intimate thing to do with someone you love.

Surely the answer, as with all sexual matters, is to make the one-to-one relationship work at home in a way that answers all one another's needs. This is especially important at a time when bisexuality seems to be booming in spite of the fears associated with AIDS.

WHAT MEN THINK ABOUT WOMEN'S SEX ORGANS

For the purposes of this section we'll confine our discussion to women's genitals and their breasts if only because the unseen parts of a woman's sex organs feature so little in men's thinking – at least not in the sexual arena.

The vagina

Most people in our culture are brought up to think that genitals are, at least to some extent, 'dirty'. Both the sexes have pretty negative views about women's vulvas with some women talking to therapists in terms of 'drains' and other similar words. Men pick up this message fairly early in their lives, often in talk with other boys in their early teens. Stories of a woman's genitals having teeth engender fears and threats of penile mutilation. Some men with impotence see putting their penis into a woman's vagina as akin to putting their head into a lion's mouth and only the most careful and sometimes protracted therapy can dissuade them from this view.

Into the lion's mouth

Pubic hair

Some men find a woman's pubic hair 'untidy', 'threatening', or even 'mystical'. The very fact that so much about a woman's sex organs is hidden also further mystifies the matter and as a result some men are quite scared and certainly ignorant of what they are really all about.

The clitoris

I am often amazed at the intelligent, middle-class men I see who have only the faintest clue as to what their partner's genitals look like. Is it any surprise then that so many women find that their men simply don't know what to do in order to stimulate their clitoris? Those men who do know a little get their information from books. Far more men are ill at ease stimulating their woman's clitoris than is generally realised by women. Most feel very much in the dark about what it is and what to do with it. A very common view among men is that the clitoris is really a secret sort of thing that shouldn't be exposed to knowledge or gaze and that somehow, as if by magic, things just happen to it during a woman's sexual arousal. Some men even feel that it is abnormal to have to do anything to it and that to do so is perverted in some way. Many more say that caressing it is the sort of thing teenagers do when they cannot have 'real sex' and that this is not their way of behaving at all. Clitoral stimulation then is seen by many men as juvenile and not what 'real men' do.

Having said this, those who *do* stimulate their partner's clitoris usually find it highly exciting for them (the men), especially if it results in the woman having orgasms. This gives them a great sense of power and control at the same time as making them feel warm about seeing their partner enjoying herself so much.

The subject of women stimulating themselves to orgasm in front of their man is a very vexed one. Some men are delighted and see it as a sign that the woman is highly aroused and very much in love with them. Others, however, feel somewhat threatened by it and feel that it is definitely not something that any 'nice' woman would do. Most men have never experienced a woman caressing her clitoris in front of them yet many such men say that they like the idea. According to most men clitoral stimulation during intercourse is acceptable if it is done by the man. This is undoubtedly because men still like to think that they are making things happen in bed and that women have orgasms only if they, the men, make them happen. In this context she should keep her hands to herself and not trespass on 'his territory'.

The vulva

The smell of a woman's vaginal area is an intoxicating and pleasant one if she washes daily (more often during a period) yet most men are wary of unpleasant smells from the vulval area and even very keen oral sex enthusiasts talk of their misgivings unless the woman's vulva is squeaky clean. The French certainly knew what they were about when they brought bidets into popular use.

Women's vulvas vary greatly in appearance, as do men's penises. Vulvas vary greatly But to some men the appearance is somewhat daunting if it differs greatly from other vulvas they have known. So it is that men talk of every vulva having its own personality and this indeed seems to be true. Given the very considerable variations in anatomy of the area some individual vulvas will appeal to a particular man while others will not. Some men are put off by certain features, such as long inner lips, whilst others are turned on by them. Much of this is highly mysterious to the average man, however, who either 'fancies' or is 'turned off' by a particular woman's genitals. Certainly the aroma of a particular vulva can greatly appeal to one man and not at all to another – undoubtedly the pheromones contained in the secretions are a vital part of the 'chemistry' that attracts a particular man to a particular woman.

A woman's cycle

Most men continue to be baffled by and ignorant of sanitary protection and to some the menstruating woman is still something of a creature who really ought to be shut up in a shed, as in certain pre-literate cultures! The whole subject is a no-go one for many men yet for a quarter of their partner's reproductive life it is a state in which she, and he, finds herself. Few men know much about their partners' periods but perhaps this is as much the woman's fault as it is the man's, if research that shows that the most private thing a woman does is changing a tampon is anything to go by.

I find this rather difficult to equate with men and women coming closer together in modern marriage. Probably the only way that men and women will become better acquainted is through a better under-standing and knowledge of one another yet the average man knows next to nothing about his partner's reproductive cycles. Couples who

There is no better way to learn about a woman's sexual response than to watch her masturbate.

use the cervical mucus method of contraception say how much more aware they both become of her cycles. Such a couple might also feel the woman's cervix for its consistency, the size of the opening, and so on. This, with the knowledge of her breast size and consistency, all builds up to give a picture of her total hormonal pattern throughout any one month, year after year. Such couples get to know, just by the feel of the woman's genitals and breasts, exactly at what stage in her cycle she is and on this they can plan for a healthy and enjoyable sexual life. He, for example, knows that as her breasts feel at all enlarged and lumpy she is coming up to a pre-menstrual phase and so goes easy on breast play. Between them they know when the best times of the month are for her most to enjoy intercourse, perhaps avoiding certain positions at particular times if she finds them uncomfortable at that part of the cycle. And so it goes on. A couple like this read the ebb and flow of the woman's hormones and their effects not only on her reproductive organs but also on her sexual life.

Biology test

For many readers this must sound like having to take a high-school biology test on the woman – and in a way it is. But the effort is well worthwhile if only because those things that remain mysterious to us hold a power over us that is demeaning to intelligent individuals living in the closing years of the twentieth century. It never ceases to amaze me how many of the men I see think that all of this is somewhat weird and mystical. They spend hours, or years, over a lifetime learning about the intricacies of a gearbox or their fishing gear; and will design complex business organisations or engineering structures; yet they remain almost totally ignorant of something whose workings affect their everyday lives so intimately. Such a man then whines when his wife pushes him away from her breasts when he goes to squeeze them at the sink on leaving for work. He goes off thinking that she's moody again, or that he has done something for which this is some sort of punishment whereas the fact is that she is three days before her period and they are tender as hell. She thinks that he must know this after all this time but he doesn't because he isn't tuned into her cycles and her hormones.

To such a man, and there are millions of them, a woman is either available for sex or she is not. When she *is* the world is OK and when she is not things are pretty bleak. To even quite intelligent men then, the working of their women's bodies is a true mystery and one which they cannot see themselves as being able to unravel. Of course this need not be so and many, if not most, relationships would greatly benefit from a lot more communication on this whole subject.

Highly successful couples are finely attuned to one another both physically and mentally. A man in such a partnership can look at the state of his partner's skin and hair and know where she is in her cycle. From this he can predict how receptive sexually she'll be, what sort of love-making she'll want and won't want; which positions she'll find pleasant; what times of day are best to make love; what sorts of foods she'll best like; how best to help her with the children; and so on. A man like this knows if she is having a particularly heavy period; will be able to make life better for her when she has pain during the first day

It started off as a friendly squeeze but he forgot the time of the month and she's upset.

or so of her bleeding; will know what to expect and what to do to help if she has pains mid-cycle; and so on. And all of this without having to be told.

If men want women to be their best friends – and numerous studies show that they do and are – then they must start to take some responsibility for them on a day-to-day basis and this includes their bodies, their moods and their hormones.

Breasts

Talking of bodies, when it comes to breasts men's views are somewhat strange. Most men, when asked in the pub, would have one believe that breasts need to be big, pointed and firm – indeed very like the 'knockers' they see on page three every day in the tabloid newspapers. Reality is, however, somewhat different, as is so often the case with men and sex.

About five years ago I asked three hundred women more than eighty questions about their breasts. Around two thirds were dis- Two thirds of women are satisfied with their breasts in one way or another yet half of their dissatisfied partners were 'satisfied' with them and a further twenty-three per cent 'fairly satisfied'. Clearly women are much more concerned about their breasts than are their menfolk. Perhaps women have fallen for the nonsense that men give out when talking with other men. Clinical experience shows that most men are delighted with their partner's breasts and that the only common turn-off is hairy nipples – and there are even fans of these.

But if men tend to like their women's breasts what they do with them during sex is not always what women want. Men tend to kiss and suck their partner's breasts when making love; but what women really like is kissing and gentle stroking.

Male misunderstanding of female orgasm

Men seem to have some pretty unrealistic notions about female orgasm. These then infect the whole sexual arena, often to the detriment of both men and women.

We have seen already that to men sex *is* intercourse. By this definition sex almost always involves an orgasm for the man. However, it less commonly results in an orgasm for the woman.

Clitoral stimulation is usually needed

There can now be little doubt that the vast majority of women obtain their orgasms from clitoral stimulation. Whether this stimulation is applied directly by the man or the woman to her clitoris or whether the clitoris is stimulated indirectly by the tugging of the inner lips of her vulva as the man thrusts in and out with his penis is somewhat beside the point. Some women can undoubtedly obtain enough rhythmic friction of the clitoral area by indirect stimulation (for example by penile thrusting alone) but this is uncommon. Others without doubt can have an orgasm from nipple or breast stimulation alone and yet others when their G-spot is massaged. However, all these methods probably result in orgasm for only the minority of women. The vast majority require direct, or nearly direct, clitoral caresses if they are to have an orgasm.

To many women the having of an orgasm during intercourse (or indeed before or after it) is something of a bonus. They enjoy sex a lot whether or not they have one. To most men, however, sex *means* having an orgasm (for them) and more recently, with all the pressure from the women's movement, for their partner too.

On the one hand we have millions of men who are striving, often at great price, to produce orgasms for their women, usually in ways that will never do so; and on the other those men who believe that if they were able to last long enough and were able to thrust in just the right way their woman would come just as they, the men, do as a result of penetration and thrusting. In other words a real man would be able to know what magic key would fit his woman's lock or would, by being so manly, be able to make her have an orgasm during intercourse even if he didn't have the key.

For most women intercourse doesn't end in an orgasm on most occasions unless the man takes an active part in making something happen. This is seen by many men as a sign that their woman is frigid in some way because the myth of super sex has it that any half-way sexy woman who fancies a man will have ready orgasms with him as soon as he starts to thrust in and out of her.

Until the beginning of this century nobody talked much about women's orgasms and when they did they assumed that what made men orgasm should have the same effect on women. Women's masturbatory practices that involved caressing the clitoris were said by Freud and his followers to be 'infantile' and many 'experts' taking up this lead believed that women who stimulated their clitoris to orgasm were somehow lacking in adult femaleness. This lead to the long-running battle of the experts over clitoral-versus-vaginal orgasm. The fact is that the overwhelming majority of women need direct, or nearly direct, clitoral stimulation if they are to have an orgasm.

Given that this is true why is it that for so many years women themselves have kept quiet on the matter and allowed their men to labour under the misunderstandings that they have?

First, until very recently women were owned by their men (first by their fathers and then by their husbands) and even today a man cannot technically rape his wife. She is his sexual possession and legally he can do with her what he likes – at least sexually.

Second, women have had, until recently, no rights over their own bodies; their husbands controlled their fertility and the State and the Church also had vital supporting roles to play.

But perhaps the most vital part of the story lies in the social and emotional position women have, until recently, found themselves in. They were clearly second-class citizens and particularly so in bed. Having said this, women have always had sexual power over men in many subtle ways but until the last half-century or so men did not tend to look at their wives for sexual high-jinks. A wife was looked to to provide bread-and-butter intercourse (or, more likely, copulation) and was, of course, the home of 'reproductive sex' but other women were turned to for excitement or sexual fulfilment. That the same woman could, at the same time, be performing both roles but in different plays is the very stuff of comedy through the ages.

But the notion that any individual married woman can be both whore and mother, lady and sex siren, is a relatively new one as modern marriage makes us seek everything from our one, life-long partner.

Other women for 'sexy' sex

MEN AND CONTRACEPTION

Given that men equate fertility with virility it is hardly surprising that the whole subject of contraception and men is a touchy one. Little research has been done in this area and men's views on the subject are scarcely known, except by those working in the field of sexual and marital medicine who have made a point of asking.

It would seem sensible and fair in today's world for contraception to be a shared responsibility. However, today's man rarely, if ever, goes to a family planning clinic – only about one and a half per cent of all attenders are men and those that do attend are usually in the company of their partners. Yet the most commonly-used contraceptive is still the condom – a predominantly male method – albeit often obtained by women.

Women don't trust men

The truth of the matter is that women simply don't trust men when it comes to contraception. After all, it is they, the women, who bear the brunt of the pregnancy and mothering. Indeed, at one time when the male pill looked like becoming an imminent reality there was quite a lot of resistance from some women at even the thought of men taking control of fertility again.

I say 'again' because men have always played a big part in contraception historically. In 1960 the withdrawal method was the only method used by up to two thirds of couples in France, Italy and Hungary and until the coming of the Pill the condom and withdrawal were the two most widely used methods of contraception. Both were male methods. In developing countries today about forty per cent of all those who use contraception use male methods.

With the coming of the Pill in the sixties women had, for the first time, a real method of contraception that they could control. It was this that started the shift towards contraception being seen as 'women's business'. Even so sales of condoms still soared. As recently as 1970 condom users still outnumbered Pill takers and more than half of all couples used a male method of contraception. By the mid-70s things were changing with the Pill becoming the most popularly used method. This didn't last long though as women became aware of the dangers of the Pill. However today low-dose multi-phasic Pills have helped redress the balance and manufacturers claim that more women now use the Pill than men use condoms.

But men, to be fair, don't have such a range of contraceptive methods that are available to them. The condom continues to be a subject of ridicule to many ('it's like wearing your wellies in the bath'), although certain other countries have reversed this situation and made condoms seem fashionable. AIDS is also changing attitudes towards the condom and people now talk about them in a way that would have been unthinkable even five years ago.

Vasectomy, whilst popular, is a non-reversible method and withdrawal is pretty unsatisfactory for both men and women. But things are changing in society in a way that will see considerable changes in attitudes to contraception among men.

First, there is an increasing emphasis on equality between the sexes and study after study shows that men express the view that they should take a serious role in contraception. That they tend *not* to do so when it actually comes to the crunch is another matter. It is true that there is more 'togetherness' in contraception than before.

Second, if women want more shared involvement and responsibility they'll have to involve men from very early on in the decision-making process. Men are playing an increasing role in childcare today and there is evidence that shows that the quality of men's lives is more greatly affected by children than is that of women. Several studies have found that couples with children are generally less satisfied with their lives than are those without and one survey found that this was especially true for the men. If men's lives are so greatly affected, and perhaps for the worse, by having children (or more children) then clearly they should be more involved at the very basic level of decision-making. All too often they are not.

Happier without children

Contraceptive methods and what men think about them

As I have already pointed out, few studies have looked at what men think about contraception. Almost all the work has been done with women. However, those of us working in the field have some pretty good ideas about men's views. Given that most women never talk about the details of contraception with their men this can come as a real eye-opener to many.

The male Pill

Such men as I have discussed the matter with find the idea none too attractive. Given that they, the men, will not have to bear the main physiological brunt of the results of forgetting the Pill many honest ones say that they think they'd probably forget to take it regularly. If it were available as a depot form of injectable drug some would be more happy because they could then forget about it for several months.

Most men think that any side-effects at all would be unacceptable and given the general move away from drugs and medications by society as a whole, it is doubtful whether any 'drug' however good, would be popular in an increasingly health-conscious culture. Also, many men raise the fact that given that they produce sperms all the time they would have less lee-way for method failure compared with a woman who ovulates only once a month.

It is my professional view, after listening to men on the subject, that the male Pill is unlikely to be a winner with men.

The Condom

The pros and cons

Most men do not like using a condom or sheath and given the choice would rather not do so. Those that favour them argue that they are cheap; effective if used with a spermicide; have no medical side effects; protect them at least to some extent against VD and particularly AIDS; can be helpful if the man comes too soon (by reducing penile sensitivity); are good if the woman has a vaginal infection such as thrush; increases the acceptability of anal sex; can be fun to put on as part of foreplay especially if the condom is one of the ribbed or 'recreational' types; are widely available and don't have to be obtained through a doctor or clinic; and that they can be carried around as a back-stop to be used in casual sexual encounters when the contraceptive safety or venereal disease status of the woman is in doubt.

These advantages are formidable and explain why it is that the condom has always been and continues to be, popular.

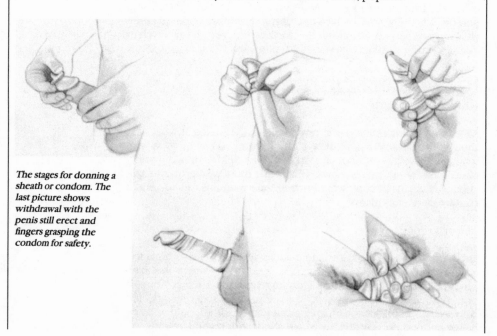

The stages for donning a sheath or condom. The last picture shows withdrawal with the penis still erect and fingers grasping the condom for safety.

However, the majority of men say that they lose at least some sensation and that it calls for a halt to the proceedings as they put one on. A condom also has to be used properly if it is to be effective and there is no doubt that many an unwanted pregnancy occurs because the man or his partner do not know how to use a condom. The basic principles are as follows: Always use a new condom, don't re-use them; ensure that the penis doesn't come near the vagina unless the condom is on – even the first few drops of semen before a man comes can contain sperms. The condom should be applied only when the penis is fully erect. Hold the teat firmly so that the air is squeezed out and then unroll the condom along the length of the penis. When it is on the penis it should show the packing rings clearly. After intercourse grip the base of the condom so that it is not left inside as the penis is withdrawn. Be sure to withdraw while the penis is still erect. Never use Vaseline or other greasy lubricants as these can damage the rubber and be careful with your finger nails.

All this calls for at least some care so it is not too surprising that there are failures with sheaths.

With the current fears about AIDS the condom will, in my view, become an even more popular item and will further take women away from the Pill. Today's woman who has more than one regular and totally trustworthy partner will probably think it wise to equip herself with a condom to use on any occasion on which casual sex might occur. In this sense the condom is now becoming more of a 'protective', as it used to be in the old days when its main value was as a protection against syphilis.

Back to the 'protectives' again

Vasectomy

Although many men are concerned about their potency after a vasectomy there is no evidence that it is adversely affected by the operation. Large studies have found that only those men with existing problems or potential problems at the time of the operation have sexual problems after a vasectomy and that men with healthy sex lives and stable relationships have nothing to worry about. This means that for the best outcome sexually a couple needs careful psychosexual counselling before the operation but this is often either unavailable or skimpily carried out.

Some men like vasectomy because it allows them to take the responsibility for contraception, after perhaps many years of seeing their partner do so. This seems to many men to redress the balance. It is also popular because it is, to all intents and purposes, completely effective. Once done it needs no further 'maintenance' or supervision. It gives a man the peace of mind that he will not sire children he doesn't want either within or outside his marriage and that he cannot be 'tricked' into having an unwanted pregnancy by his partner who may, for quite unconscious reasons, want to have another baby.

However, some men are unhappy about vasectomy because it is not reversible and thus becomes a once-and-for-all decision. Many men worry about what would happen should their wife and children all be killed in a car crash, for example. A very few men bank sperms against this eventuality but this is rare in the UK. As long as vasectomy is still an irreversible procedure most men will have at least some qualms about it.

Having said this many men in their late thirties or early forties are sure that they would not want more children with any future partner. Given that men seem to fare worse in the happiness stakes once they have children this is hardly surprising. However, in a world of easy divorce at least some come to regret their decision to have the operation because the unthinkable (wanting more children) becomes a reality with a new loved one and the loss of his own children to his ex-wife.

A vasectomy is not immediately effective; tests have to be done for some weeks afterwards to ensure that all the sperms stored before the procedure have been exhausted. During this time the man (or his partner) has to use another method. This is usually not a problem but it can be because some women take it upon themselves, often quite consciously, let alone unconsciously, to go for a 'last throw of the dice' before their man becomes sterile for ever. This worries some men whose partners are not as happy about the procedure as they are.

Withdrawal

This age-old method is not much liked by men because it goes against a man's instinctive desire to thrust deeply into the vagina just before his climax. The sense of let-down for both the man and his partner can be very unpleasant and for this reason few men choose the method if they have a choice. All that can be fairly said in its favour is that it doesn't cost anything and that it is better than making the woman pregnant. Most men who use this method say how unrelaxing it is to have to be constantly vigilant in case they lose control and start to ejaculate inside the woman. Given that a loss of control is one of the most exciting and intimate parts of making love this is a drawback.

Terribly unsafe

But the biggest problem with the method is that it is so unsafe. Getting the timing right can be difficult, even for an experienced couple, especially if they are totally absorbed in the matter in hand. The intercourse positions which can be used are also restricted because the penis has to be removed at a moment's notice. If the woman is worried that the man might not withdraw in time she is very unlikely to relax thus making intercourse uncomfortable, or even painful, for her. Lastly, there are few men who have the lasting power to enable their partner to climax with the penis inside which means that most such couples end up with the woman unsatisfied during intercourse and looking to masturbation afterwards to finish the act for her.

None of these factors makes the method suitable for the inexperienced couple or for the man who has not learned with some certainty when his ejaculation is imminent.

Obviously, from what has been said, this method is highly unsatisfactory from most points of view – not the least of which is that it is very unsafe. The safety can be somewhat increased if the couple keep a spermicide handy to put into the vagina after intercourse should there be any doubt that sperms could have been spilled.

The Pill

Increasing numbers of men today are concerned for their partner's health on the Pill. For the majority though, it is still the contraceptive of choice because it is not related to intercourse; it ensures that his woman is permanently 'available'; it is very effective if taken properly; it enables a woman to plan her periods thus making sex on holiday or honeymoon a possibility when otherwise it would not have been; it can reduce her period pains; and finally it makes periods shorter and lighter which is nice for the man because his partner is sexually unavailable for less of the month.

Men worry about their partner

The Pill then has many advantages for the man and indeed for his partner but for many the potential hazards are too much of a gamble and as a result many thousands of couples choose not to use it.

The Pill is, *par excellence* the female method of contraception that 'excludes' or excuses men from the burden of unwanted pregnancy. The man plays no part whatever in the day-to-day use of the method; it is totally the woman's affair. He is unaware that she is using it when actually making love and for these and many other reasons it is easy to see why it is that the man whose partner is on the Pill is often the most delighted of all men, provided, of course, that it suits *her* health.

The diaphragm

This is a greatly undervalued form of contraception. It is cheap and easy to use; it is nearly as safe as the Pill if used with a spermicide; there are no side-effects; it can be used to hold back menstrual flow, if only for a few hours, so as to make love-making more pleasant during a period; and it can become part of an inventive couple's love-making to put it in.

Indeed, there are very few drawbacks to the diaphragm from a man's point of view. Some women are very sensitive on the front wall of their vagina (around the G-spot) and find that the rubber of the diaphragm gets in the way of having this stimulated. If this is so another method will have to be found. Some men complain that they don't get the same sensations they used to because they cannot feel their partner's cervix against the tip of the penis. If this is a real loss an alternative method will have to be used but this is rarely a reason to abandon the diaphragm.

Depending on the sexual lifestyle of the couple the woman can insert her diaphragm every night when she brushes her teeth on the basis that she'll then be ready for sex should the matter arise. For the couple who don't make love a lot this is a waste of time and effort. For this latter group of women, sex or at least foreplay, often gets interrupted as she breaks off to go to the bathroom or wherever to put the device in. This is less attractive to most men but is a small price to pay for the safety and flexibility of the method. In fact, the diaphragm is ideal for the couple who make love very rarely or only sporadically and unpredictably. For the highly active couple the diaphragm can be a nuisance because if they want to make love again within a few hours of the last time the woman has to insert more spermicide into the vagina (leaving the diaphragm in place) and this can be messy for both her and her man.

Some men are concerned that their partner might not be using a contraceptive either at all or perhaps might be doing so unreliably. For the man who doesn't trust his partner contraceptively, and there are many more of these men than would at first seem likely, the diaphragm is a visible sign that something is being done. Having said this I have female patients who have made holes 'accidentally' in their diaphragm before making love. A man married to a woman who is determined to get pregnant come what may simply cannot win.

The sponge

This relative newcomer to the contraceptive scene is useful only in those couples in whom the woman's infertility is already on the wane. It is not safe enough to be used alone if the woman definitely does not want to get pregnant. From a man's point of view it is easy for the woman to use; is safe and is a good non-permanent barrier method. It does, however, cover the cervix thus reducing sensations to both man and woman if this is usually a source of excitement for them; is somewhat messy to put in; has, like the diaphragm, to be left in place for six to eight hours after intercourse; is fairly expensive insofar as it can only be used once; and may have side-effects from the spermicide that is absorbed through the bloodstream of the vaginal wall.

Check during foreplay

Oral sex with a sponge in place is not so pleasant for the man as it is with a diaphragm and it cannot be used to hold back menstrual flow. As some women find it difficult to ensure that it properly covers the cervix thereby assuring protection I suggest to couples that the man feel that it is covering the cervix, as a part of foreplay. This puts his mind at rest too.

Natural methods

These include the calendar methods; the Billings method; various combinations of cervical mucus awareness and temperature taking; and so on. In really careful hands a combination of cervical mucus monitoring and taking the woman's temperature every morning before rising can give a safety level nearly as good as the diaphragm. But in most relationships all these methods are unreliable. They are certainly not to be recommended in unstable relationships.

All the natural methods are women's methods. The man therefore has to rely on the woman's honesty that she is where she says she is in her cycle. Such methods are not suitable for the days around ovulation so some other method will have to be used during this time.

For the very 'together' couple who are stable in their relationship and who want to work together at making contraception a joint effort and who perhaps make the cervical mucus assessment a part of their love-making, such methods can work and work well. The aware and sensitive man can, by learning about these methods, come to have considerable insights into the workings of his partner's body and there are many such men who can tell by the state of her breasts, her cervix or her vaginal secretions exactly where she is in her cycle. Such closeness and intimacy is not likely to suit everyone but for those who like it it is a major feature of their man-woman relationship that brings them even closer.

Tubal sterilisation

This operation is the female version of a vasectomy. Like the male procedure it must be regarded as permanent and is virtually one hundred per cent effective. Also, like a vasectomy, once it is done it doesn't call for any further thought.

However, many men are concerned about their partners having their tubes tied because the operation, while not major and often done on a day basis, is much more serious than a vasectomy. Any surgical operation has the potential for complications and tying a woman's tubes is no exception. Another weighty matter for many men is that if they are the one in the partnership who doesn't want to have more children it makes them uneasy that their partner is the one to take the irrevocable decision to be sterilised.

The decision as to which member of a partnership should undergo the sterilisation procedure is a difficult one at the best of times. On occasions one or other partner has very strongly-held views about which way the matter should go and this will usually decide it. For example, some women say that they think their man would be 'less of a man' in some way if he had a vasectomy. It really doesn't much matter what the unconscious reasons are for this – the fact remains that the woman will probably never be happy if her man were to go ahead with the operation knowing that she had such strong views against it.

It appears from clinical experience that most couples come to some sort of agreement fairly easily on the subject if only because at this stage of their reproductive lives they have decided that they definitely do not want any more children and because some sort of once-and-for-all answer seems attractive. It is thus a matter of deciding which of the two is to be sterilised. Any couple who finds that the subject raises problems within the relationship should probably seek professional help because it is often a sign that other matters need attention. One of the most common problem areas is that the couple do not agree that they have in fact completed their family. Often time is the best healer in such situations. Even a delay of six months in making the decision can make all the difference. On balance it is best not to force the issue quickly because the partner who ends up being sterilised 'against their will' under however subtle pressure, can end up feeling very bitter, sometimes for a lifetime.

Who should be 'done'?

Intra-uterine device (IUD)

Men have few commonly-aired views on the subject of the coil, IUD or loop. From the man's point of view it is a trouble-free method that, once in place, can be forgotten for long periods of time. It doesn't really interfere with love-making though a few men say that they don't like the 'tail' of the device in the vagina. This can be a good method for the older couple who have almost certainly completed their family.

There are, however, several disadvantages to the IUD and many men are not happy to subject their partners to them. The main problem is that of sub-clinical infection of the uterus. This can cause reduced fertility or even complete infertility. There are now some US gynaecologists who will not prescribe an IUD for any woman who seriously thinks she might want to get pregnant in the future. Such doctors use the method more as a form of 'permanent-yet-potentially-reversible' procedure rather than as a method of family planning.

Quite a large minority of women with an IUD have heavier periods than they used to and some have 'spotting' of blood in between periods. This can be annoying to both the woman and her partner and can sometimes be enough to make the man unwilling for his partner to continue using the method.

Although the device has to be inserted by a doctor in the first place this creates no problems for the average man. However, an IUD can be expelled without the woman knowing it and this makes it less than totally safe for the couple who definitely do not want to have more children. It is always said that a woman should feel for the tail of the device each month after a period but studies have found that in the majority of those who cannot feel it the IUD is still in place and doing its job.

On its way out

All in all then the IUD is probably a method that will become less popular as the years go by and undoubtedly this will be, at least to some extent, because couples will be increasingly unwilling to expose the woman to what they perceive to be unacceptable risks.

The subject of men and contraception is a thorny one, as we have seen. Given that there are no signs that contraception thirty years from now is going to be much different from what it is today and might even be more restricted, it looks very much as though the matter will continue to present problems in many relationships. The irony is that it is often those women who are most vociferous about wanting to retain control over their fertility that, in subtle ways, make their man feel that he should be taking more of the responsibility.

In this sense some men simply cannot win. And this is set against a strong cultural view that a man's potency is somehow inextricably linked to his fertility. Because of these and other factors I hope that I am not being unduly pessimistic when I say that I see very little change occurring in the area of men and contraception – at least not in the foreseeable future.

MAKING CHANGES

The reader who has come this far in the book will, I hope, have more insight into her man's sexuality than when she started. She will also have picked up some commonsense tips that have occurred to her as she has worked through the previous chapters.

In this section I want to look briefly at some practical things that can be done to help improve on what any couple reading this book might already have going for them in their relationship.

Communicating about sex and emotions is one of the great minefields that couples have to learn to negotiate if they are to have a happy relationship in or out of bed. Because this is so central to all that follows I have started the section with some hints as to how to make things happen, especially with a view to encouraging the man who finds it difficult or impossible to talk about intimate matters. This leads naturally on to a discussion of intercourse. As I have already shown, many couples copulate all their married lives and many women, especially, become bored or annoyed by it. So in this section I look at how copulation can be transformed into intercourse and why it is worth bothering to do so.

The next part deals with pleasing your man in bed. Most women truly want to please their men yet somehow fall short of doing so for many reasons.

Lastly, almost all men have at least some sexual mishaps or problems during their relationship with a woman and it is helpful for her to know how to handle them. Very often a simple problem can be defused at an early stage and even quite major difficulties can be sorted out by a couple themselves provided they know what to do and have sufficient goodwill.

This section cannot hope to be an exhaustive guide to making love and sex better but it will, I hope, help the reader to expand in a practical way some of the areas that have been discussed in passing in the rest of the book.

Nothing in this area of life is simple or clear-cut and each woman will have to find her own way around her particular problem areas. Hopefully this section will provide at least a simple structure around which she can work in finding her own answers in her own way.

COMMUNICATING ABOUT SEX AND EMOTIONS

Verbal communication

Partly because sex is a secret area of our lives, especially in a culture that makes it all seem somewhat furtive, naughty and forbidden, and because boys are brought up to deny their feelings, talking about sex and emotions can be a real problem for even the loving couple who find communicating about other things quite easy. As a result it gets put off and off until what started as small problems grow into major battle zones that either one or the other dare not enter. First, let's look at some basic rules that seem to help when starting to talk about sex and emotions.

Make time for something to happen

Many's the couple I see who complain that they have trouble talking about these subjects yet they simply don't give themselves a chance because they are always busy, find any excuse to avoid getting together to talk, and put communication at the bottom of their priority list. They are often quite happy to *do* things together but less so to sit back and think about them or discuss them.

I know it will sound silly to many a reader but what I find works in practice is to make an appointment with one another in your diaries or on the family calendar and to decide on an agenda for what is to be discussed. Each bring a few subjects to the 'meeting' and take it in turns to talk about a subject on your list. This might seem very contrived but it works and can often be the only way of actually getting the ball rolling.

RIGHT: *This couple are on a sensual holiday (see page 189). They are enjoying one another's company and refreshing their relationship.*

It is often best to have this discussion away from home on neutral ground perhaps on a walk, in the car on a long journey, at a pub, or wherever suits you best. Here are some useful tips as to how to conduct such a get-together – tips that have been learned from helping couples trying to get it right.

Don't forget that your partner is probably your best friend

We have seen throughout the book how it is that men have a lot invested in their partners. Ironically it is this very investment that often puts them off communicating anything much. They have so much to lose if their partner takes something badly, turns on them and criticises them or actually wants to call an end to the relationship, that they often back off and say nothing. This infuriates the woman, who usually wants nothing more than to 'get it off her chest'.

Don't blame the one you love

When things go wrong in life we tend, understandably, to take it out on those whom we love most. Clearly they are most available but more than this they can, many of us wrongly believe, be taken for granted. Certainly a good relationship can withstand *some* knocks but few can take a beating very often and not suffer. Often things we do or say to our partner are reflections of other things that are wrong in our lives. So it is that a man may row with his wife, getting angry with her at the slightest provocation, yet the trouble really lies at work where his boss is being a real nuisance to him. He cannot shout and yell at the boss or he'll lose his job but he can let go at his wife instead. She, however, doesn't realise that she is standing in for the boss on these occasions and wonders what on earth is going on.

This makes it vital to try hard to express only emotions and concerns that are to do with your partner and your relationship and to be honest about other troubles or relationships that are clouding the issue. We all tend to displace our emotions to some extent and a woman frustrated with her toddler will, for example, sometimes bring out her feelings on her husband. Try to guard against this when having your heart-to-heart talks and always ask yourself, 'Is what I am accusing him/her of really about our relationship or is it something that I should be sorting out with someone else?'

Unfortunately, in such discussions or rows damaging phrases such as, 'How would you understand, you're only a man' come out almost without thinking. There is no answer to such a remark because the man can do nothing to change his sex and now sees himself as written out of the conversation because of it. Such comments are hard to forget and make real communication impossible.

When having your discussions about sex and emotions be honest certainly, but remember that we all have a limit to what we can take and that a man, particularly, finds it difficult to accept endless blows, criticism, bad temper, sulking, or whatever because it reminds him of his mother. Although it can be difficult, it is vital for the woman to remember that men are exceptionally likely to react badly to motherly behaviour even where it doesn't exist, and so should modify their behaviour accordingly. This is not to say that men need to be feather-bedded on this matter but rather that the woman who behaves in a way that reminds her man of his mother will discourage him from being open and communicative. Few couples are good at all this when they first try and it takes practice and time to put these skills to the test. As the years go by successful couples find communication skills that work well for them.

Prevent arguments from becoming rows

Almost any area to do with sex and emotions is open to considerable differences of opinion. There are, after all, few absolute truths when it comes to human behaviour. One partner's opinion is of about as much value as the other's. The very nature of sex and emotions means that they raise old, unconscious wounds and hurts that have often lain dormant for years.

When we get married we marry one another's parents and when sitting in on marital rows it is not difficult to hear the parents arguing rather than the partners. This makes discussing these things potentially explosive if only because we all realise, however unconsciously, that much of what we come out with is almost automatic – we have been primed to think and talk that way over our years at home. In this way things get said that we don't actually believe in the here-and-now yet they *are* said and cause great hurt.

Even what starts off as a sensible discussion can start to range far and wide to include just about everything and all the old grievances get dragged up. The end of this is one or the other storming out, someone sleeping in the spare bedroom, or someone getting verbally or physically violent.

The secret here is to keep strictly to the subject under discussion, and possibly closely related ones, and to keep wild generalisations to an absolute minimum. It is obviously nonsense to generalise about all men or all women and it is harmful and unfair to do so about our partner. 'You always go on at me about money' and similar remarks yield little fruit and cannot be answered. In this way things get said that you wish had not been and the hurts don't go away that easily.

As a rule try to listen about as much as you talk and don't shout your partner down. Make it a rule that one has their say first and then the other says their piece uninterrupted. Once you have both had your say try to summarise the main points. I find it is useful to put things down on paper. This clarifies the matter and makes each partner see how close they are on many points.

Listen as much as you talk

Here's another useful tip. Try to see what it is about the subject being discussed that you *can* agree on. Draw up a list of these points of agreement and then look at what you *cannot* agree on. Now see how each of these latter points could be tackled in turn by each of you, separately perhaps, so that you can enlarge your list of agreed areas.

Something that can work well is to write a letter to your partner after such a discussion outlining your thoughts on the matter. This has the advantage of being more calm and collected; enables you to think out your arguments, and your partner's more clearly; and prevents you from flying off the handle when something hurtful, however true, is said. This is especially likely to occur with men who are being criticised, however justly, because most men, while feeling perfectly justified in criticising their partner's behaviour are unable to accept her criticism in return. In most heart-to-heart discussions or arguments men act as if they expect the woman to pull her punches and shield her man from the realities. This letter-writing approach is

Discussing even quite serious matters can take place when doing something else together – it isn't necessary to sit opposite one another at home.

valuable to men who, because of their model at work like to see things set out systematically and in a 'business-like' way and is useful to women because it forces them to structure their views or complaints in a way that is understandable by their man.

When writing this letter be positive whenever possible and be personal. Don't say 'Men make women feel like little girls when they do X' but 'When you do X I feel just like a little girl and it makes me upset and angry'. And so on.

Whether the matter is raised in the discussion you set up or whether it comes out of a letter you write to one-another, don't make the mistake of ignoring what appears to you to be a 'silly' matter. Even if an apparently silly thing upsets your partner it is of concern to you because of its importance to him. 'If my partner has a problem, however unrealistic it appears to me, it is *my* problem', is a good rule to follow.

Don't make assumptions about your partner from your knowledge of yourself

Definitions of love

We all tend to make thoughtless remarks and assumptions about others, and perhaps especially about our partners because we think we know them so well. So men, for example, think that their wife's views about sex are those of her mother. They then act as if she were 'nice' and so deprive her of the benefit of being able to express her own sexuality. It can even appear that it is she who is at fault whereas this is not so. A common trap that most of us fall into, if only from time to time, is that we assume our definitions of love, sex and emotional matters are those of our partner. This leads to comments such as, 'If you really loved me you would do A, B and C, but you would not do X, Y or Z'. This would be fine provided that both partners agreed on what A, B, C, X, Y and Z were but they don't. They are thus working from different scripts but appear to be acting in the same play. A good example of this is that many women claim that their men never tell them that they love them. The man, on the other hand, says that he doesn't *need* to tell her in as many words because it must be obvious that a man who helps with the children and does so much DIY around the home *must* love his wife or he wouldn't do it. She, on the other hand, sees such things as his marital duty, not a sign of his love for *her* as a unique individual and so fails to see that the new greenhouse he so painfully erected for her, taking up the whole of his Sunday, was his way of saying 'I love you'.

Unfortunately, so ingrained are many of these assumptions that we might need to sit down with a professional to work them out. Simple discussion can work wonders but it may lead to a questioning of the very basis of the relationship. In a sense everything we do domestically could be seen as an expression of our love for our partner – from looking after the children to planning holidays together. Yet most of us make assumptions about what our duties and rights are within a relationship and then run our lives along these lines irrespective of what our partner believes. Rather than make assumptions on sexual and emotional matters, try hard to define what you both mean. 'When you say that oral sex is not loving, what exactly do you mean?' is the sort of question that needs to be asked if any headway is ever to be made in such areas. The revelations that follow should prove invaluable to the one who asks the question, especially if they are prepared and clever enough to read between the lines of the reply.

Never use threats to get your own way

This is particularly damaging because you might be called on to live up to your threat. And you might regret it. The best way of handling things is to leave your options open in case you change your mind, however far in the future. Something that never ceases to amaze me in marital work is that so many people give the impression that their views are set for life and that they somehow have to make a stand on them on the grounds that nothing *will* change. But things *do* change, and quite quickly if there is good will between a couple. What most of us respond to rather badly is a threat or implied threat yet to be fair many a hurt individual expressing a deep emotional pain *appears* to be issuing a threat or ultimatum whereas they really are not. We all have a final position on everything and shouldn't be asked to move it at once. However, this so-called 'final' position *will* change from month to month, or year to year, in a way that can make the unthinkable not only possible but positively enjoyable a few weeks or months later.

Even 'final' positions change

That this can and does happen is plain in marital therapy. Very often one or other partner will say something as if it were written in stone for all time only to go totally against it a few weeks later, and of their own free will.

All of this makes the issuing of threats fruitless and harmful. Just remember that there are few things worth putting your relationship on the line for, if only because the line changes with time and you could come to regret it.

Don't punish your partner

Many couples when setting out to talk about sex and relationships end up punishing one another both deliberately and unconsciously. The tables can turn many times with each hurting the other in some way or another. Such a couple give one another the cold shoulder in and out of bed; sulk; talk hardly at all; allow standards of housekeeping to fall to levels that few would find acceptable; involve the children in the fight; ration sex; or worse still, perhaps, have sex but very grudgingly as a chore.

This sort of behaviour makes true communication almost impossible. Someone has to give in if life is to return to normal and this is humilating to the one who does the backing down. If ever you feel like punishing your partner stop for a moment and see how you could improve your communication skills perhaps by using some of the following suggestions.

Keep 'no-go' areas to a minimum

LEFT: *Talking about deep things on neutral ground can often work well if only because one or both of you can walk away without having to leave your house.*

Very few couples can talk about sex and emotions without coming across at least some 'no-go' areas. These are subjects as different as the woman's breasts; oral sex; the children's schooling; religion; the 'in-laws' and so on that, when addressed, lead to hostility at worst or uneasiness at best. Life for such a couple proceeds tolerably normally until they come across one of their 'no-go' areas. They then avoid it by changing the subject or by going silent. The couple who have very few such areas can function well and can talk about most things with ease but those, and they are many, whose marriage is riddled with such areas, find that they really cannot communicate on anything much because as soon as they start to get just below the surface they hit a 'no-go' area and have to retreat. Such a couple skim over issues in life all the time and as a result never truly communicate about anything.

Many 'no-go' areas aren't that serious when it comes to it but I find it helpful for couples to list their 'no-go' areas to see what they have in common with their partner. The thread that underlies them might be a single matter that can be sorted out by the couple themselves or by a therapist.

A common 'no-go' area for a man is the woman's emotions. We bring up boys to see women as unfathomable creatures and then wonder why it is that men treat women so badly when they grow up. A major part of a woman's very being is denied by the average man and women, not unreasonably, become frustrated and angry as a result.

The man's inability to function with ease, or even at all in this area makes him retreat from it on the basis that if he can't win he isn't going to play the game. Such a man often does well with professional help and many others come to learn about their partner's feelings if the woman can assure him that he has something to gain from tackling the matter.

Many men fear that they'll be taken over by this mass of feelings about which they understand so little. Of course when it comes to it they are not and things usually work out well if the woman treads cautiously. What she needs to do is to allow her man to express *his* emotions in a way that feels safe to him. Once he has aired his emotions and found that the world hasn't caved in he can then begin to cope with hers.

Men fear feelings

Invest some thought in your relationship

This is especially important for men who tend not to do it naturally but applies equally to women, of course. Most men spend very little time thinking about their relationships, or at least in thinking about how to improve them. Not only should sex be spontaneous and 'natural', but a relationship that is 'any good' should somehow just fall into place and succeed. Or so many men think.

It is a lucky couple for whom this occurs and I think it is rare. Most of us need to work at our relationship and this means learning and re-learning day by day.

Getting married or settling down with someone isn't an end, as many see it, but a beginning. The beginning of a long journey in an uncertain world that changes its rules at the blinking of an eye. The couple who study one another and make a serious investment in their relationship find communicating about even very complex things much easier than the couple who expect big returns from little or no investment.

While it is obviously important to feel things for one another, feelings alone are not enough. We are intellectual creatures too and crave an understanding of life. A book like this can only be a start but it is nevertheless *a* start to understanding your man. The French have a good saying, 'To understand all is to forgive all'. I feel this applies very aptly to the man-woman relationship. Yet so many people, and men in particular, behave as though their relationship didn't warrant the slightest study or effort.

All of this sounds a real chore and even a bore to many men especially, but they have often not realised that by truly understanding someone else they can come to understand themselves. And self-knowledge is at the heart of a successful life. As the Greeks put it so succinctly, 'First, know thyself'. The way many of us get to know ourselves is through a loving, caring relationship that endures for many years. But it needs working at, like many other things in life. Women are, by and large, prepared to put an effort into understanding sex and relationships and realise that it is central to life that they do so. Men still tend to see such knowledge and insights as something 'too feminine' or even that they are, as some patients tell me, biologically unable to grasp such matters because they don't have the right hormones!

Physical communication

Feeling and doing

But so much for thinking and talking about sex and emotions. Let's now look at what else a couple can do to enrich their communication. Because after all, communication isn't only about thinking and talking it is also about feeling and doing. Many's the couple who have never really given themselves the opportunities they deserve to learn more about how to love one another. Because so much emphasis is placed on genital behaviour in our culture the pleasures of simply being together and feeling loving and caring towards one another are ignored.

Many people start off their marriage being very close and good will and romance are there in plentiful supply. As the years pass though work, children, money and other things put stresses on the relationship in such a way that makes communication difficult or even impossible. After all, with the best will in the world a couple has to want to share something sexual or emotional for it to happen.

Even if we do have areas of difference on matters to do with sex and emotions, and most of us do, we can still be loving in non-genital ways most of the time. When couples are having trouble communicating I try to get them to go back to courtship behaviour. In this they stop having intercourse, give one another little presents; phone up 'for no reason'; spend more time together; leave notes about the place with loving messages; and so on. Just stopping genital activity can work wonders as it takes the pressure off one or other to perform. This kind of behaviour re-kindles the flames of courtship and encourages the couple to find non-genital ways of pleasing and pleasuring one another.

This then is the basis for a loving relationship that involves cuddling, kissing, and courtship behaviour short of intercourse. It is the basis for making love all day that I see at the heart of any relationship in which communication stands a chance of occurring. Obviously we cannot and wouldn't wish to spend all day having intercourse but making love to one another in this way keeps both partners aware of the value they are to one another and in fact makes everything they do together a part of their love-making. Even painting the kitchen ceiling takes on a new meaning when looked at in this way and the couple who really want to make the effort will see rewards very quickly.

Such a couple might not actually make love, in the sense of having intercourse, very frequently yet they'll be happy with one another and able to communicate freely because they are on the same 'wavelength' so much of the time. Such a couple shares a secret language, think the same things some of the time, share their fears before they blossom into real worries or problems and, of course, share their pleasures too.

Sharing a 'wavelength'

Some people see all this as unnatural and claim that a relationship that needs this kind of investment of time and effort deserves to have died anyway. That this is untrue can be seen all around us. Most of us are lazy and would like everything to go well without much effort but there are few short-cuts when it comes to the man-woman relationship, at least if it is to be a fruitful one lasting many years.

A way of overcoming the barriers that many couples find beset them when they try to go back to courtship and loving behaviour is to take a sensual holiday.

A sensual holiday

This is an evening, a day, a weekend or longer in which you decide to throw out the old routines and roles and start all over again learning and teaching one another to be intimate. It's a kind of planned return to courtship. Of course couples have always tried to get away together to recharge their emotional and physical batteries but a sensual holiday is more than this, it's a time to devote yourselves to yourselves alone and to develop your intimacies and sensitivities. It is also a time for romantic behaviour and games.

Because of these 'goals' a sensual holiday cannot just happen – it needs planning for. Some couples take it in turns to plan the holiday so that each gets a chance to make happen what he or she best likes. This planning enhances the pleasure, of course. So a man might buy his partner a set of lovely underwear, or arrange for flowers to be delivered to the house (if the holiday is an evening at home); or a woman might set up for them to see a play or something else that she knows her husband would really enjoy. It's best for the more outgoing partner to start the ball rolling by organising the first sensual holiday as this encourages the less able partner to be more imaginative both generally and when they come to take their turn at planning their sensual holiday.

One fun thing to do is to prepare some love tokens ahead of time and give them to your partner. You simply dream up the things you'd most like to do or have done to you and put them on slips of paper. Give your lover these slips a day or two beforehand so that he or she can prepare if necessary. Anyway the anticipation is half the fun.

Some ideas might include a night in a hotel; champagne breakfast in bed; quickie sex in a semi-public place; one sensual massage; one evening of total submission to your wishes; an evening pretending to be a whore with your partner; or whatever turns you on.

But although sex and romance should be at the heart of your sensual holiday it need not be totally centred on such pleasures. How about spending a day in a picture gallery; or climbing or sailing, if that's what interests you. Whatever you do, get out of your rut of unromantic love-making and try new places, positions and activities.

Teasing can be fun. Make an arrangement to have no genital contact when away on a sensual weekend until say, tea-time on Saturday. This builds up the tensions and calls on all your old courting skills to pleasure one another without having intercourse. Do something wild that you wouldn't normally do. For example, just as you are going into a restaurant for a lovely evening out tell your man that you have no underwear on and, if possible, give him a glimpse of the fact as you get out of the car.

Obviously every couple will find their own way of making a sensual holiday work for them. The idea is to be adventurous, to break out of old bounds, to spend time together doing things each of you likes and to rekindle the romance that you so enjoyed in the past.

On return from your 'holiday' try to set aside some time to chat about it within a few days. Say what you liked and what didn't work well for you. Make plans for the next time and agree who'll arrange it. Looking forward to the next holiday will keep each of you on your toes and will tend in itself to make communication easier than before.

Now that we have looked at how talking can help, and have seen how increasing your loving feelings for one another can make communication easier let's finally look at a very valuable technique that I teach all my couples because it is so valuable a tool in learning to communicate better.

Sensual massage

This is a type of massage performed first by one partner then by the other though not necessarily at the same session.

The practicalities are simple but getting good at it takes practice and some skill. Set aside some time when you'll both be alone. Have a bath, together or separately, take the phone off the hook, warm the room and if you like, have a small alcoholic drink to relax you. Put a sheet on the floor or on the bed and warm up some massage oil by placing it near a fire or radiator. Any oil will do but it's best, if you can afford it, to use proper massage oil or, even better, aromatherapy oil. The essence of sensual massage is that a couple learns to communicate their needs and the results of what their partner does accurately and honestly. It does not involve the genitals or breasts and should not be thought of as a type of foreplay. If it is, even the most diligent of couples will see it as a means to an end which it is not – at least not to intercourse. Later, once you have learned the techniques and are at ease with communicating with one another without talking, it is possible and delightful to massage one another before making love but at the start this is not helpful.

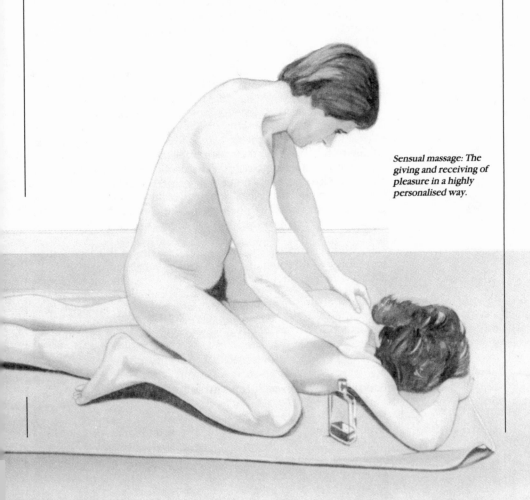

Sensual massage: The giving and receiving of pleasure in a highly personalised way.

There are no rules as to how to do the massage but there are plenty of books which describe how to do it in practical terms. What you actually *do* is beside the point really so long as it is enjoyable for the receiver. Be careful not to fall into the trap of one always being the receiver and the other the giver. It's very easily done and says a lot about the relationship, I find. Once you get going you should find that sensual massage is not something that is done *to* the other but rather is something that you both share. At the end cuddle up and go to sleep in the early days, or later have intercourse if you feel like it. By the receiver giving almost constant feedback and instructions to the giver in the early days of learning the massage, he or she finds that their partner can and will listen to what they say, take it in and act on it.

Any preconceived notions as to what the receiver might like or dislike are ignored and current information only is used as the basis for action. These things in themselves are valuable communication skills in any relationship, as the reader will readily see. As time goes by the needs of one or the other may change and the ability of the partner to respond to the new needs once again creates a flexibility of thinking and action that benefits the whole of the couple's relationship.

Also, and on a very practical note, it is very hard or near impossible to be horrid to someone you are massaging in this caring and intimate way two or three times a week.

Don't talk at first

At first I always suggest that a couple speak only about the massage while they are doing it. This focuses attention on what is going on and is vital if they are to learn how to do it well for the other. However, once a couple have the massage technique mastered as a 'natural' response after some practice, it can then become a time for sharing fears, worries or pleasures. Some people feel emotionally released when they are being massaged and so feel more able and willing to be open with their partner. Sitting opposite one another talking about something that hurts emotionally can be very difficult for all but the closest of couples but to share at this intimate level with the lights low, some soft music on, the smell of the massage oil, and one's partner's hands and body soothing away the cares of the world can make sharing even the most worrying of emotions possible.

A couple that enrich their lives along the lines of this section will inevitably end up communicating better about almost everything. In such a setting emotions can be confronted by even the most resistant of men and the man who had previously thought of his partner as something very different from himself comes to realise just how similar she really is. It is this similarity that forms the very basis for true communication. For in communicating with others we communicate with ourselves.

From copulation to intercourse

There is little doubt that intercourse is the most intimate form of physical communication that occurs between human beings. However, many couples rarely have intercourse, they are usually copulating and often communicate very little as a result.

The bad habits of copulation start in the teens when furtive, guilt-ridden and hurried sex creates poor learning conditions.

This, coupled with men's ideas about intercourse, makes it likely that most couples entering their long-term relationship will start off on a somewhat bad footing because they will already have rushed into copulation rather than grown slowly into intercourse. Bad habits die hard in sex, as elsewhere in life, and many couples never get off the narrow tracks they lay for themselves in their late teens and early twenties.

All is not necessarily lost though because it is possible to change what we do and how we do it. This is what this section is about.

The journey to intercourse from copulation starts with better communication generally. In fact the preceding sections of this part of the book are the foundations for intercourse. A couple who cannot share their intimate thoughts with one another are unlikely to have intercourse – they will always tend to 'fuck'. The dissatisfactions that this sort of behaviour produces, especially among men, are too great to be ignored and lead men to disruptive behaviour that endangers their partners, their families and themselves.

It starts out in bed

Let's assume then that you and your partner have successfully negotiated most, if not all, of the stages of communication outlined on the previous pages. You now talk to one another about your emotions and about your sexuality; can feel at ease being romantic and loving without genital activity; and are frequently perking up your physical relationship with sensual holidays and similar intimate occasions.

You are now ready to start on your programme that leads to intercourse. Obviously any such guide can only be a general approach to the subject and each individual couple will find their own way through to the end-point they want, but this is a scheme that works and has been proven to do so for many couples. Feel free to modify it to suit your needs according to your existing skills and abilities *but* do not miss out stages just because you think they don't seem like what you'd normally do. Progress in this area, as in most areas of life, means stepping out of the normal pattern and trying something that will effect a change.

Stage One

Learn about one another's genitals

It is an interesting fact that many couples have never really looked at their partner's genitals. Here's how to go about it.

Start off by revealing your genitals to your man. I find things work best this way round because women are, by and large, less shy about such revelations and are more used to having their genitals dealt with in ante-natal clinics, family planning clinics, at GP surgeries, and so on.

Put some time aside and, perhaps after a cuddle, lie down naked
at least from the waist down. Ensure that you have a good light and
then get your partner to look at what he can see. A mirror can also be
useful so that you can look and lead the man in his discovery.

Get him to start by looking at the pubic area generally. See the distribution of the hair. Get him to feel the hair and tell him about how it grows, the colour compared with that on your head, and how you keep it trimmed. Ask him what he likes about it, and what he doesn't. Most men, once they get into the swing of it, become intensely interested and for many a woman this will be the first time that anyone has had a conducted tour of her genitals which in itself will be interesting to her.

LEFT: *A careful detailed examination of his partner's genitals could be one of the best investments he'll make in their sex life.*

Next, the man should open the lips of the vulva and note their consistency, size and extent. The outer lips are thicker and more fleshy and the inner ones thinner. The inner lips come together at the top to clothe the clitoris in a little hood.

Finding the clitoris can be tricky for many men and this might call for some help from you. Get your partner to find the tip of the organ and then to run his finger-tip along the shaft. Show him exactly which parts you caress when you masturbate and tell him which bits are too tender to touch. Now open your lips for him to see the little hole that is the urinary passage just below the clitoris. This lies between the clitoris and the vaginal opening.

Next, he can look carefully at the vaginal opening. The appearance of this area differs from woman to woman and many men are surprised just how different things can be. The little tags of skin around the opening are the remains of the hymen that was broken on first intercourse or when you first used a tampon.

Now the man can insert a finger gently into the vagina to feel its walls. You could contract your pelvic muscles too so that he can feel just how strong they are. Now he can advance his finger (two might be easier) until he can feel your cervix deep inside the vagina. The indentation is the opening to the cervix canal up which sperms swim to get into the uterus. The canal is very narrow indeed – not even as wide as a pencil – but becomes greatly enlarged in late pregnancy and during labour so as to be able to let a baby come out.

Lastly on the tour of your genitals you could get him to massage the front wall of your vagina firmly to see if it is pleasant for you. This is the area that has been called the G-spot but is probably just a sensitive part of the wall that gives some women an orgasm when stroked. It is usually best to stroke the area between 11 and 1 o'clock assuming that the clitoris is at 12 o'clock.

Find the G-spot

If, as a result of all this, you are now feeling aroused you could, of course, go on to have sex, but if you want to you could go straight on to examining your partner's genitals.

Start off with him lying down comfortably in a good light so that you can see everything clearly. Look at the distribution of the hair and see how different it is from your own. Next, look carefully at his scrotum and feel the testes inside. These are soft but firm and can be made to move closer to the body by touching them, arousing them, or making them cooler. At this stage don't stimulate them in any particular way, just get to know the feel of them in some detail.

The main structure of the testis itself is a sort of oval ball and at each end there are small tubular systems that you can easily feel. Go now to the top of the testis and feel the narrow but hard tube that runs up into the groin. This is the vas deferens. It is cut when a man has a vasectomy. Most of the contents of a man's scrotum are sensitive to pain and now could be the time to squeeze various parts of his scrotum to see what is painful and what is pleasant. Some men like to have their balls squeezed as they become aroused and a few enjoy very firm pressure indeed as they near ejaculation. Don't go this far yet.

Next look at the penis. See how the foreskin is attached and how it pulls back. Look at the little fold of skin on the underside of the tip. This is the fraenum and is the most sensitive part for most men. Almost any stimulation here will make most men become aroused, if the stimulation is done how he likes it. Look at the hole at the tip of the penis. This is where urine and semen come out. Now feel the shaft of the organ and lastly end up by feeling right down to the 'root' of the penis between the bottom of the organ and the man's anus. Stimulating this area firmly can be very pleasant for many men.

Stage Two

Learning about arousal

Now that you are both familiar with one another's genitals you can go on to learn what happens as each of you becomes sexually aroused. Again, take it in turns and take care to look in detail at what is happening.

Start with you. The idea on this occasion is to have an orgasm with your man watching minutely everything that you do. This obviously might mean making things a little less 'medical' than on the anatomical discovery occasion. So if you want to have a little drink, to spend some time kissing and cuddling do so but be sure that your partner has had a detailed look at your vulval area before you start. Even a short cuddle will make you start to become aroused and appearances will change very quickly.

He should now keep very much in the background as if you were masturbating alone and let you get on with it without interruption. He should be able to answer questions such as how and where exactly you stimulate yourself; what your body position is; how many fingers you use; how fast you caress your clitoris; how this speed changes as your arousal progresses; whether or not you put anything inside your vagina as you become aroused (many women put a finger or two inside); how your vulval area swells and changes in colour; how much vaginal fluid you produce as arousal progresses; what else you do to the rest of your body (for example caressing your breasts or nipples); the changes that occur in the rest of your body, especially those in your breasts; what you do actually as you climax; how the rest of your body behaves at this time; what the very first signs of an impending climax are (many women start involuntarily to twitch their toes, for example); how long you go on stimulating yourself once an orgasm sets in; whether or not you go for another climax; and lastly, how things

subside as you recover from your climax and get back to normal again.

Needless to say, the man who can answer all these questions, perhaps after a few sessions of observation, will be vastly better equipped to stimulate you than he was before. You too will feel that much less inhibited in asking him to do perhaps even new things to increase your enjoyment and quality of orgasm.

On another occasion this can all be repeated with the man. Questions you should be able to answer include: How he starts to stimulate his penis, or genitals generally; what other areas he stimulates; exactly how he holds his penis; how fast he moves his hand; whether he stops and starts his hand movements; the amount of

Learning how to masturbate her man teaches her a lot and enables her to pleasure him when intercourse is off the menu.

pressure he exerts on the penis; the changes in his scrotum; his facial changes; the size and force of the initial spurt of semen; the number and force of subsequent spurts; at what stage he stops manipulating himself; and so on.

After each such session it helps to cuddle one another and to talk about the experience. This gives you both a chance to talk and listen to the effects that the doing and the watching had on you. *You* may want to talk about your shame and your *man* about his amazement that you masturbate at all. Now is a good time to share your masturbation histories including when each of you first started; how you learned to masturbate; how things have changed over the years; when and how you masturbate today; what your best fantasies are; and so on.

He shows her how to squeeze the top of his penis to slow him down and prevent him ejaculating too soon.

Stage Three

Sharing fantasies

Many people have sexual fantasies that they use either when masturbating or at other times as a kind of day dream. About half of all women, for example, claim to have fantasies of other men or situations when making love with their husband. Many people imagine, quite

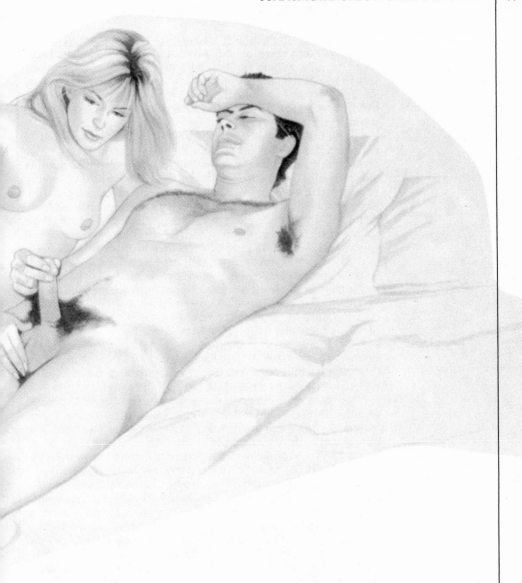

wrongly, that all fantasies are suppressed wishes or desires but some are simply a form of exploration and for most their fantasies either could not be acted out, perhaps because they could not be made to happen, or would not, in practice, be much fun if they were to become a reality.

Sharing fantasies is a tricky affair and should be undertaken with caution. Just because we have a fantasy doesn't mean that we have to dump it on our partner, however we might justify it. There are some fantasies that are probably better not shared – at least not until you are both very secure in one another's love at a very deep level. Fantasies about people you both know socially, for example, are usually best kept to yourself, if only because many women, knowing men as they do, fear that today's wishful thinking might just become tomorrow's fact. If this were to involve the girl next door or your best friend things could get tricky.

The trouble is knowing what to share and what not to. If in doubt, keep quiet and bide your time. If you declare a fantasy it puts considerable pressure on your partner to accept it, with all that that might entail. The knowledge that one cannot, for whatever reason, answer such a need for one's partner can niggle away and do harm. Men particularly, as we have seen, think that a woman who 'really loves them' will do anything for or with them including answering their fantasy wishes. Of course many women cannot answer such needs and anyway do not see it as a realistic test of their love that they do so.

The secret of sharing fantasies is to be sure that it is a game that you both want to play. Neither should be cajoled into it but having said this it takes some small amount of bravery to set the ball rolling. Revealing fantasies is usually best started on a particularly steamy occasion and it hardly matters who takes the lead. There are all kinds of ways of learning what might be of interest to your partner but keeping an eye on what interests him in fiction, on TV, or at the cinema, is a good start. A more sophisticated game is to write a short (one-page) outline for a sexy video or film. This reveals all kinds of underlying fantasy material which can be built on over the years.

Much of value can come out of sharing fantasies. With care and sensitivity it is possible to learn a lot about what best excites your partner. Fantasies that are revealed can be built into love-making in various ways, perhaps in a diluted form. Many a woman is too shy to ask directly for what she best likes and many a man finds difficulty too if the needs he has could be seen as being less than masculine.

Two examples are the woman who likes to be dominated and taken forcibly and the man who likes to take the back seat from time to time. Such a woman might have rape dreams or fantasies of being sexually taken by many men. The lover of such a woman can take his cues from these revelations and perhaps increase his ardour or even inject a little sadism into their love-making. The man who wants to be the less active partner, albeit only from time to time, and has fantasies of women taking the initiative could be seen by his partner as being somewhat 'unmanly'. If she loves him though and wants the best for him sexually she'll use this knowledge to increase her level of activity and take the lead more frequently.

Remember, just because your partner declares a fantasy need doesn't mean that it has to be satisfied exactly as in the fantasy. Be clever and see what the underlying principle is and try to satisfy it in a way that *is* acceptable to you. A good example of this is the man who has fantasies of anal sex yet his wife doesn't want to indulge in it. She can, with little effort and only the minimum of anxiety, start to adopt rear-entry position for vaginal intercourse so that he can fantasise that

Shy women don't ask

This rear-entry position suits him well because he can fantasise that he is having anal sex with her which she, in fact, will not allow.

he is making love to her anally. This could well satisfy his needs and allow her to keep her own views and tastes intact.

The sharing of fantasies is just one more step in the progression from copulation to intercourse because it makes the encounter between the couple unique and tailored to their own individual needs. Sharing fantasies also opens up a whole new area of games that a couple can play. These games then add to their fantasy life and over some time the couple build a whole library of games and fantasies that can arouse and please them whatever the occasion.

A couple who share fantasies in this way are now communicating at such a deep level and with such trust that copulation is already unlikely to be their normal fare. They are well on the way towards intercourse.

Mutual masturbation, a popular favourite especially for those couples who are not sure of their partners' sexual history.

Stage Four

Mutual masturbation

A vital part of learning about one another is knowing how to masturbate each other really well. There is no way that this can be learned
except by observation and practice. There is only one expert on
masturbation and that is the individual him or herself and he or she it
is who has to be the teacher. You'll have learned a lot by watching one
another in Stage Two and now is the time to put it into practice. There
are several basic rules that are worth following if masturbating your
partner is to stand a chance of going well.

Getting the position right is critical. Many couples say that masturbating one another is a nuisance but often the reason is that they do not
ever find the best position in which to do it. Get comfortable with your
partner once he is in his position. When starting off masturbating a
man it is often best to use a non-threatening position in which he faces
away from you (see illustration).

Getting the mood right. This really helps. Obviously you'll want to be
un-interrupted but perhaps having a small alcoholic drink to relax you
both would make all the difference. Make the room warm. Dim the
lights, have some music on and perhaps share a sexy magazine or
video beforehand. Have a bath together, cuddle up a little first, and so
on. Don't do it in the dark or you'll miss out on so much. Watching
your partner can be very exciting and you'll learn a lot too.

Use plenty of lubrication. Whichever way around the stimulation is
occurring be sure to have plenty of wetness. If you aren't already wet
with your natural vaginal secretions do some more kissing and
cuddling, with or without breast play, or use some commercial
lubricant such as KY jelly. Saliva is always available and is less sticky
than commercial lubricants. It is also at the right temperature.

You can masturbate your man using talc or baby oil but talc
should not be used on your genitals because it can get inside your
vagina and cause problems.

The secret is to keep either the penis or the clitoris well
lubricated at all times if you want to be sure of success.

Tell one another about it. You'll have already laid the foundations for
this with your arousal exercises in Stage Two so now things should
come easily. The one who is taking the active role should listen
intently to the receiver and be guided exactly in minute detail as to
what he or she wants. It is probably most important to be aware of
what is NOT wanted because even a small wrong detail can mar the
whole event. After some experience of one another actual talking
becomes a thing of the past and grunts, groans, moans, and other
appreciative noises and movements take their place.

Bathing together is a delightful prelude to almost any sexual encounter.

Remember your partner's special needs. Cast your mind back to when you were a spectator at your partner's masturbation and see what he best wanted done other than just genital stimulation. Many women like their breasts or nipples caressed; and some men want their anal area, or their scrotum caressed. Concentrating on the penis or clitoris might not produce the best results, or indeed any result at all.

Find out what your partner best likes and then stick to it. Be guided both by arousal experiences and by what your partner tells you and find out what gives him the best results. As this is a book for women perhaps I should point out a couple of complaints men have about their women masturbating them.

Many men complain that women don't hold their penis properly when masturbating them. Watch how he does it himself and then model your grip on that. Women generally try to hold the penis like a pencil rather than a milk bottle. Grip it firmly and then move your hand up and down as he best likes it.

Once you have found what your partner best enjoys don't deviate from it too much. Most people, of either sex, say that they like predictability when it comes to masturbation.

Learning how to masturbate one another really well is useful not only as a part of transforming copulation into intercourse but as a way of relieving one another when intercourse isn't possible.

Stage Five

Enriching it all

This stage is a building one in which you now expand your fantasies; use erotica; share sexy thoughts; experiment with other erotic pas- Share sexy thoughts times such as stripping; sexy undies, new locations, using sex toys, and bathing together; increase your romantic activities; and anything else that makes the whole business of sexual arousal and release more pleasant and rewarding.

This is time to start experimenting with making one another last longer. A man can be aroused to fever pitch and then allowed to go soft, only to be re-aroused, perhaps orally. This can be repeated several times until he is confident that he can last for any length of time he or his partner wants. She can be teased too in the same way though many women find that they don't have the same problem with coming too quickly that men do.

Stage Six

Having intercourse

This stage should be a natural extension of the previous stage rather than a set-up special day. By now the chances are high that a couple who have prepared themselves in this way will greatly enjoy true intercourse, the ultimate in sharing communication. Although this will tend to be a time of exploring new sexual positions, genital gymnastics is not the aim. Make it a time of slow and intimate revelation of how better to please one another. If this happens to include different or novel sex positions, so be it.

Stage Seven

Taking it in turns

Even a couple who have come this far may still fall into the trap of one always being the 'doer' and the other the 'receiver', so the last stage but one in the journey to intercourse is for the couple to exchange roles from time to time. Each partner takes it in turn to lay down the rules of foreplay, penetration, positions, and so on. The other adopts the role of sex slave and does exactly what is ordered. Such behaviour prevents stereotyping and boredom and allows the less dominant partner to have a real say in what happens. It also allows the partners to experiment with what each wants against a background of complete security and trust within the sexual relationship.

Stage Eight

Progress checks

No matter how much we love one another or how much we have invested in creating the best possible sexual environment, life takes its toll of us all and things slip back towards copulation if we are not careful. The sensible couple takes every opportunity to update their love-making by experimenting, building on what they had, reviving old and favourite pastimes in and out of bed, taking sensual holidays together, and constantly reviewing their sexual life.

Against this background of intercourse a couple can, of course, enjoy the occasional 'quickie' or abandoned bout of copulation. It can be highly exciting, especially if it is unplanned and takes place in an unlikely location. Nothing I have said in this section about love-making becoming more of a studied art form should make the reader think that spontaneous love-making should become a thing of the past. Rather it has been about ensuring that intercourse becomes the norm rather than 'screwing' with all its boredom, predictability, and unsatisfactoriness.

Bored no more

A man who complains of always wanting more sex, as many men do, is soon cured of his malaise if he embarks on the course outlined in this section of the book. Instead of having 'one boring partner', which is what he thought he had, he now finds that he has an infinitely varied fare on offer in the hands of a 'mistress' that other men would envy. And any man who can romp with a 'mistress' who is also his best friend and companion is likely to be a very happy man. He will also, on balance, want to ensure that his partner is a very happy woman.

...an needn't just mean
...s. Use your body, your
...and to best advantage.

Use your hands

Having now driven him wild by *not* touching his genitals and having excited him by using your body in ways he had never even thought of, it is time to turn to his penis and the area around it. Most women enjoy handling their partner's penis every bit as much as their men do. Although I have said that we are now going to start on the penis, and that this is what most men will be waiting for, make him wait some more while you stroke all around the area for a while. Don't forget the area between the root of the penis and his bottom and slowly and teasingly caress everywhere but the penis and scrotum themselves.

PLEASING YOUR MAN IN BED

Although it might seem strange, pleasing your man in bed starts *out* of bed. Few men can separate the woman they know and relate to out of bed as housewife and mother perhaps, from the one they know in bed, their mistress. This means that pleasing your man in bed is part of an ongoing process of love-making. Whilst it is certainly true that a man can make love passionately to a woman that gives him trouble occasionally, few men can function really well or enjoyably if there is constant tension, argument, put-downs, or behaviour that is more appropriate coming from a mother.

It will be plain to any reader by now that men do not, as is commonly claimed, simply want 'a good fuck'. Most need to feel that they are loved and wanted which means that they want the woman to take the initiative at least some of the time. We have seen in several places throughout the book that many men complain that they have to make all the running and that this makes them feel that their partner cannot really love them. Most men would, on occasions, like their women to take the lead and at least some of the responsibility.

Women should take the initiative

Although it is clear that men differ greatly in what they best enjoy in bed few can resist the times when their partner makes their genitals the centre of attention and makes them feel loved and wanted.

This is so attractive to a man because he is then not at the centre of the stage and doesn't have to worry about 'performing'. He can simply lie back and enjoy being spoilt, perhaps on the understanding that he won't have to 'pay for it' by returning the compliment later, unless, of course, he wants to.

Here then are some tips about what men say they best like in bed with a woman.

Use his brain

Most men find a naked woman attractive but as many find a woman who'll excite their mind just as alluring. This is, perhaps, even more

Aural sex

arousing in certain ways because 'nice' women don't 'talk dirty' or express their fantasies and needs and they certainly don't seek to turn their man on with uninhibited talk of *his* sexual fantasies.

A good way to start getting your man aroused is to indulge in aural sex. This involves telling him sexy stories that you know excite him because they contain his, or your, favourite fantasy material. Remember to change the story each time, if only by a little detail, so that he doesn't become bored with it and its predictability. Most couples find that feeding *his* fantasies works best but having said this many's the man who is driven wild with desire for his partner as she reveals *her* fantasies as she whispers in his ear as they cuddle.

There are several tips for the creation of successful fantasy stories like this. The first is to put lots of detail into them. Men like detail so describe the setting; the woman in the story; the clothes she is wearing, or isn't; be sure to tell him what the woman is feeling about it all; and go into graphic detail about the actual process of the sexual encounter, including the genital details of both parties involved. Even a macho type of man wants more than crude dirty talk and will respond to carefully contrived situations and detail in the story.

The second thing to remember is to customise the fantasy to him and his particular tastes. If you have been together for some time you'll probably know a lot about what he best likes, but if you haven't there are lots of ways of discovering. You could get some men's magazines and ask him to outline any section of the stories that really turn him on. You could suggest that he reads a sexy book you have enjoyed or have heard about and do the same. How about getting him to tell you about his old flames? Be on the look-out all the time for clues as to what excites or interests him in the press, the magazines, on TV, or at the films. Sometimes you can pick up clues from the sexy jokes he tells. Work out what the basic building blocks of his fantasy world are and then weave a story, preferably as you go along, so that it comes over as natural.

While it is impossible to generalise, it is probably safe to say that as men age they need more stimulating inputs in the stories. This might take the form of stories about things that previously wouldn't have been necessary or even interesting to him. For older men subjects such as dressing up, masochism, bondage, games with sex toys, group sex, and so on might be welcome by way of extra stimulus.

If any of this seems too difficult for you, and it might be if your personal sexuality is somewhat inhibited, try practising by reading out aloud a few raunchy sections from a sexy book whilst you are on your own. Some women find that once they have become used to hearing their own voice saying such things they can more easily deal with them in bed with their man. The best way of making things happen easily is to get aroused *yourself* before embarking on your first session of story telling. Most women find that their reticence soon disappears as they too become embroiled in the excitement of the occasion.

Clearly this is a game that any two lovers can play and is one that further individualises their love-making in a way that makes it of more value to them. It'll certainly make you more valuable to your man.

There is perhaps just one note of cauti
subject. It is probably not sensible to incluc
things in your stories just in case it fires your
could harm him or someone else. This is not to
should be tame or squeaky clean because that
the object but simply that it is probably not he
further his fantasies of rape; having sex w
women, except in play; and so on.

Having said this very few men actually
anyway – most are more than delighted with
everyday sexual escapades.

Use your body

Most men say that seeing their partner partly d
turn-on. Find out what he best likes by being w
his fantasies and then dress up in things that p

Most women use far too few parts of the
man. Whether you are partly dressed or totally
how you caress his eyes and his body with you
about getting undressed and if the aim is to ex
you 'accidentally' expose yourself in ways that

Once you start to caress him, go slowly.
intercourse far too quickly yet at the same tir
string things out. Don't let him hurry you. Ru
and if he isn't undressed do it for him gently. D
at this stage at all. Many men like their wor
complain that they come too quickly or that
soon.

Slowly and seductively rub yourself aga
hands on various parts of you that you want hi
your lips and mouth to caress him all over. Ger
of course kiss his mouth in the way that he bes
with your hair all over his body. Few men ca
when it trails over their genitals which you ar
touch. Kiss his body with your hair and roll him
it all to his back too.

Now that he is ready to be aroused by t
coming into contact with his, lie on him and r
him slowly and gently. Rub him with oil if you l
in using your body. Be adventurous and use yo
to massage his back, or your feet to massage hi

Experiment with all kinds of sensation p
parts of your body and find out what he best er

He'll now be ready for you to start on his

Masturbating your r
stimulating his peni
hair and your free h

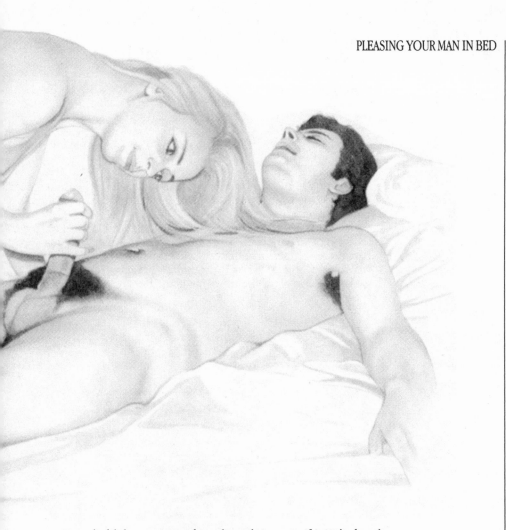

Next, hold the penis gently and watch it grow, if it isn't already erect. You'll know from your previous exercises just how he likes it held best and caressed so be guided by this. Always do what he liked best when you were learning and then add in some extras of your own to really turn him on. Try, for example, massaging the penis with one hand, then with both hands; roll it like a roll of plasticine; cover it in oil and rub it; or soap it in the bath. When the penis is wet it is much more excitable so be careful because you'll find the man will climax much more easily.

It's not just the shaft of the penis that men like caressed. Try *Drive him wild* rubbing the root firmly down to the anus. Next, pull back the foreskin if the man isn't circumcised and run your fingers, well lubricated, around the head of the penis and especially along the little ridge called the fraenum (see page 141). These manoeuvres will all produce exquisite sensations that will drive the average man wild with desire for you.

Now you can transfer your attention to the scrotum. Cup it in your hand and gently squeeze the balls. The amount of pressure any one man enjoys can only be found by trial and error and by and large it is more easily tolerated as he becomes more aroused. Some men like the pressure to start off being gentle and to be very hard as they ejaculate. The pressure can be constant; can be of increasing strength, or can be applied on-and-off in a teasing way. Some men enjoy the scratching of a finger nail along the skin of the scrotum. A teasing tickle can be good too.

Now you can run your fingertips around his anal area and see if he likes it. He probably will, as many men enjoy anal stimulation, if only to this extent.

For those who like more exciting anal stimulation it makes sense for the man to have bathed well beforehand and that the woman not have any infections of her fingers and ensure that her nails are short. We saw on page 158 how to stimulate a man's prostate gland by massaging it with a finger in his anus. Be sure to use plenty of

lubrication when doing anything other than the most superficial of anal play. If both of you are sure of one another there is absolutely no danger from AIDS when indulging in this sort of love-play but if you are with a new partner or have any reason to distrust your existing partner it's probably best to keep away from anal play altogether. This is certainly a wise precaution if your partner is bisexual.

Use your mouth

Orally caressing your partner's penis is a very intimate thing to do and as such is seen by most men as highly arousing and a sign that you really love him. You'll already have caressed his body, bitten him gently, and licked him and kissed him so extending this attention to his penis should come fairly easily as a continuation of all this other oral

This classical 69 position is a favourite for some but many say they like to be either giving or receiving in such an intense way rather than doing both at once.

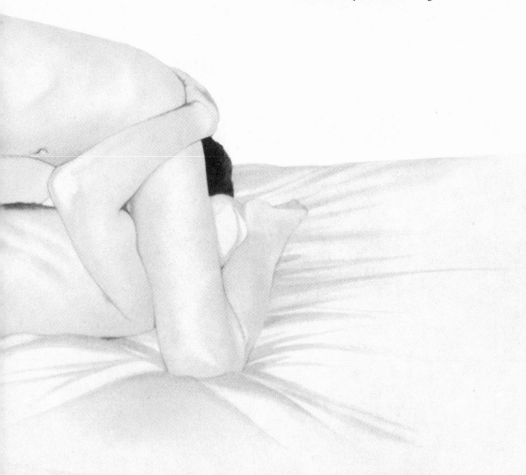

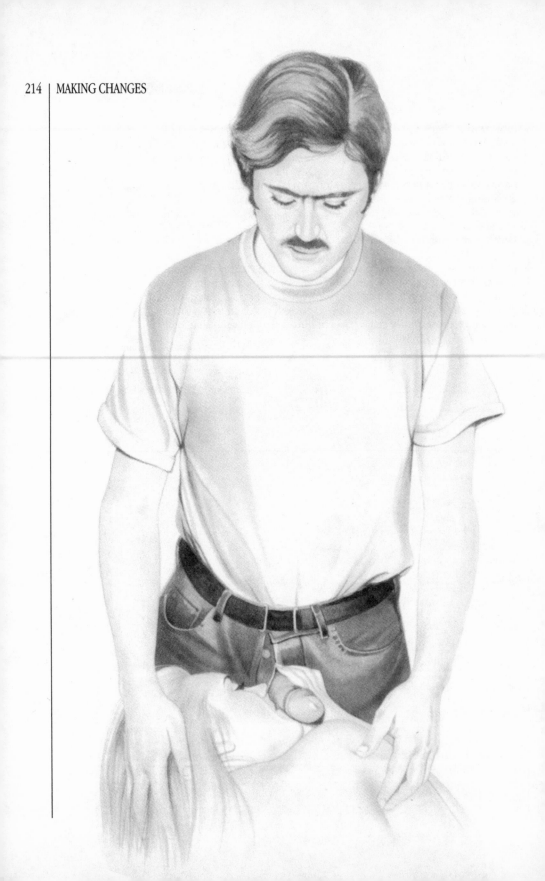

love-making. What most men like about a woman's mouth around their penis is that it is rather like a vagina but because her tongue is so active she can make things even more stimulating for him than she can with her vagina.

There are numerous things that men enjoy when it comes to oral sex but here are just a few of the favourites. Lick the penis head as if it were an ice cream. Stimulate the tip with your tongue and push the tip of the tongue into the slit on the head. Gently flick the vertical ridge of tissue underneath the head with your tongue tip. Whirl your tongue around the penis head while it is deep inside your mouth. Suck hard on the penis. Push the penis in and out of your mouth whilst at the same time whirling your tongue around the head.

How you position your partner to do all this is up to you, obviously, but it is very relaxing if he is lying down. If you are feeling more adventurous how about kneeling down in front of him and taking the penis in your mouth. Most men find this highly stimulating. Or, get him to sit in a chair and then take his penis into your mouth as you kneel down in front of him. Try the 69 position—in which you face his feet and he can kiss your bottom or vulva while you suck him.

For the true enthusiast put something really tasty on the penis and lick it off. Cream, jam, yoghurt, or anything that you enjoy the taste of will do no harm.

If you are going to suck a man's penis though you should have a secret sign that tells you he is about to ejaculate if you do not want him to come in your mouth. You might not want this to happen because you want to have intercourse and are using oral sex only as a form of foreplay, or you might have an aversion to semen in your mouth. Semen tastes different from man to man and in the same man from occasion to occasion so just because you haven't liked the taste once in the past doesn't mean that you never will with a new, or even the same, partner. If you want to let the man ejaculate into your mouth but not swallow the semen you could discreetly spit out the fluid into a paper hanky kept handy for the purpose.

There are some other helpful courtesies and 'rules' that are worth thinking about when it comes to fellating a man. First, make sure that he is immaculately clean. If you have any reason to believe that he has a venereal infection don't do oral sex. If you have cold sores around your mouth stay away from oral sex. Under normal circumstances wash him yourself – perhaps you could bathe or shower together, or get him to do it. Washing the penis can be made into a stimulating part of foreplay.

Some courtesies

Second, when sucking a penis be sure not to bend it too far downwards because this is painful. A man likes his penis to be aimed up towards his tummy.

Third, find a really comfortable position. Too many women become bored, annoyed or tired when doing oral sex on their man because they haven't taken the trouble to find a comfortable position that suits them. Neck ache is the enemy to guard against but once you have the knack it is not a problem.

Fourth, keep your teeth out of the way. Open your mouth really wide and cover your teeth with your lips if necessary. Some men are so thick that this can be difficult and you may have to confine yourself to sucking the tip only.

Fifth, don't forget that the rest of his body will still want caressing too. Keep both your hands in action all the time to make it really good for him.

Don't forget that you can use your tongue and mouth on his scrotum too. Nip the skin gently; poke your tongue into the deep parts of his scrotum; or even take one ball into your mouth if you both like it.

Most couples will indulge in such oral sex as a part of foreplay or even as part of oral intercourse but for a real treat, how about sucking your man one morning before he wakes up when he has a morning erection?

Use your vagina

There are many things that a woman can do with her vulva and vagina other than simply going straight for intercourse. How about using your vulva to stroke his penis as you rub your body up and down his? Part the lips of your vulva and rub their insides up and down the penis.

Next dip the penis into the mouth of your vagina just a little and, perhaps with you on top, control its entry so that you drive him wild. Don't let him go too deeply into you, tease him for a while. A popular manoeuvre is for the woman to sit on top of the penis either facing him or facing his feet and to squeeze it with her pelvic muscles. Some men can be brought to orgasm by this alone.

'Kiss' with your vagina

If you are fellating your man you could use your vagina to 'kiss' him on his mouth.

Another arousing pursuit is to make him watch you play with yourself. Sit him up comfortably and then start to caress your vulva and clitoris while he watches but is forbidden to touch. Put a finger or two inside your vagina and give him the secretion to smell or to lick if this is what he likes. An extension of this is to use a dildo or vibrator in your vagina as you masturbate. This excites most men to the point of distraction.

Use your imagination

Most men admire a woman who is experimental and creative in bed. Here are some ideas that are a sure-fire hit with most men.

Take some photographs of his penis in various stages of erection. Polaroids are best because few laboratories will process pictures of an erect penis. Some women have fun decorating the penis with whipped cream or flowers before they photograph it.

A very few men like to be depilated. If you are shaving a man's pubic hair off be careful and be doubly so if using a depilatory cream. The latter hurts a lot if it comes into contact with the sensitive anal or penile skin on its head. Rings around the penis have been used for thousands of years to make it harder. These are fine if they are specially made for the purpose. They can be bought from sex shops and by mail order from catalogues. Never use one that you have adapted for the purpose because if you cannot easily release it the man may have extreme difficulty in removing it and the penis might be damaged. Never use metal rings of any kind.

Some men enjoy a vibrator being used on the penis, scrotum, testes, penis root or anus. By and large men are not very turned on by vibrators but it can enhance things for a few.

Penis 'exercises' can be fun and have been practised by couples for centuries. Hang a small towel or something similar on the penis when it is totally erect and give your man points for how heavy a

Fun with a polaroid camera as you create your own pin-ups.

weight he can maintain for a given period of time. As you 'train' him reward him suitably for his improvement and you'll be rewarded too as you notice how much stronger he is when he makes love to you.

The games a loving and experimental couple can play with a man's penis are numerous and great fun but here are some words of caution. First, if there are any changes that make you suspicious that he might have any sort of disease encourage him to see a doctor before involving his penis too intimately in your love-making. Second, never blow down a man's penis. Third, never put anything into the urinary passage because things can become stuck there and be very difficult, even for a doctor, to remove. Fourth, never kiss a man's penis if you have cold sores around your mouth; and last, never bite the penis however carried away you become during oral sex. The erect penis is full of high-pressure blood and bleeds profusely.

Fulfilled and delighted

A man whose partner is willing and able to indulge in many, or even some, of these arousing pursuits will be delighted and very unlikely to even think about looking elsewhere for sexual fulfilment. For some women though such a programme of arousal for their men will prove unacceptably distressing because they will be too inhibited to stimulate him in the way he likes best. But such a woman shouldn't despair because, as clinical experience shows, what seems impossible today can become tomorrow's daily fare, in the couple who are exploring and growing together.

It is the experience of most people working in sexual and marital medicine that the couple who really want to please one another and answer one another's sexual needs have few barriers, if any, to doing such things, if only from time to time. No woman would want, and few men could stand, the whole 'treatment' I have outlined here at any one love-making session but that is not the point. Such a programme of stimulating arousal can be used in part from time to time; in a progressive way that keeps the man hungry for more; to enlarge his abilities to enjoy his orgasm; to be sure to be able to arouse him even when evidence to the contrary is plentiful (such as when he is worried, tired or unwell); to increase the value of his partner to him; and to make other members of the opposite sex seem a waste of time.

In an age when AIDS is making people think more than twice about casual sex and promiscuity the couple that can provide one another with a sexual menu that keeps all this going will be set up for life. Many men say that they'd *like* to be monogamous but that frankly they don't see their partner ever being able to satisfy all their needs. When I hear this in the consulting room I take it as a challenge to help the woman become exactly what her partner wants and needs. She often enters into the spirit of the thing with some gusto and finds that other women do indeed become less attractive to him.

If the man is following a similar programme of sexual pleasures and fulfilment aimed at his partner it is easy to see how a couple who have this kind of sexual life together rarely have problems but for those that do the following chapter gives some tips as to how you can help your man overcome them.

HELPING YOUR MAN OVERCOME HIS SEXUAL PROBLEMS

A lmost all men have a sexual failure or mishap from time to time. Unfortunately, given the way we bring up boys, most men over-react even to quite minor sexual problems.

Let's look at some of the more common things that can go wrong. There are really only three that are amenable to self-help by a man's partner. Clearly a professional would look at these rather differently and in much more depth but here we shall concentrate only on what a woman can do personally to help.

The three conditions worth looking at in this context are impotence; premature ejaculation; and retarded ejaculation.

Impotence

First I should say that impotence is not a word to be applied to the occasional failure to erect that can occur if a man is tired, worried, or drunk. Impotence is a much more specific condition in which a man persistently, or recurrently, fails to obtain or sustain an erection long enough to complete intercourse. There are scores of causes for the condition, some of which are physical, some to do with drugs and medications, and others that originate in the mind, often in the unconscious.

Some men are potent in intercourse and mutual masturbation but not in self-masturbation. Others find that they are potent only if they have fantasies of heterosexual intercourse that doesn't go as far as penetration. Such men, when asked in therapy to fantasise penetration, lose their erection at once. Such men are quite clearly avoiding intercourse, however unconsciously.

The young, sexually inexperienced man often suffers from impotence, often to his horror, but can usually overcome the problem because his drives are so high and his partner so willing.

More mature men may find that they function well in the marital bed but cannot do so outside it, in an affair, for example.

Scores of causes

Older men may find that they suddenly become impotent after many years of normal functioning. They think it is simply a part of ageing but this isn't usually so. What happens is that their sex drive falls below the level of their inhibitions and they fail to erect. This is often worsened by their partner's inability, or unwillingness, to offer additional stimulation and nothing much happens. Not a few older men **Impotence after abstinence** become impotent after a long period of abstinence, for example if they or their partner have been ill or in hospital for some time.

Relationship problems are also a common cause of impotence. Such men erect perfectly well outside marriage but not within it. The opposite occurs with some frequency in other men. Such men see their wives as too 'nice' and so cannot bring themselves to have intercourse with them. They can do it perfectly well with another woman who is, by definition, a tart.

Sorting out the cause of impotence can be a long and complex affair, even for a sexual and marital therapist. Here are my tips on how you could help your partner to regain his potency.

My top ten tips for overcoming impotence

1. Help your man by talking about it honestly without apportioning blame and without criticism.

2. Stop having intercourse (or trying to).

3. Go back to courtship behaviour.

4. Reveal more about your sexuality to your man.

5. Encourage him to masturbate until he is competent at it again.

6. Once he is confident that things can be controlled, if only by him, *you* can now start to masturbate him.

7. Look at the left hand column of the list on the following pages and avoid anything obvious that seems to be causing the trouble.

8. Work through the section of this book from page 207, so that you start to think intercourse instead of copulation.

9. Be patient. You are building something of value for the future, not just sorting out a current problem.

10. Start having intercourse again.

If this doesn't do the trick, and it often will, work through the specific causes in the list that follows and see what results you have.

CAUSES OF IMPOTENCE	THINGS YOU CAN DO TO HELP
Penile abnormalities such as a torn foreskin, tight foreskin or any painful infection of the penis.	Seek medical advice. In the meantime avoid stimulating the penis and concentrate on other sexual activities.
Diabetes.	Ensure that your man has all the medical help he needs. Talk to your local diabetics specialist and see what suggestions he has. Contact a self-help group. Ensure that your partner does everything he should to control his diabetes. Use all your skill as a lover to excite him the best you can. If he becomes completely impotent in the later stages of the disease get a dildo for him to use on you as he makes love to you in other ways.
Arterial disease; diseases of the spinal cord; after certain operations (lumbar sympathectomy, kidney transplant, pelvic surgery for cancer, prostatectomy); disordered hormone production and psychiatric illnesses such as severe depression.	Talk to your specialist dealing with the problem. Sometimes the impotence is temporary and amenable to some improvement by medical treatment but on other occasions it is permanent and has to be lived with. Again sex aids can be helpful.
Drugs such as excessive tobacco; hashish; hard drugs; alcohol; medical drugs; especially those for high blood pressure, and anti-depressants.	Cutting down or stopping smoking can greatly help. Encourage him to stop taking hard and soft drugs and get him to professional help as soon as possible. Help him cut right down on drinking. Talk to your doctor about the medical drugs he's on and see if there could be a way around them. For example, it is possible to use natural methods for controlling blood pressure that can reduce or even cut out the need for drugs. Perhaps psychotherapy would be better than anti-depressants. It'll certainly produce less impotence!
The man unconsciously equates his partner with his mother thus making her prohibited on the grounds that he cannot have sex with his mother. This can occur after the wife has had a baby.	Encourage him to seek professional therapy of some kind.
Fear of intimacy.	Embark on the training outlined on pages 178–206 to help him become more at ease with being intimate.
Guilt about sex.	Seek a professional therapist

CAUSES OF IMPOTENCE	THINGS YOU CAN DO TO HELP
Inability to relax. He has considerable concern about his erections and his performance generally.	Learn sensual massage together (see page 190). Spend more time together perhaps on a sensual holiday (see page 189). Help him to sort out his job or other worries if you can and encourage him to take up a sport or hobby to take his mind off the pressures of life. Try to go for a month without having intercourse. Return to courtship behaviour and take the pressure off 'performance' sex.
Anxiety about a recent disease (such as a heart attack or operation).	Men all too easily think that anything medical will wreck, or has wrecked, their potency. This is usually mistaken. Seek medical reassurance from his specialist or by reading more about the condition. Work on the assumption that in all but the most extreme of illnesses it should be safe to have sex and that only rarely do illnesses have a long-term adverse effect on sex.
Fear of women, their genitals, their 'pureness', their criticism, or their assertiveness.	Seek professional help. You'll be unlikely to be able to do much yourself because you might be seen to be at the heart of the trouble, however unjustifiably.
Apprehension of catching VD, getting the woman pregnant, and of other negative consequences of intercourse.	All these are especially likely to occur during extra-marital intercourse. Reassurance about your safety from VD and your contraceptive reliability will certainly help. If you are involved in an extra-marital affair then the adverse consequences are very real and the man's unconscious is speaking through his penis. Perhaps the course of action needs questioning again.
Misperceptions about female sexuality.	Many men have strange views about what women are really like. Sometimes you'll be able to sort this out for yourself just by talking things over and by being more honest about your real needs. If this kind of disclosure brings no result, seek professional help.

CAUSES OF PREMATURE EJACULATION	THINGS YOU CAN DO TO HELP
He has always come too quickly because of poor training in his youth.	Reassure him. Do Stop-Start exercises until he learns to hold back.
He feels unsafe.	Look together at what the causes might be. Is it a fear of being overheard by the children or perhaps being interrupted by them? Is the sex extra-marital and thus guilt-ridden or unsafe? Is he afraid of hurting you after a baby, episiotomy, or gynaecological operation? Is it the first time you as a couple are making love? Try to sort out what is worrying him and seek a way around the problem, if possible. He'll probably need lots of reassurance from you if his fears are about your genitals.
He is 'trigger-happy' because he hasn't had an orgasm for some time.	Some couples find that if the man doesn't have fairly frequent orgasms, especially if he is young, then when they make love they almost always find him coming too soon. Make love more frequently or get the man to masturbate an hour or two before having intercourse.
Bad problems in the relationship leading the man unconsciously to want to punish his partner.	Seek professional help.

Some useful games for premature ejaculators

It was the internationally renowned sex research team of Masters and Johnson who first made these techniques popular in the sixties and they have rightly remained as the mainstay of do-it-yourself treatment for premature ejaculators. The US team claimed very high success rates but at home, without any other professional inputs, such rates are bound to be unobtainable. Having said this, many couples, even if they do little or nothing else to alter their relationship, can cure the condition at home in the privacy of their bedroom.

Start off by cuddling one another and ensuring that your man at least becomes aroused. Now place him in a position in which he is comfortable and in which you can easily and comfortably caress his penis. The aim is to make the game pleasurable and informative for both partners. Few women fail to enjoy the sight of their man aroused, especially if they have been responsible for his arousal, and it is a good opportunity for her to get to know about the changes in his genitals, and indeed in his whole body, during the arousal cycle.

Her interest and arousal with its implied acceptance of his sexuality will help him to relax and to become uninhibited and enjoy his orgasm.

The squeeze technique in action. A sure-fire way of gaining ejaculation control.

In the stop-start game the woman caresses the man's penis and genitals generally to bring him to an erection while the man himself relaxes and concentrates on his feelings and sensations. When he is about to reach the point of no return he signals her to stop. The erection will now subside and when it does she can start again until he is once more fully erect. This cycle is repeated several times until, when the couple decide that the man has had enough, they masturbate him to climax.

A variant of this game is the squeeze game. In this the woman not only stimulates the man as above but when she stops doing so in each cycle she also squeezes the rim of the penis head between her thumb and two fingers of the same hand. The squeeze is applied for ten seconds or more until the penis becomes limp.

Whichever method is used the first stage in the cure is to enable the man to be confident that he can recognise the sensations in his genitals, or indeed in the rest of his body, that immediately precede orgasm.

Now the whole thing can be made more real by lubricating the penis with talc, KY jelly, baby oil, or massage oil. This makes the arousal quicker and more like that which occurs in the vagina. Control is now much more difficult for the man so more caution is required as you stimulate him.

Continue these games over some weeks until the man is completely happy that he can come when he wants rather than being overtaken by his orgasm and ruled by his penis. As he gets better you'll be able to set a time, say ten or fifteen minutes, at which the man will be 'allowed' to ejaculate. He and you can then work towards that. The really skilled couple can produce several erections one after the other and bring the man to a climax almost to a countdown.

Confidence will by now be so high that you'll be ready to progress to intercourse.

Next time you produce an erection for him, suddenly and without warning straddle his penis and just let it sit there inside you while you stay immobile. If he now feels that he is about to ejaculate get off him at once and squeeze him so that he goes off the boil, as before. Repeat this several times but ensuring that you do not go on to let him ejaculate inside you. When he is totally happy about this you can start to work your pelvic muscles on his penis so that he obtains extra stimulation. Slowly build up the vaginal activity until he can tolerate a lot of it and not come until you tell him to.

Now the game is nearly over and you can have intercourse normally in any position you choose. At first thrusting may have to be kept to a minimum but you'll soon get the hang of what works yet is not too exciting for the man.

Although all of this might sound somewhat mechanical, and it is, it is worth doing for almost any couple, let alone the one whose man is plagued by premature ejaculation. Not only is it fun to do but few Fun to do couples end up unhappy with a man who can last for a long time and can ejaculate at a time that pleases them both. Over-training can, on occasions, produce the opposite problem – retarded ejaculation. This is usually fairly easily overcome though by removing the brakes a little and making things more abandoned.

Retarded ejaculation

This is a condition in which the man finds it difficult or impossible to have an orgasm in the vagina. He can usually masturbate well but may have pain on vaginal intercourse. Some men have a headache or pain in the groin and others say that there is something wrong with their semen. Others claim that they have a 'blockage' somewhere or say that it feels as if their penis is in a vice-like grip. The pain, or these other unfortunate sensations, make it impossible for the man to climax inside his partner. Usually no physical cause can be found by a doctor though rarely there is one.

As with all male sex problems this can sometimes be a form of sex avoidance, however unconscious. During treatment such men sometimes turn into premature ejaculators, once more avoiding sex but in another way.

My top ten tips for overcoming retarded ejaculation

1. Help your man by talking honestly and openly about it without apportioning blame.

2. Stop having intercourse.

3. Go back to courtship behaviour.

4. Reveal more about your sexuality to your man.

5. Encourage him to feel at ease about masturbating in front of you and show him that you don't think his semen as dirty or unacceptable.

6. Over several occasions get closer and closer to him while he masturbates and eventually you'll be able to masturbate him without him feeling ill at ease about it.

7. Work through this section from page 207 until you both think about intercourse instead of copulation.

8. Be patient. You are building something of value for the future, not simply dealing with a problem in the here-and-now.

9. Get your man excited and have him ejaculate on to your tummy or breasts. Help him by reassuring him that you are happy about it.

10. Have intercourse, preferably in a way that pleases him.

This should deal with the problem in most cases but if you still have troubles with your man's inability to ejaculate inside you work through the following list and see what you can do for yourself.

CAUSES OF RETARDED EJACULATION	THINGS YOU CAN DO TO HELP
Spinal injuries and operations on the pelvic organs (all rare).	Seek specialist advice from your partner's hospital doctor.
The man unconsciously perceives you as a mother.	Stop acting like one! If necessary, seek professional help to do this, and as a couple try to help him overcome any predisposition he might have to see you as a mother even if you do not think you behave like one.
He thinks of his semen as a form of excretion.	Show him that you like it by letting him ejaculate over you. Touch it, even lick it if you want to. Anything that shows him that you are not revolted by it, which is what he expects you to be, will work wonders.
Fear of getting you pregnant.	Use a better method of contraception that reassures him. Get him involved.

CAUSES OF RETARDED EJACULATION	THINGS YOU CAN DO TO HELP
Fear of having an orgasm with a woman.	Encourage him to masturbate on his own with you out of the room. Slowly over some weeks come into the room as he becomes very aroused and watch from a distance. Next, come closer on the following occasion. Repeat this until he is happy to have you sitting on the bed next to him as he ejaculates.
Fear of losing control.	Reassure him that you like to see him being uninhibited and being himself. Show him how *you* enjoy losing control by masturbating in front of him, perhaps with rather more than usual abandon.
Belief that sex is for reproduction only and that any form of non-procreative sex is somehow unnatural, perverted or wrong.	Seek professional help.
Recent orgasm.	Discourage him from masturbating himself. This might be important in the older man who could be resistant to re-stimulation for up to forty-eight hours after his last orgasm.
Increasing age.	Offer much more stimulation of all kinds.
Some drugs, especially anti-depressants.	Have him talk to his doctor about changing to something else. Psychotherapy has no similar side-effects and probably cures depression better anyway.
Too much alcohol.	This might need professional help or assistance from a specialist group such as Alcoholics Anonymous if real progress is to be made with all but the most 'social' of drinkers. Alcohol at almost every level of intake has bad effects on male sexual arousal and function.
Relationship problems.	Seek professional help if working through this section from page 207 does no good.
Vagina too large or too wet.	Get your man to enter you while you are still not too aroused and thus drier. Do pelvic muscle exercises to strengthen your vaginal area and thus be able to grip the penis and give him better sensations.

BIBLIOGRAPHY

Although, as I pointed out in the Introduction, the literature on male sexuality is not as voluminous as that on female sexuality it is still large, if somewhat specialised. I have drawn on many sources to write this book but here I list only some books that might be of interest to readers. Learned research papers are, by and large, unavailable to the public and so are not included, though they are, of course, much more numerous.

Abrahamsen, D. *The Psychology of Crime*. Oxford University Press, 1960.

Alfred Marks Bureau. *Sex in the Office: An Investigation into the Incidence of Sexual Harassment*. Alfred Marks Bureau, London, 1982.

Allan, G. *A Sociology of Friendship and Kinship*. Allen & Unwin, London, 1949.

Altman, C. *You Can Be Your Own Sex Therapist*. Berkley, New York, 1976.

Altman, D. *The Homosexualization of America*. Beacon Press, Boston, 1983.

Ambrose, P., Pemberton, R., & Harper, J. *Surviving Divorce: Men Beyond Marriage*. Wheatsheaf Books, 1983.

Arcana, J. *Every Mother's Son*. The Women's Press, 1983.

Archer, J. and Lloyd, B. *Sex and Gender*. Penguin, London, 1982.

Ashley, M. *The Natural Superiority of Women*. Collier Macmillan, 1974.

Balint, A. *The Psycho-analysis of the Nursery*. Routledge & Kegan Paul, London, 1953.

Beall, Nand McGuire, J. *Fathers: a Psychological Perspective*. Junction Books, London, 1982.

de Beauvoir, S. *The Second Sex*. Penguin, London, 1972.

Bednarik, K. *The Male in Crisis*. Greenwood Press, U.K., 1982.

Bell, A. and Weinberg, M. *Homosexualities*. Mitchell Beazley, 1979.

Bell, D. Being a Man: *The Paradox of Masculinity*. The Lewis Publishing Company. Brattleboro, VT. 1982.

Bengis, I. *Combat in the Erogenous Zone*. Wildword House, London, 1973.

Benson, L. *Fatherhood: A Sociological Perspective*. Random House, New York, 1968.

Bernard, J. *The Future of Marriage*. Yale University Press, 1982.

Berne, E. *Games People Play: The Psychology of Human Relationships*. Penguin, London, 1970.

Berne, E. *Sex in Human Living*. Penguin, London, 1973.

Biller, H. *Paternal Deprivation*. D. C. Heath, 1974.

Biller, H. and Meredith D. *Father Power*. David McKay Co., New York, 1975.

Block, I. *Sexual Life in England Past and Present*. Arco, London, 1958.

Block, J. *Friendship: How to Give It. How to Get It*. Macmillan, New York, 1980.

Blood, R. Jr. and Wolfe, D. *Husbands and Wives*. Greenwood Press, U.K., 1978.

Bowlby, J. *Childcare and the Growth of Love*. Penguin, 1965.

Bowlby, J. *Attachment and Loss, 1: Attachment*. Hogarth Press/Institute of Psycho-Analysis, 1982.

Bowskill, D. & Linacre, A. *Men, the Sensitive Sex*. Frederick Muller, 1977.

Bradford, D., Sargent, A. and Sprague, M. *The Executive Man and Woman: the Issue of Sexuality* in F. Gordon and M. Strober (Eds) *Bringing Women into Management*. McGraw-Hill, New York, 1975.

Bradman, T. *The Essential Father*. Unwin, 1985.

Brecher, R. and Brecher E. *An Analysis of Human and Sexual Response*. Andre Deutsch, London, 1967.

Brenton, M. *The American Male*. Fawcett, 1970: George Allen & Unwin, 1967.

Broby-Johannsen, R. *Body and Clothes*. Faber, London, 1968.

Brothers, J. *What Every Woman Should Know About Men*. Granada, 1982.

Brownmiller, S. *Against our Will: Men, Women and Rape*. Simon & Schuster, New York, 1975: Penguin, London, 1977.

Brownmiller, S. *Femininity*. Hamish Hamilton, London, 1984.

Buber, M. *I and Thou*. T. & T. Clarke, Edinburgh, 1980.

Burt, A. *Ah! Men*. A. & W., New York, 1980.

Carter, A. *The Sadeian Woman*. Virago, London, 1979.

Cauthery, P. and Stanway, A. *The Complete Guide to Love and Sex*. Century Hutchinson, 1983.

Cauthery, P. and Stanway, A. *The Complete Guide to Sexual Fulfilment*. Century Hutchinson, 1985.

Cauthery, P. and Stanway, A. *Love and Sex over Forty*. Chartsearch, 1986.

Cherfas, J. and Gribbin, J. *The Redundant Male*. Paladin, 1985.

Chesler, P. *About Men*. Simon & Schuster, New York, 1978: The Women's Press, London, 1979.

Claremont de Castillejo, I. *Knowing Women*. Hodder, London, 1973.

Comfort, A. *The Anxiety Makers*. Delta, 1967: Panther Books, London, 1968.

Comfort, A. *The Joy of Sex*. Crown, 1972.

Curle, A. *Mystics and Militants*. Tavistock, 1972.

Daley, E. *Father Feelings*. Morrow & Co. New York, 1978.

Dobbert, J. *A Man's Place: Masculinity in Transition*. Englewood Cliffs, NJ: Prentice-Hall, 1979.

Dodson, F. *How to Father*. W. H. Allen, London, 1974.

Dollimore, J. *Masculinity and Homophobia, in Literature Teaching Politics*, Bristol Polytechnic, 1985.

Douglas, A. *The Feminisation of American Culture*. Alfred A. Knopf, New York, 1977.

Dowling, C. *The Cinderella Complex: Women's Hidden Fear of Independence*. Summit Books, New York, 1981: Fontana, London, 1982.

Dworkin, A. *Pornography: Men Possessing Women*. The Women's Press, Lauda Lederer (ed). London, 1981.

Dworkin, A. *Woman Hating*. Dutton, New York, 1974.

Easthope, A. *What a Man's Gotta Do*. Collins, London: Paladin, 1986.

Ehrenreich, B. *The Hearts of Men: American Dreams and the Flight from Commitment*. Pluto Press, London, 1983.

Eichenbaum, L. and Orbach, S. *What Do Women Want?* Michael Joseph, London, 1983: Fontana, 1984.

Eisner, B. *The Unused Potential of Marriage and Sex*. Little Brown, Boston, 1970.

Ellis, A. *Sex and the Liberated Man*. Secaucus, NJ. Lyle Stuart, 1976.

Ellman, B. *Thinking About Women*. Harcourt, Brace & World, 1968.

Ernst, S. L. and Goodison, L. *In our Own Hands: A Book of Self-Help Therapy*. The Women's Press, London, 1981.

Ewing, W. *Changing Men: Mission Impossible?* The Research Center on Women, Denver, 1978.

Farrell, W. *The Liberated Man: Beyond Masculinity: Freeing Men and Their Relationships with Women*. Random House, New York, 1975.

Fast, J. *The Incompatibility of Men and Women*. M. Evans, 1971.

Fasteau, F. *The Male Machine*. McGraw-Hill, New York, 1975.

Figes, R. *A Book of Men: Visions of the Male Experience*. Stonehill, New York, 1978.

Fisher, S. and Fisher, R. *What We Really Know About Childrearing*. Simon & Schuster, New York, 1976.

Ford, A. *Men*. Weidenfeld & Nicolson: Corgi, 1986.

Ford, C. and Beach, F. *Patterns of Sexual Behaviour*. Eyre & Spottiswoode, London, 1952: Methuen, 1965.

Foucault, M. *The History of Sexuality*. Penguin, London, 1981.

Freud, A. *The Ego and Mechanisms of Defense*. Hogarth Press, London, 1968.

Freud, S. *The Dissolution of the Oedipus Complex*. Collected Papers Vol XIX, Hogarth Press, London, 1929.

Freud, S. *Three Contributions to the Theory of Sex*. E. P. Dutton, New York, 1962.

Friedan, B. *The Feminine Mystique*. Norton, New York: Gollancz, London, 1963.

Friday, N. *Men in Love: Men's Sexual Fantasies: The Triumph of Love over Rage*. Delacorte Press, New York: Hutchinson, London, 1980.

Fromm, E. *The Art of Loving*. Allen & Unwin, London, 1975.

Fromm, E. *Man for Himself*, Rinehart, 1947.

Gagnon, J. and Simon, W. *Sexual Conduct*. Hutchinson, London, 1974: Aldine, Chicago, 1975.

Gardener, L. *Whisper in his Ear*. Futura, London, 1984.

Gatley, R. and Koulack, D. *The Single Father's Handbook*. Anchor Press/Doubleday, New York, 1979.

Gavron, H. *The Captive Wife*. Routledge & Kegan Paul, 1972.

George, V. and Wilding, P. *Motherless Families*, Routledge & Kegan Paul, 1972.

Gilder, G. *Sexual Suicide*. Quadrangle, New York, 1973.

Goldberg, H. *The Hazards of Being Male: Surviving the Myth of Masculine Privilege*. Sanford J. Greenburger Associates, 1976.

Goldberg, H. *The New Male: From Self-Destruction to Self-Care*. William Morrow, New York, 1979.

Goldberg, S. *The Inevitability of Patriarchy*. Morrow, New York, 1975: Abacus, London, 1979.

Goldstein, M. and Kant, H. *Pornography and Sexual Deviance*. University of California Press, 1973.

Gornick, V. and Moran B. *Woman in Sexist Society*. Basic Books, New York, 1971.

Green, R. *Sexual Identity Conflict in Children and Adults*. Basic Books, New York, 1974.

Greenwald, J. *Creative Intimacy*. Simon & Schuster, 1975.

Griffin, S. *Pornography and Silence*. The Women's Press, London, 1981.

Groth, A. and Birmingham, H. *Men Who Rape: The Psychology of the Offender*. Plenum Press, New York, 1979.

Hapgood, F. *Why Males Exist: An Inquiry into the Evolution of Sex*. Mentor Books, New York, 1979.

Harris, T. *I'm OK – You're OK*. Cape, London, 1973.

Hartnett, O., Boden, G. and Fuller, M. *Sex Role Stereotyping*. Tavistock, 1979.

Hearn, J. *Making Friends, Keeping Friends*. Doubleday, New York, 1979.

Heath, S. *The Sexual Fix*. Macmillan, London, 1982.

Henriques, F. *Prostitution in Europe and the New World*. MacGibbon & Kee, London, 1963.

Herzog, E. and Sudia, C. *Boys in Fatherless Families*. US Department of Health, Education and Welfare, Washington DC, 1970.

Hite, S. *The Hite Report on Male Sexuality.* Knopf, New York, 1981: Macdonald, London, 1981.

Hocquenghem, G. *Homosexual Desire.* Allison & Busby, 1978.

Hodder, E. *The Step-Parents' Handbook.* Sphere Books, 1985.

Hodson, P. *Men.* Ariel Books, 1984.

Horner, M. and J. M. Bardwick, E. Douvan, M. S. Horner & Dr Gutman, *Feminine Personality and Conflict.* Brooks-Cole, New York, 1970.

Howard, J. *Please Touch.* McGraw-Hill, New York, 1970.

Howeed, L. *The Future of the Family.* Simon & Schuster, 1972.

Hunt, M. *Sexual Behaviour in the 1970s.* Playboy Press, Chicago, 1974.

Ingham, M. *The Male Myth Exposed.* Century, 1984.

Ingham, M. *Men.* Century Hutchinson, London, 1984.

Johnston, H. *Executive Life Styles: A Life Extension Report on Alcohol, Sex and Health,* Cromwell, New York, 1974.

Josephson, E. and Josephson, M. *Man Alone: Alienation in Modern Society.* Dell, New York, 1962.

Julty, S. *Male Sexual Performance.* Grosset & Dunlap, 1975.

Kaplan, A. & Bean J. *Beyond Sex Role Stereotypes: Toward a Psychology of Androyny.* Little Brown, Boston, 1974.

Kass D. and Strauss, F. *Sex Therapy at Home.* Simon & Schuster, New York, 1975.

Katz, J. *Gay American History: Lesbians and Gay Men in the USA.* Cromwell, New York, 1976.

Kiell, N. *Varieties of Sexual Experience.* International University Press, 1976.

Kiley, D. *The Peter Pan Syndrome.* Dodd, Mead, New York, 1983: Corgi, London, 1984.

Kiley, D. *The Wendy Dilemma.* Arrow Books, London, 1985.

Kinsey, A., Pomeroy, W. and Martin, C. *Sexual Behaviour in the Human Male.* Saunders, Philadelphia, 1948.

Komarovsky, M. *Dilemmas of Masculinity: A Study of College Youth.* Norton, New York, 1976.

Korda, M. *Male Chauvinism: How it Works!* Random House, 1973: Barrie & Jenkins, 1974.

Kronhausen, E & P. *Pornography and the Law.* Ballantine, 1959: NEL, London, 1967.

Kuhn, A. *Women's Pictures.* Routledge & Kegan Paul, London, 1982.

Laing, R. *The Divided Self.* Penguin, London, 1961.

Laver, J. *Modesty in Dress.* Heinemann, London, 1969.

Lazarre, J. *On Loving Men,* Virago, 1981.

Lederer, W. *The Fear of Women,* Grune & Stratton, New York, 1968.

Leefeldt, C. and Callenbach, E. *The Art of Friendship.* Pantheon, New York, 1979.

Lewinsohn, R. *A History of Sexual Customs.* Longmans, Green. London, 1958.

Lewis, C. *Becoming a Father.* Open University Press, 1986.

Lorenz, K. *On Aggression.* Harcourt, Brace & World: Methuen, London, 1966.

Lynn, E. *The Father: His Role in Child Development.* Wadsworth, Belmont CA, 1974.

M. *The Sensuous Man.* W. H. Allen, London, 1971.

Maccoby, E. and Jacklin, C. *The Psychology of Sex Differences.* Oxford University Press, 1975.

McKee, L. and O'Brien, M. *The Father Figure.* Tavistock, London, 1982.

Malinowski, B. *The Sexual Life of Savages.* Routledge & Kegan Paul, London, 1929.

Martin, W. and Mason, S. *Leisure and Work.* Leisure Consultants Ltd, Sudbury, Suffolk, 1982.

Masters, W. and Johnson, V. *The Pleasure Bond.* Bantam, New York and London, 1975.

Masters, W. and Johnson, V. *Human Sexual Response.* Bantam, London, 1980.

Masters, W. and Johnson, V. *Human Sexual Inadequacy.* Bantam, London, 1980.

Mead, M. *Male and Female.* Penguin, London, 1962.

Metcalf, A. and Humphries, M. *The Sexuality of Men.* Pluto Press, London, 1985.

Miller, J. *Towards a New Psychology of Women.* Penguin, London, 1978.

Miller, S. *Men and Friendship.* Houghton Mifflin, Boston: Gateway, London, 1983.

Millett, K. *Sexual Politics.* Abacus, London, 1972.

Money, J. and Ehrhardt, A. *Man and Woman, Boy and Girl.* Johns Hopkins University Press, Baltimore, 1972.

Montagu, A. *The Natural Superiority of Women.* rev. ed. Collier Macmillan, London, 1974.

Montague, A. *Touching: the Human Significance of the Skin.* Harper & Row, New York, 1972.

Morris, D. *The Human Zoo.* Cape, London, 1969.

Morris, D. *Intimate Behaviour.* Cape, London, 1971.

Morris, D. *The Naked Ape.* Cape, London, 1967.

Naifeh, S. and Smith G. *Why Can't Men Open Up?* Warner Books, 1984.

NALGO Liverpool. Equal Opportunities Working Party. *Report on Sexual Harassment.* Liverpool Nalgo, 1982.

Nicholson, J. *Men and Women: How Different are They?* Oxford University Press, 1984.

Oakley, A. *Sex, Gender and Society.* Temple Smith, 1972.

Odenwald, R. *The Disappearing Sexes.* Random House, New York, 1965.

Papalia, D. and Olds, S. *A Child's World: Infancy Through Adolescence.* McGraw-Hill, New York, 1975.

Parke, R. *Fathering.* Fontana, London, 1981.

Penney, A. *How to Make Love to a Man.* Dell, New York, 1981: Macmillan, London, 1982.

Pietropinto, A. and Simenaur, J. *Beyond the Male Myth*. Signet, 1977.

Pietropinto, A. and Simenaur, J. *Husbands and Wives*. Berkeley, New York, 1979.

Pleck, E. and Pleck, J. *The American Man*. Prentice-Hall Spectrum Books, Englewood Cliffs NJ, 1980.

Pleck, J. and Sawyer, J. *Men and Masculinity*. Englewood Cliffs, New Jersey: Prentice-Hall, 1974.

Pleck, J. *The Myth of Masculinity*. MIT, 1981.

Pomeroy, W. *Boys and Sex*. Delacorte, New York, 1969: Penguin, London, 1970.

Prince, P. *The Good Father*. Cape, London, 1983.

Rapoport, R. and R. *Dual-Career Families*. Penguin, 1971.

Rapoport, R., Rapoport, R. and Strelitz, Z. with Kew, S. *Fathers, Mothers and Others*. Routledge & Kegan Paul, London, 1977.

Read, S. *Sexual Harassment at Work*. Hamlyn, Feltham, 1982.

Reich, W. *The Function of Orgasm*. Farrar, Straus & Giroux, New York, 1969: Souvenir, London, 1983.

Reich, W. *The Sexual Revolution: Toward a Self-Governing Character Structure*. 4th ed. Farrar, Straus & Giroux, New York, 1969: Souvenir, 1983.

Reich, W. *Reich Speaks of Freud*. Penguin, London, 1975.

Reisman, J. *Anatomy of Friendship*. Irvington Publishers, New York, 1979.

Reynaud, E. *Holy Virility*. Pluto, London, 1983.

Rich, A. *Of Woman Born*. Virago, London, 1977.

Roberts, Y. *Man Enough*. Chatto & Windus, 1984.

Roeber, J. *Shared Parenthood. A Handbook for Fathers*. Century, London, 1987.

Roen, P. *Male Sexual Health*. Morrow, 1974.

Rose, F. and Bennet, G. *Real Men: Sex and Style in an Uncertain Age*. Doubleday, New York, 1980.

Rubin, M. *Men Without Masks, Writings from the Journals of Modern Men*. Addison-Wesley, Reading, Mass, 1980.

Rubin, T. and Berliner, D. *Understanding Your Man: A Woman's Guide*. Ballantine Books, New York, 1977.

Ruitenbeek, H. *The Male Myth*. Dell, New York, 1967.

Russell, G. *The Changing Role of Fathers*. Open University Press, 1983.

Russianoff, P. *Why Do I Think I Am Nothing Without A Man?* Bantam, New York and London, 1982.

Rutter, M. *Maternal Deprivation Reassessed*. Penguin, 1972.

Sanders, D. *The Woman Book of Love and Sex*. Sphere, London, 1985.

Sarnoff, S. and I. *Masturbation and Adult Sexuality*. Evans, New York, 1979.

Schwenger, P. *Phallic Critiques*. Routledge & Kegan Paul, 1984.

Sexuality and Man. S. Scribner's Sons, New York, 1970.

Shwa, G. *Meat on the Hoof*. St Martin's Press, 1972.

Sheehy, G. *Passages: Predictable Crises of Adult Life*. E. P. Dutton, New York, 1976: Bantam, 1982.

Sinfield, A. *What Unemployment Means*. Martin Robertson, Oxford, 1981.

Skynner, R. and Cleese, J. *Families and How to Survive Them*. Methuen, 1983.

Sorensen, R. *Adolescent Sexuality in Contemporary America*. World, New York, 1973.

Stanway, A. *Infertility, A Commonsense Guide*. Thorsons, 1980.

Stanworth, M. *Gender and Schooling*. Hutchinson, London, 1983.

Stearns, P. *Be a Man! Males in Modern Society*. Holmes Meier, New York, 1979.

Stekel, W. *Auto-Erotism: A Psychiatric Study of Onanism and Neurosis*. Grove Press, New York, 1961: Nevill, 1951.

Stoller, R. *Sex and Gender: On the Development of Masculinity and Femininity*. Science House, New York, 1968: Hogarth, London, 1968.

Sutton-Smith, B. *Child Psychology*. Appleton-Century-Crofts, New York, 1973.

Tannahill, R. *Sex in History*. Hamish Hamilton, 1980.

Tanner, J. *Foetus into Man*. Open Books, London, 1978.

Thornes, B. and Collard, J. *Who Divorces?* Routledge & Kegan Paul, London, 1979.

Tiger, L. *Men in Groups*. Random House, New York, 1969. M. Boyars, 1984.

Tolson, A. *The Limits of Masculinity*. Harper & Row, New York: Tavistock, London, 1977.

Tripp, Ca. *The Homosexual Matrix*. McGraw-Hill, New York, 1975: Quartet, London, 1977.

Turgenev, I. *Fathers and Sons*. Heron Books, Geneva, 1962: Bantam, London, 1959, 1981.

Vanggaard, T. *Phallos: A Symbol and Its History in the Male World*. International University Press, Independence, Missouri: Cape, London, 1972.

Wagenvoord, J. and Bailey, P. *Men: A Book for Women*. Avon, New York, 1978.

Walters, M. *The Nude Male*. Paddington Press, London, 1978: Penguin, 1979.

Weeks, J. *Sex, Politics and Society*. Longman, 1981.

Weeks, J. *Sexuality and its Discontents*. Routledge & Kegan Paul, 1985.

West, D. *Homosexuality*. Penguin, Harmondsworth, 1960.

Westropp, H. and Stanaland, W. *Phallicism in Ancient Worship*. Curzon Press, 1972.

Wilson, E. *What is to be Done about Violence Against Women?* Penguin, London, 1983.

Woodman, M. *Addiction to Perfection: The Still Unravished Bride*. Inner City Books, Toronto, 1982.

Zilbergeld, B. *Male Sexuality. A Guide to Sexual Fulfilment*. Souvenir, London, 1979.

INDEX